30 Minute Meals

A COMMON SENSE GUIDE

30 Minute Meals

A COMMON SENSE GUIDE

bay books

CONTENTS

GLOSSARY
Terms used in recipes for cooking sometimes seem mysterious but once understood, help you cook with confidence. Knowing the function of common ingredients also helps you on your way.

Al dente Meaning 'to the tooth'. Pasta and risotto rice are cooked until they are al dente the outside is tender but the centre still has a little resistance or 'bite'. Pasta cooked beyond this point goes soggy.

Anchovies A small fish from the herring family found mainly in southern European waters. Although anchovies can be eaten fresh, they are rarely found outside Mediterranean fishing ports as they are delicate and need to be eaten or processed quickly. More commonly, anchovies are cured and packed in oil, salt or brine and are readily available in cans or jars.

Antipasto The Italian version of hors d'oeuvre, this literally means 'before the meal'. Antipasto in restaurants is generally served on platters on a large table and each diner makes a selection. At home, antipasto can be served on a large platter or a series of smaller plates.

Arborio rice A short-grained plump rice imported from Italy. Used in both sweet and savoury dishes, arborio rice is particularly suitable for making risotto because the grains absorb a lot of liquid and become creamy but still retain their firmness. Available in most supermarkets.

Artichoke The edible flower of a member of the thistle family. The largest are usually boiled, but the smallest and most tender can be eaten raw as antipasto. Common varieties include Romanesco (large and purple), Precoce di Chioggia (large and green), Violetto Toscano (small and tender enough to eat raw) and Spinoso di Palermo (a purple variety from Sicily).

Bamboo shoots Crunchy in texture and with a subtle, refreshing taste, these are the edible young shoots of certain types of bamboo. Spring bamboo shoots are pale, fibrous and chunky; winter shoots are thinner with a finer texture and more pronounced flavour. Fresh bamboo shoots are hard to get and, if not already prepared, must be peeled then parboiled to remove toxic hydrocyanic acid — boil whole or in chunks for 5 minutes or more until they no longer taste bitter. Canned and bottled bamboo shoots are the ones most often used.

Banana leaves The large flexible leaves of the banana plant are used throughout Asia to wrap foods for steaming or baking. They keep the food moist and impart a mild flavour. Remove the thick central stalk, rinse the leaves well and blanch in boiling water to soften. Foil can be used instead.

Barbecued Chinese pork (char siu) These are strips of pork fillet which have been marinated in five spice powder, soy sauce, sugar and red colouring (usually from annatto seeds) then barbecued over charcoal.

Beef marrow The marrow extracted from the hollow centre of large beef bones. These bones can be bought from butchers — ask for them to be cut into short lengths or cracked open so you can scoop the marrow out easily.

Besan (chickpea flour) This is a pale yellow flour made from ground chickpeas and used most commonly in Indian cuisine, giving a unique texture and flavour. Often used as a thickener in sauces and batters.

Black beans One of the most popular flavours in the cooking of southern China, black beans are dried soy beans that have been cooked and fermented with salt and spices. They are soft with a sharp, salty taste. Wash thoroughly before use and lightly crush or chop to release the aroma. Black beans are available in cans or packets; once opened, be sure to refrigerate in an airtight container.

Bocconcini and **ovolini** These are soft, moist, mild, almost white cheeses. Ovolini is a small version of bocconcini. If bought unpackaged from delicatessens, refrigerate in the whey that they come in and use within 3 days. Those sold in sealed bags have a use-by date on them — use within 3 days of opening. Bocconcini (fresh baby mozzarella) means literally 'small mouthful' and is used to describe various foods, but generally refers to small balls of mozzarella, about the size of walnuts.

Bok choy (pak choy) Also known as Chinese chard and Chinese white cabbage, it has fleshy white stems and leaf ribs and green flat leaves. It has a slightly mustardy taste. Separate the leaves, wash well and drain. The white stems can be sliced thinly and eaten raw. Look for firm stems and unblemished leaves. A smaller type is called baby bok choy or Shanghai bok choy.

Borlotti (cranberry) beans Slightly kidney-shaped, this large bean is a beautifully marked pale, pinkish brown with burgundy specks. Popular in Italy, borlotti beans have a nutty flavour and are used in soups, stews and salads. They are sometimes available fresh, otherwise dried or canned can be used.

Broad (fava) beans Unlike many other beans these have to be podded before use. Peel the beans out of the fuzz-filled pods and either cook them as they are or pod them again by removing the leathery, grey outer layer from each bean. Broad beans can be bought frozen when they are not in season.

Burghul (bulgur) Also known as cracked wheat, burghul is wheat which has been hulled, boiled or steamed, then dried and cracked. It is a staple in the Middle East and requires little or no cooking. Sold coarsely or finely ground.

Calasparra rice This white medium-grained Spanish rice is traditionally used to make paella. If it is not available, arborio, carnaroli or vialone nano can be used instead.

Cannellini beans Cream, almost white, beans which are usually used dried rather than fresh. They need to be soaked for a few hours to soften them before using them in recipes. Tinned beans can also be used — add them at the end of the cooking time or they will disintegrate.

Cannelloni tubes Pasta which have a hole big enough for filling with meat and vegetable sauces. After filling, they are baked with a sauce poured over the top to keep them moist.

Capers The pickled buds of a shrub which grows wild in many parts of the Mediterranean. Capers have a sharp, sour taste and are sold in seasoned vinegar or packed in salt which needs to be rinsed off before use. These are available preserved in brine, vinegar or salt, and should be rinsed well and squeezed dry before use. Baby capers are tiny and are used whole. Some larger capers need to be chopped.

Cardamom This very aromatic spice of Indian origin is available as whole pods, whole seeds or ground. The pale green oval pods are tightly packed with sweetly fragrant brown or black seeds. When using whole pods, lightly bruise them before adding to the dish.

Cavolo nero A type of cabbage with long leaves that are so dark green they appear to be almost black. If unavailable, dark green Savoy cabbage can be used.

Cheddar cheese It comes in various strengths including mild, semi-matured, matured (tasty) and vintage (extra tasty). The milder ones are paler yellow in colour. They are all quite firm but the more mature ones are often more crumbly.

Chickpeas One of the most versatile and popular legumes in many parts of the world, chickpeas were first grown in the Levant and ancient Egypt. There are two kinds of chickpea, the large white garbanzo and the smaller brown dessi. Some of the most popular Middle Eastern dishes, including hummus, have chickpeas as their basis. They can be boiled, roasted, ground, mashed and milled and are available dried or canned.

Chillies (dried) Chilli flakes are dried red chillies that have been crushed, usually with the seeds (leaving in the seeds increases the hotness). Store in a cool, dark place in an airtight container. Common dried red chillies will vary in size and degree of heat, depending on which type has been dried. Soak in hot water until soft, then drain well before adding to dishes. If preferred, remove the seeds before soaking to reduce the fieriness. The tiny chillies are very hot.

Chillies (fresh)

Bird's eye chillies These are the hottest chillies. From 1–3 cm (½–1¼ in) long, they are available fresh, dried or pickled in brine.

Small red chillies Approximately 5 cm (2 in) long and also very hot. Used to make chilli powder and chilli flakes.

Medium chillies About 10–15 cm (4–6 in) long, they are the most commonly used in Indonesian and Malaysian cooking.

Long thin chillies These are hot but not overpowering.

Large red and green chillies About 15–20 cm (6–8 in) long, these are thicker than medium chillies. The ripe red ones are very hot.

Chilli powder This is made by finely grinding dried red chillies and can vary in hotness from mild to fiery. Chilli flakes can be substituted, but not Mexican chilli powder, which is mixed with cumin.

Chinese cabbage (wong bok) Also known as celery cabbage and napa cabbage, has a long shape and closely packed broad, pale green leaves with wide white stems. It has a delicate mustard-like flavour. This is the vegetable used in cabbage rolls.

Chinese dried mushrooms Also called Chinese dried black mushrooms, grow on fallen decaying trees. Their distinctive woody, smoky taste is intensified by the drying process, and they are rarely eaten fresh.

Chorizo A Spanish sausage, with many regional varieties, based on pork, paprika and garlic. Chorizo is sliced and served as tapas and is also cooked in paellas, stews and soups.

Choy sum Also known as Chinese flowering cabbage, it is slimmer than bok choy and has smooth green leaves and pale green stems with clusters of tiny yellow flowers on the tips of the inner shoots. The leaves and flowers cook quickly and have a light, sweet mustard flavour; the stems are crunchy and juicy.

Ciabatta Slipper-shaped Italian bread with a rough, open texture. The loaves are made from a very wet dough, which allows large bubbles to form and also gives a thin crust. Ciabatta is best eaten on the day it is bought or made. Stale ciabatta can be used for bruschetta and crostini.

Coconut cream Also known as thick coconut milk, it is extracted from the flesh of fresh coconuts and has a thick, almost spreadable consistency. It is very rich.

Coconut milk Extracted from fresh coconut flesh after the cream has been pressed out and has a much thinner consistency. Once opened, the milk or cream does not keep, so freeze any leftovers. (Coconut milk is not the clear, watery liquid found in the centre of fresh coconuts — this is coconut water or coconut juice.)

Conchiglie A shell-shaped pasta which comes in various sizes. Large shells are excellent for baking with fillings such as seafood whereas small shells can be used in casseroles and soups or can be served cold in salads.

Coriander (cilantro) Also known as Chinese parsley. All parts of this aromatic plant — seeds, leaves, stem and root — can be eaten. The leaves add an earthy, peppery flavour to curries, and are used in salads and as a garnish, and the stems and roots are ground for curry pastes. Dried coriander is not a suitable substitute.

Cotechino A sausage made from pork and pork rind. Cotechino has a gelatinous texture and is often flavoured with cloves and cinnamon. It needs to be cooked before eating. Cotechino can be bought from Italian butchers and delicatessens.

Couscous This cereal is processed from semolina and coated with wheat flour. Instant couscous cooks in 5 minutes. Couscous is used in much the same way as rice is in Asia — as a high-carbohydrate accompaniment to meat and vegetable dishes.

Crisp fried garlic and onion These are very thin slices of garlic cloves and onions or red Asian shallots that have been deep-fried until crisp. They are used as a crunchy, flavoursome garnish, and can be added to peanut sauce. Available in packets or they can be prepared at home.

Cumin These small, pale brown, aromatic seeds have a warm, earthy flavour. In its ground form cumin is an essential component of curry pastes and many other spice mixes. Black cumin is smaller and darker than common cumin and sweeter in taste.

Curry leaves These small, shiny, pointed leaves from a tree native to Asia have a spicy fragrance and are used in southern India, Sri Lanka and Malaysia to impart a distinctive flavour to curries and vegetable dishes. Use as you would bay leaves, and remove before serving. Bay leaves are not a substitute.

Daikon Much used in Japanese and Chinese cooking, this carrot-shaped white radish can be up to 30 cm (12 in) long, depending on the variety, and has a similar taste and texture to ordinary radish. It is added to stewed dishes, grated and mixed with finely chopped chillies as a relish, pickled in a solution of soy sauce, or thinly sliced as a garnish. The leaves can also be eaten raw in a salad or sautéed.

Dashi Made from dried kelp (kombu) and dried fish (bonito), this is the basic stock used in Japanese cooking. It is available as granules or a powder which are dissolved in hot water to make up the stock.

Eggplant (aubergine) Native to Asia, eggplants come in a variety of shapes, sizes and colours. Tiny pea eggplants are small, fat, green balls which grow in clusters, and can be bitter in flavour. They are used whole in Thai curries or raw in salads. Slender eggplants, also called baby and Japanese eggplants, are used in Indian curries and vegetarian cooking, where they readily absorb the flavours; the common eggplant used in Western cooking can be substituted.

Farfalle This is a small butterfly- or bow tie-shaped pasta.

Fenugreek An important ingredient in Indian cooking, the dried seeds from this plant of the pea family are small, oblong and orange-brown. They are usually gently dry-fried, then ground and added to a curry paste; in Sri Lanka a few seeds are often used whole in seafood curries. Use sparingly, as the flavour can be bitter. Pungently flavoured fenugreek leaves are cooked in vegetable dishes or ground as part of a tandoori marinade.

Feta cheese A soft, white cheese ripened in brine. Originally made from the milk of sheep or goats, but often now made with the more economical cow's milk. Feta cheese tastes sharp and salty and can be eaten as an appetiser, cooked or marinated. It is an ingredient in traditional Greek salad.

Fish sauce This thin, clear, brown, salty sauce with its characteristic 'fishy' smell and pungent flavour is an important ingredient in Thai, Vietnamese, Laotian and Cambodian cooking. It is made from prawns (shrimp) or small fish that have been fermented in the sun. Its strong flavour diminishes when cooked with other ingredients. It is also used in dipping sauces. There is no substitute.

Five-spice powder This fragrant, ready-mixed ground spice blend is used extensively in Chinese cooking. It contains star anise, Szechwan peppercorns, fennel, cloves and cinnamon. Use sparingly, as it can overpower lesser flavours.

Frisée Part of the chicory family, frisée is also known as curly endive or endive. Frisée is a winter salad green and has a mild, bitter flavour. It is well-matched with robust flavours such as bacon, walnuts or mustard.

Fusilli This is also known as twist or spiral pasta — good in salads and with meat sauces as the meat gets caught in the spirals.

Gai larn Also known as Chinese broccoli or Chinese kale, has smooth, round stems sprouting large dark green leaves and small, white flowers. The juicy stems, trimmed of most of their leaves, are the piece of the plant which is most commonly eaten. Gai larn has a similar flavour to Western broccoli, but without the characteristic large flower heads.

Galangal root Similar in appearance to its close relative ginger, but it is a pinkish colour and has a distinct peppery flavour. Use fresh galangal if possible. When handling take care not to get the juice on your clothes or hands, as it stains. Dried galangal, sold in slices, must be soaked in hot water before use. It can also be bought sliced and bottled in brine. Galangal powder is also known as Laos powder.

Garam masala This is a mixture of ground spices which usually includes cinnamon, black pepper, coriander, cumin, cardamom, cloves, and mace or nutmeg, although it can sometimes be made with mostly hot spices or with just the more fragrant spices. Commercially made mixtures are available, but garam masala is best freshly made.

Garlic Used in large quantities in all Asian cooking except Japanese. Asian varieties are often smaller and more potent than those used in Western cooking. The pungent flavour is released when a clove is cut; crushing releases maximum flavour. The strength diminishes with cooking. Pickled garlic is used as a garnish and relish.

Garlic chives Also known as Chinese chives, these thick, flat, garlic-scented chives, stronger in flavour than the slender variety used in Western cooking, are particularly prized when topped with the plump, edible flowerbud.

Ginger This spicy tasting root, used fresh, is an indispensable ingredient in every Asian cuisine. Look for firm, unwrinkled roots and store them in a plastic bag in the refrigerator. The brown skin is usually peeled off before use. Ground ginger cannot be substituted for fresh.

Gnocchi Small savoury dumplings made with vegetables or semolina. They are poached and served with sauces.

Gorgonzola A soft, creamy, blue-veined cheese with quite a pungent smell and a strong bite to its taste. It adds richness to pasta dishes but you can choose a milder-flavoured blue cheese, if you prefer a more subtle taste. It melts well and is often used in sauces. If not available, use another blue cheese.

Gremolata or **gremolada** Used to garnish osso buco, is a mixture of finely chopped parsley, lemon zest and garlic.

Gruyère A form of firm Swiss cheese, pale yellow in colour. Gruyère varies from dry and strong-flavoured to a more mild creamy style. The creamy one is preferable in most sauces. Gruyère is an excellent melting cheese which draws hardly any threads. You can use a cheddar as a substitute if you prefer.

Haloumi A salty Middle Eastern cheese made from ewe's milk. The curd is cooked, then matured in brine, often with herbs or spices. It is most often grilled or fried but can also be used in salads or on bread.

Hoisin sauce From China, this thick, red-brown sauce is made from soy beans, garlic, sugar and spices and has a biting, sweet-spicy flavour. It is used in cooking and as a dipping sauce, usually with meat and poultry dishes.

Juniper berries Blackish-purple berries with a resinous flavour. Used in stews and game dishes. To release their flavour, crush the berries in a pestle and mortar or with the end of a rolling pin slightly before use.

Kaffir lime Native to Southeast Asia, this variety of lime tree has fragrant green leaves and bears a dark green, knobbly fruit. The leaves and fruit rind are added to curries and other dishes to give a citrus tang (the fruit is not very juicy and is seldom used).

Remove the coarse central vein from the leaves and tear or shred; pare or grate rind from limes. Leaves and limes are available fresh from Asian food stores; leftover fresh leaves can be frozen in airtight plastic bags. Also available are dried leaves and dried rind; these must be soaked in water before use. Fresh young lemon leaves and strips of zest from a standard lime can be substituted, but the flavour will not be quite the same.

Kecap manis Also known as sweet soy sauce, this thick, dark, sweet soy sauce is used in Indonesian cooking as a seasoning and condiment, particularly with satays. A substitute can be made by gently simmering 250 ml (9 fl oz/1 cup) dark soy sauce with about 6 tablespoons treacle and 3 tablespoons soft brown sugar until the sugar has dissolved.

Kefalotyri cheese A very hard, scalded and cured sheep or goat's milk cheese with a mild flavour. Its use depends on its age. When young, it is a table cheese, at six months old, it is used in cooking, and when more mature, it makes an excellent grating cheese. Parmesan or pecorino can be substituted.

Lasagne sheets Flat or ridged sheets of pasta. Layered with sauces and then baked. Some need pre-cooking before layering. Follow the manufacturer's instructions.

Lemongrass This long, grass-like herb has a citrus aroma and taste. Trim the base, remove the tough outer layers and finely slice, chop or pound the white interior. For pastes and salads, use the tender, white portion just above the root. The whole stem, trimmed, washed thoroughly and bruised with the back of a knife, can be added to simmering curries and soups (remove before serving). Dried lemongrass is rather flavourless so it is better to use lemon rind, although this will not duplicate the flavour of lemongrass.

Lentils du Puy This tiny, dark green lentil is considered a delicacy in France and is relatively expensive. Unlike most other lentils, lentils du puy keep their shape and have a firm texture after cooking. They are used mostly for making salads and side dishes.

Macaroni Straight or curved (elbows) short lengths of pasta with a hole through the centre. Often used in baked dishes.

Marsala A fortified wine from Marsala in Sicily that comes in varying degrees of dryness and sweetness. Dry Marsalas are used in savoury dishes and drunk as an aperitif. Sweet ones are suitable for putting in dessert dishes such as zabaglione and are also served with desserts.

Mascarpone A cream cheese originally from Lombardia. Made with cream rather than milk, it is very high in fat. Mascarpone is generally used in desserts such as tiramisu or instead of cream in sauces. Widely available, it is usually sold in tubs.

Mirin A sweet spirit-based rice liquid used predominantly in Japanese cooking in basting sauces and marinades, but also good in salad dressings and stir-fries. Sweet sherry can be substituted.

Miso A staple of the Japanese diet, this is a protein-rich, thick, fermented paste made from soy beans and other ingredients, including wheat, rice or barley. It has a pungent, wine-like taste. Generally, the lighter the paste, the milder the flavour. It varies in colour from white, yellow, light brown to brown and red. The many varieties include red, brown, light brown, yellow and white, each having a distinctive flavour and varying in texture from smooth to chunky. Miso is used in soups, sauces, marinades and dips.

Mozzarella cheese A soft, smooth cheese, pale yellow in colour. It has a mild, sweet flavour and is excellent for recipes that have the cheese melted on top and for use in salads.

Nigella seeds Also called black onion seeds, these seeds have a nutty, peppery flavour. They are used in the Middle East and India as a seasoning for vegetables, legumes and breads. Often confused with black cumin.

Nori This is the most common form of dried seaweed used in Japanese and Korean cooking. It comes in paper-thin sheets, plain or roasted. Before use it can be toasted lightly over a naked flame to freshen and produce a nutty flavour. Keep in an airtight container or in the freezer.

Okra Also known as ladies' finger, this vegetable of African origin is a narrow, 5-sided seed pod, pointed at one end and containing small white seeds; it has a gelatinous quality when it is cooked. It is much used in Indian cooking where it is added to curries and stir-fries, stuffed with spices and deep-fried, or pickled. It is available fresh in summer, and it is also sold frozen, dried and in cans.

Olive oils Extra virgin and virgin olive oils are pressed without any heat or chemicals and are best used in simple uncooked dishes and for salads. Pure olive oil can be used for cooking or deep-frying. Different varieties of olives are grown all over Italy and the oil of each region has a distinctive taste. Tuscan oil tends to be full-bodied and peppery; Ligurian oil is pale and subtle; Pugliese and Sicilian oils are fruity and sharp. Try different types to find a variety you like on salads.

Olives Table olives are the fruit of an evergreen tree. There are many types, all named for different reasons. For example, Ligurian are named after the region they come from and Sicilian after their curing style. Others, including Cerignola, have names which refer to the variety of olive. Green and black olives are different in flavour but can be used interchangeably in recipes unless the final colour is a factor. Jet-black pitted olives are often dyed and have a duller flavour so avoid these if at all possible.

Oyster sauce This is a thick, smooth, deep brown sauce with a rich, salty, slightly sweet flavour. Although it is made from oysters and soy sauce, it does not have a fishy taste. Commonly used in Cantonese cooking, oyster sauce is also used in Thai dishes that have a Chinese influence. It is a rich, thick, salty sauce made from dried oysters, and it is used for both flavour and colour. Readily available in supermarkets, once opened it should be stored in the refrigerator. Vegetarian oyster sauce has a similar taste and is made using mushrooms as its flavour base instead of oysters.

Palm sugar Made from the boiled down sap of several kinds of palm tree, including the palmyra palm and the sugar palm of India, palm sugar ranges in colour from pale golden to deep brown. It is sold in block form or in jars. Palm sugar is thick and crumbly and can be gently melted or grated before adding to sauces or dressings. Soft brown sugar can be substituted.

Pancetta Cured belly of pork, somewhat like streaky bacon. Available in flat pieces or rolled up (arrotolata), and both smoked and unsmoked. Generally used, either sliced or cut into cubes, as an ingredient in many dishes.

Parma ham This prosciutto comes from traditionally reared pigs fed on the whey from making Parmigiano Reggiano. It has a sweet taste and is only flavoured with salt. Can be identified by the stamp on the skin showing the five-pointed star of the Dukes of Parma. Other prosciutto can be used if Parma ham is unavailable.

Parmesan cheese A hard granular, light yellow cheese with a very strong flavour which blends extremely well with meat, tomato and vegetable sauces as well as some creamy sauces and soups. It is not generally used with mushroom sauces or seafood. Parmesan cheese keeps for months if wrapped tightly before refrigeration.

Parmigiano-reggiano The best type of parmesan with a good strong flavour. It is available at most delicatessens. The rind should have its name marked on it. If you can't get it, try Grana. If you can't find either of these, use the block parmesan available from the dairy section of most supermarkets. Avoid ready-grated parmesan.

Passata Meaning 'puréed', this most commonly refers to a smooth uncooked tomato pulp bought in tins or jars. Best without added herbs and flavourings.

Pecorino cheese A hard granular cheese, pale yellow, darkening with maturity. It has a stronger, more piquant, tangy taste than parmesan and can be used as a substitute for parmesan if you enjoy the biting flavour. Like parmesan, it stores for a long time. Made from sheep's milk and always by the same method, although the result varies according to the milk and ageing process. Pecorino Romano is a well-known hard variety from Lazio and Sardinia. One of Italy's most popular cheeses, virtually every region produces a version.

Penne Straight short lengths with a smooth or ridged surface, with a wide hole through the middle. Ends are cut at an angle. Retain sauce well.

Plum sauce This sweet-sour sauce is used in Chinese cooking and as a dip with fried meats and snacks. It is made from plums, garlic, ginger, sugar, vinegar and spices.

Polenta The name of the dish and also the ingredient itself, which is ground corn. The cornmeal comes in different grades of coarseness. Finer varieties are better in cakes, and coarse ones to accompany stews. There is also a white cornmeal. These ground, dried corn kernels are a staple in Northern Italy. Polenta is most often made into a porridge and flavoured by mixing in butter and Parmesan. After it is cooked, it can also be spread into a thin layer in a dish, then allowed to set before frying or grilling and being served with vegetables or with toppings as an appetiser.

Porcini The Italian name for a cep or boletus mushroom. Used in Italian and French cooking, these have a brown cap and a thick white stem. Also known as cep mushrooms, they come fresh or dried. Usually bought dried and reconstituted in boiling water, but available fresh in the spring and autumn. Soak dried ones in warm water, then rinse.

The strained soaking water can be used. Dried porcini have a strong flavour and should be used sparingly. Good in risottos and omelettes.

Preserved lemons These are lemons pickled in salt and spices. They need to be rinsed before use and the pulp removed and discarded. They are used mainly in North African cuisine to flavour couscous and traditional tagine dishes.

Prosciutto The Italian name for ham. Prosciutto crudo is cured ham and includes Parma ham and San Daniele. Prosciutto cotto is cooked ham.

Provolone Curd cheese made from cows' milk. The curds are spun and worked into large pear- or tube-shaped cheeses, then immersed in brine and bound with string. Available fresh or matured and eaten as a table cheese or used in cooking.

Purple or holy basil (bai kaphrao) Narrow, dark, purple-reddish tinged leaves with a pungent, clove-like taste. It is added to stir-fries and strong flavoured curries.

Radicchio A salad leaf of the chicory family with slightly bitter red leaves. There are several varieties: radicchio di Castelfranco, di Chioggia and rosso di Verona are similar to a red cabbage with round leaves; radicchio di Treviso has longer, pointed leaves. Bear in mind the bitterness before adding too many leaves to a mixed salad; you may need sweeter green leaves to offset the flavour.

Ras-el-hanout A North African spice blend comprising up to twenty-seven ingredients including powdered cumin, cinnamon, cardamom, ginger, turmeric, nutmeg, cloves, rosebuds, peppercorns and oregano. Traditionally, it also contains aphrodisiacs such as the Spanish fly beetle.

Ravioli and **tortellini** Pasta shapes with a variety of fillings including vegetable, chicken and meat. Buy them fresh or dried or make your own. They are cooked separately and usually served with mild sauces that don't overwhelm the flavour of the filling.

Red Asian shallots Small reddish-purple onions, these grow in bulbs, like garlic, and are sold in segments that look like large cloves of garlic. They have a concentrated flavour and are easy to slice and grind. If unavailable, substitute French shallots or brown or red onions.

Rice vinegar This clear, pale yellow, mild and sweet-tasting vinegar is made from fermented rice. Diluted white wine vinegar or cider vinegar can be substituted.

Rice wine Chinese rice wine, also known as Shaosing, is amber-coloured with a rich, sweetish taste. It adds flavour and aroma to a variety of Chinese dishes and is also used in marinades and sauces. Dry sherry can be substituted, but grape wines are not suitable.

Ricotta A moist, fine, white cheese with a sweet, delicate flavour. The texture is quite creamy. Made by recooking the whey left over from making other cheeses and draining it in baskets. It is produced as a by-product of many different types of cheese and varies in fat content. Hard, salted versions are available and there is also a ricotta made from buffalo milk. Fresh ricotta cut from a wheel has a better texture and flavour than that sold in tubs It is very good for use in the fillings for pasta dishes such as cannelloni and is quite often used in the cooking of sweet dishes.

Risotto rice Round-grained, very absorbent rice, cultivated in northern Italy. Risotto rice comes in four categories, classified not by quality but by the size of each grain. The smallest, Riso comune (common rice) is very quick to cook (12–13 minutes), and is ideal for rice pudding. Semifino rice includes varieties like vialone nano and cooks in about 15 minutes. Fino takes a minute longer and has more bite. The largest, Superfino, includes arborio and carnaroli and takes about 20 minutes.

Rocket This salad green, also known as arugula, rugula or roquette is native to the Mediterranean. The peppery flavour increases as the leaves grow. Served over cooked pizzas, or in a mixed green salad.

Romano cheese A hard granular cheese with a biting flavour. It has small holes throughout and is golden yellow, darkening with maturity. Sometimes it is used as a substitute for parmesan cheese. Like parmesan, it is often finely grated or shaved for use as a garnish to enhance the flavour of pasta dishes.

Rosewater This distilled essence, extracted from roses, is used in the eastern Mediterranean to perfume sweets such as Turkish delight and other sweet dishes, as well as drinks.

Saffron powder and threads Made from the dried, thread-like stigmas of the saffron crocus, this costly spice adds a vivid yellow colour and subtle flavour to food. It is available as bright orange threads (sealed in small glass jars or tiny plastic packets) or ground into powder (the powder is often adulterated and of inferior quality).

Sambal oelek This is a hot paste made from fresh red chillies mashed and mixed with salt and vinegar. It is used as a relish in Indonesian and Malaysian cooking, and can be used as a substitute for fresh chillies in most recipes. Covered, it will keep for months in the refrigerator. It is available ready-made.

Seaweed This can be bought fresh from some fishmongers or dried from specialist supermarkets, health-food shops and Japanese food shops. Look in the Japanese section. Soak dried seaweed to soften it.

Semolina This is the product obtained from the first milling of wheat, usually the very hard durum wheat. Semolina can be coarse, medium or fine and is used for making pasta, gnocchi and some puddings or cakes. Although it is tough and doesn't break down into mush when cooked, it still manages to produce a light texture. Semolina is good for dusting fresh pasta to stop it sticking.

Sesame oil This dark amber, very aromatic oil is pressed from toasted white sesame seeds and has a strong, rich, nutty flavour. It is used as a flavouring in Chinese, Korean and Japanese dishes. It is not used for frying. Store in a cool dark place, but not in the refrigerator where it will turn cloudy. Cold-pressed sesame oil, pressed from the raw seed, has little flavour and cannot be used as a substitute.

Sesame seeds The tiny, oval, oil-rich seeds of an annual herb, sesame seeds are used throughout Asia for their flavour and their high protein content.

White sesame seeds are the most common. Toasted and crushed, they are an essential ingredient in Japanese and Korean dressings, dipping sauces and marinades. Whole seeds are used as a garnish for both savoury and sweet dishes and breads, and pressed seeds are made into a variety of pastes.

Japanese sesame seeds are plumper and have a nuttier flavour than other sesame seeds.

Black sesame seeds have a more earthy taste. They are used in sesame and seaweed sprinkle, a Japanese condiment, and in some Chinese desserts.

Shiitake mushrooms are closely related to the Chinese black mushroom and are the most commonly used mushrooms in Japan. They have a rich smoky flavour, are grown on the bark of a type of oak tree, and are used fresh and dried. The fresh mushroom has a fleshy, golden-brown cap and a woody stem.

Shrimp paste Also known as blachan, this type of shrimp paste, used in the cooking of Thailand, Malaysia and Indonesia, is made from prawns or shrimps that have been dried, salted and pounded. Sold in blocks, it has a very pungent odour and when opened should be wrapped in plastic, sealed in an airtight container and stored in the refrigerator or freezer (this is to reduce the smell as the paste itself does not require refrigeration). Use sparingly; always roast or fry before adding to a dish.

Silverbeet Also known as Swiss chard, silverbeet is often confused with spinach. The large, crinkly leaves have more texture than spinach and are suited to longer cooking because they don't collapse like spinach. Both the leaves and stems can be eaten but need to be blanched before being braised, gratinéed or used as pie fillings.

Snake beans Also called long beans and yard-long beans, this legume grows wild in tropical Africa, where it probably originated. Growing to 38 cm (15 in) and more long, with a crunchy texture and similar taste to green beans, it comes in 2 varieties: pale green with slightly fibrous flesh, and darker green with firmer flesh. Use fresh; snip off the ends and cut into bite-sized pieces. Stringless green beans can be substituted.

Soffritto The flavour base for many soups, stews and risottos. Soffritto is a mixture of fried ingredients like onion, celery, carrot, garlic, pancetta and herbs. It means literally to 'under-fry' and the mixture should be sweated rather than coloured.

Soy sauce Soy sauce is made from fermented soy beans, roasted grain (usually wheat, but sometimes barley or rice) and salt. Dark-coloured with a rich, salty flavour, it is widely used in Asian cooking, and is essential for flavour and colour in many dishes.

Light soy sauce is thinner, lighter in flavour and pale golden in colour. It is suitable for soups, seafood, vegetable dishes and dipping sauces.

Japanese soy sauce, also known as shoshoyu, is less salty and much lighter and sweeter than standard soy sauce, but not thick. It is used in cooking and as a condiment. Refrigerate after opening.

Spring onions Also called green onions and scallions, these are immature onions which are pulled before the bulb has started to form and sold in bunches with the roots intact. Discard the roots and base of the stem, and wash stem leaves well before use. Spring onions add colour and a mild onion flavour and they need little cooking.

Squid ink Used to colour and flavour pasta and risotto. The ink is stored in a sac that can be removed from whole squid and cuttlefish or bought in sachets from fishmongers or delicatessens.

Star anise The dried, star-shaped seed pod of a tree native to China, star anise adds a distinctive aniseed taste to long-simmered meat and poultry dishes and is one of the components of five spice powder. Available whole or ground.

Sumac The reddish berry has a sour, fruity flavour and is processed to form various grades of powder. Used mainly in Syria and Lebanon for adding to or sprinkling on meat, especially kebabs, fish and vegetables, to add flavour and colour.

Sun-dried tomatoes These are widely available either dry and loosely packed, or in jars in oil. The dry variety need to be rehydrated before use. To do this, cover them with boiling water and leave for about ten minutes. If buying sun-dried tomatoes in oil, choose the variety in olive oil as you can use the oil for cooking to add extra flavour to your dish.

Tahini An oily paste made from ground sesame seeds, tahini adds a strong nutty flavour and is very popular in the eastern Mediterranean.

Taleggio cheese A mountain cheese originally from the Italian Alps near Bergamo, but now also made in other regions. Taleggio is a very good table and cooking cheese and should be eaten young — its flavour becomes more acidic with age. It is made in squares and has a pink-yellow crust and creamy centre.

Tomato passata This is a bottled tomato sauce commonly used in Italian cooking. The sauce is made with fresh, ripe tomatoes which are peeled, seeded and slowly cooked down with basil, onion and garlic. The thickened sauce is then passed through a sieve before being bottled.

Tomatoes, tinned Several types of tinned tomatoes are available. Whole ones often need to be chopped before use or broken down with the edges of a spoon as you cook them. Chopped ones are cut into small cubes. Most tinned tomatoes are a plum-shaped variety called San Marzano.

Tamarind The tropical tamarind tree bears fruit in pods like large, brown beans. The fruit is tart-tasting and has fibrous flesh and a flat stone at the centre. An essential flavour in many Asian dishes, tamarind is available in bottles as tamarind concentrate (also known as tamarind purée), a rich brown, ready-to-use liquid, and as blocks of compressed pulp that has to be soaked, kneaded and seeded.

Thai basil (bai horapha) Slightly serrated green leaves on purple stems. It has a sweet anise flavour and is used in stir-fries, red and green curries, shredded in salads and as a garnish for soups.

Tofu Also called bean curd, tofu is a processed extract of soy beans. It is an excellent source of protein, and is available fresh or deep-fried.

Fresh tofu comes in two forms: a soft, white variety, also known as silken tofu, which is cut into cubes and used in Japanese dishes; and a firmer variety which is cut into cubes, wedges or slices and deep-fried. Both are available in blocks sealed in plastic; once opened, store in the refrigerator in water that is changed daily and use within a few days. Fresh tofu has little flavour when uncooked, but absorbs other flavours.

Tofu pouches, also known as inari, are deep-fried, thin slices of tofu, crisp on the outside and dry on the inside, that can be cut open to form bags. In Japan inari are stuffed with vegetables or vinegar-seasoned rice; they can also be added whole or shredded to soups and other dishes.

Tofu puffs are cubes of tofu that have been deep-fried until they are puffed and golden. They can be cooked in their own right with a strongly flavoured sauce, used in vegetarian cooking and braised dishes, added to salads or used a garnish for soups, or cut open and filled.

Turmeric This is a bitter-tasting spice which comes from the root of a plant related to ginger. It is used for its intense, bright yellow-orange colour and, dried and ground, it is the main ingredient in many curry powders. The fresh root is used in the same way as fresh ginger root — peel away the skin and finely slice, chop or grate the flesh. Store in a plastic bag in the refrigerator.

Vietnamese mint Also called laksa leaf and Cambodian mint, this trailing herb with narrow, pointed, pungent-tasting leaves does not belong to the mint family, despite its common name. It has a flavour resembling coriander but slightly sharper, and is eaten raw in salads, or as an accompaniment to most Vietnamese dishes.

Vine leaves Young leaves from the grape vine, blanched then preserved in brine. Available in packets, jars and cans.

Wasabi Also known as Japanese horseradish, this is a pungent paste made from the knobbly green root of the wasabi, a plant native to Japan. It is used as a condiment with seafoods and is extremely hot, so use sparingly.

Water chestnuts These white fleshed roots of a variety of water grass are prized for their semi-sweet taste and crisp texture, which is retained when cooked. They are used throughout China and Southeast Asia in both savoury and sweet dishes. Available canned and sometimes fresh; cut off the woody base, peel away papery skin, and cover in water to stop discolouring.

Watercress Watercress was introduced into Asia by the British. Its peppery flavour is added to soups and steamed vegetables in Chinese cooking, and it is used in salads in Thailand, Laos and Vietnam and as a garnish in Japan.

Wrappers These are thin pieces of dough used to wrap bite-sized savoury fillings. They are available fresh and frozen; defrost before use. When filling, work with one at a time and keep the others covered with a damp cloth to prevent them from drying out.

Won ton wrappers are thin squares of a wheat flour and egg dough. Spring roll wrappers are square or round, and made from a wheat flour and egg dough.

Gow gee wrappers are round and made from a wheat flour and water dough.

Dried rice paper wrappers are paper-thin, round, square or triangular, and are made from a dough of rice flour, water and salt. Brush them on both sides with water before use so they soften and become pliable.

Za'atar Popular in Turkey and North Africa, this spice blend is a mixture of toasted sesame seeds, dried thyme, sumac and salt. The proportions vary from region to region. It is used as a seasoning for meats and vegetables and is also mixed with oil to dip bread into, or sprinkled on flatbread, such as Lebanese or pitta bread, that has been brushed with olive oil and then lightly toasted.

Zucchini The Italian name for courgettes. Varieties include the common dark green ones, pale green ones known as 'white' and yellow ones. Some are long and thin, others are ball-shaped. Tiny 'baby' courgettes are also available as are their flowers.

Zucchini flowers The yellow or orange flowers of the zucchini (courgette) plant. These can be found either attached to a stalk (male) or at the end of tiny zucchini (female). Before you use them, gently open out the flowers and check the insides to make sure there are no bugs.

KITCHEN EQUIPMENT

Stocking a kitchen is a personal thing based on how much cooking, and what kind of cooking, you like to do.

It is not always necessary to buy a whole set of knives — instead, it is better to have a few good ones that will last. Similarly, buy two or three good-quality saucepans and frying pans rather than a whole set of inferior ones. Kitchen equipment can be built up over time.

BASIC KNIVES

Kitchen knives Buy the best you can afford. Make sure they are comfortable to hold and the handle and blade are well balanced. Put them in a block to keep them sharp — if they bash around against things in a drawer they will blunt quickly. You will need one large knife for chopping, one medium knife and one small serrated knife for fruit and tomatoes — if you can, find one with a pointed end that will easily pierce the skins. A serrated bread knife is used for slicing loaves. A flat-bladed knife is not a good substitute as it squashes the loaf rather than cuts it. Use a steel to keep all your knife edges sharp, and sharpen before every use.
Scissors Kitchen scissors should have tough blades, preferably with a serrated edge. The lower handle should be large enough to grip with three fingers. Poultry shears have a cutting point near the pivot for gripping bones as you cut them.

SPECIALIST KNIVES

Specialist knives These are needed if you plan on being more adventurous with your cooking. A **mezzaluna** is a double-handled knife with one or two curved blades, which are rocked from side to side to chop herbs. An **oyster knife** is essential for opening oysters and other shellfish. Its short, flat blade with two cutting edges slides easily between shells. For basic meat preparation, a **boning knife** with a very strong, thin blade will help. A **citrus zester** and **canelle knife**

easily peel off zest in thin or thick shreds using a row of small holes or a deeper, V-shaped cutting edge.

SAUCEPANS AND FRYING PANS

Saucepans These should be good quality and the most expensive ones that you can afford. There is a huge range on the market but stainless steel with a sandwich base (stainless steel sandwiching a metal such as copper that conducts heat well) are a good bet for even heat distribution. Stainless steel is also non-reactive (it will not be affected by the use of an acid such as lemon juice). Choose pans with comfortable handles (check these do not heat up) and lids that have a tight seal. You will need one large pan and a couple of smaller ones. A pasta boiler with a fitted drainer is useful for cooking pasta.
Frying pans Like saucepans, these should be good quality. Cast-iron ones are heavy but last a very long time. Non-stick ones have to be used with wooden or plastic implements. An ovenproof handle is useful for making anything that needs to be finished in the oven or under a grill (broiler).

OVENWARE

Ovenware These should be good quality and be able to be used on the stovetop and in the oven. Casseroles need to be heavy enough to absorb and retain heat and also need tight-fitting lids so as not to let any moisture escape. Cast-iron or enamelled ones (with cast-iron or steel underneath) are generally the best as they conduct heat well. You will need several sizes as it is important that the recipe fits the casserole. Baking and gratin dishes should be fully ovenproof and able to withstand high heat. Enamel, cast-iron and stoneware are good options.
Roasting tin Should be made from stainless steel or anodized aluminium so the tins can be used over a heat source without buckling. One with a rack is useful so meat and poultry can be roasted and the fat and juices collected underneath.

GENERAL EQUIPMENT

Chopping board An essential piece of equipment, whether wooden or polyethylene. Whichever you choose, your board should be kept spotlessly clean.

Graters These vary in shape, but the important part is the cutting edge, which should be very sharp. A box grater doesn't slip easily and is good for large quantities.

Potato masher Potato mashers work on all cooked vegetables. Old-style mashers with a cut grid often work better.

Tin opener It is worth buying a good-quality one that grips properly.

Lemon squeezer Available in glass, ceramic, plastic and wood. The squeezers with a container underneath for collecting the juice are the most useful.

Sieves These come in a range of sizes. Larger colanders are best for draining. Round-bottomed stainless steel sieves have a mesh suitable for sifting and puréeing and nylon mesh sieves are for fine sifting and puréeing.

KITCHEN UTENSILS

Spoons Useful for stirring, mixing and beating. Wooden spoons are good because they do not conduct heat, do not scratch and are non-reactive. Metal spoons are used for folding ingredients. A perforated spoon is useful for draining. Ladles are made for serving liquids.

Pastry brush Made with either nylon or natural bristles and can be flat or round.

Peeler A good peeler shaves only a thin skin off vegetables.

Rubber spatula This can scrape a bowl completely clean.

Fish slice This needs enough flexibility to be able to slide under things.

ASIAN EQUIPMENT

Wok Buy a carbon steel or pressed steel wok from your local Chinatown as they conduct heat better. Season by rubbing it with salt and hot oil, then wipe it out after each use rather than washing it — this will build up a non-stick surface over time. Use with a wok charn for stir-frying. This is a shovel-like spatula ideal for tossing food around the curved side of the wok.

Chopper/cleaver Used for chopping through bones, as well as an all-purpose knife. Buy a good heavy one for chopping and a lighter one for slicing.

Metal or bamboo tongs Very useful for turning things over, or lifting things out of boiling liquids.

Clay pot Glazed on the inside and used for slow cooking as it heats up evenly all over.

Steamers Bamboo stackable steamers allow food to be cooked in steam.

SPECIALIST EQUIPMENT

Mortar and pestle A bowl (mortar) with a slightly rough surface and a crushing stick (pestle) that fits the curvature of the bowl and provides the second grinding surface. Very good for crushing seeds, spices and cloves of garlic.

Salt and pepper mills (grinders) Buy a pepper mill with a steel grinding mechanism for efficiency and an adjustable grind.

SCALES, MEASURING CUPS AND THERMOMETERS

Scales You only need one good-quality set of scales. Choose one with both metric and imperial weights.

Measuring jugs Plastic and glass jugs are best to use as you can read them easily. Choose one with the calibrations visible.

Measuring cups Often used instead of scales for dry and liquid measures. Available in fractions and multiples of cup measures.

Measuring spoons Available in sets ranging from ¼ teaspoon to 1 tablespoon. Dry measurements should be levelled off with a knife to be accurate.

Thermometers These are essential for accurate oil measurements. An oven thermometer is used to ensure that the thermostat is registering accurately. These are important to ensure good results.

Kitchen knives

Mezzaluna

Saucepans

Enamelled casseroles

Glass bowls

Wooden spoons

Metal measuring cups

Box graters

Bamboo steamer

Mortar and pestle

Food processors

Blenders and grinders

PASTA

We have finally discovered a secret the Italians have known for centuries... it is difficult to go wrong with pasta. What could be simpler or more appealing than butter and shavings of parmesan melting over a bowl of fresh tagliatelle? Pasta can be as simple or as extravagant as you like — depending upon its accompanying sauce.

PASTA BASICS

There are good reasons why pasta is such a popular food: it's cheap, it's quick and easy to prepare, it's delicious, it's nutritious and it's amazingly versatile. You can dress up pasta for a dinner party, or serve it simply, with parmesan. You can eat pasta every day of the week and never tire of it. Pasta goes well with anything, including breads, vegetables and salads.

TYPES OF PASTA

There are five main shapes of pasta: short, curly, long, filled and flat. There are good reasons for matching one pasta shape with a particular sauce. Apart from the traditional regional preference for a local shape, its ability to hold and support the sauce is all important. With up to 300 different pasta shapes, it can be confusing knowing which sauce to serve with which pasta shape. A basic rule to remember is that a chunky pasta is best with a chunky sauce and a thin pasta is best with a thin sauce. Chunky pasta shapes enable you to pick up the sauce with the pasta. Smooth, slender pasta shapes will not hold a chunky sauce but will suit a sauce of olive oil or a fresh tomato sauce. Long pastas aren't suited to chunky sauces as the chunks end up at the bottom of the bowl and won't stick to the pasta. Filled pasta should be eaten with simple sauces that won't overshadow their own flavour.

Long thin pastas such as bavettini, linguine, spaghetti, tagliarini, vermicelli and bucatini go well with simple sauces such as garlic and oil, which stick to their long lengths without falling off. Usually bought as durum wheat or dried egg pasta. Long pasta does not need to be broken before cooking but can be folded into the pan — it will soften as it hits the boiling water.

Pasta ribbons are long flat pastas such as tagliatelle, fettucine, mafaldine, tagliarini and pappardelle. They go well with creamy sauces like mushroom, prosciutto or seafood as the finer textured sauces stick better to their lengths. Flat pasta is usually available both fresh and dried. Fresh ribbons are made from egg pasta; dried pasta are made from durum wheat, with or without egg.

Pasta shapes are usually made from durum wheat. They include spiral shapes like fusilli, shell shapes like conchiglie, as well as rotelle (wheels), lumache (snails), orecchiette (ears), farfalle (butterflies), casareccie (small twists) and ditali (thimbles). They go well with thick, chunky meat or tomato sauces, which get caught in their shape.

Tube-shaped pastas include short tubes such as maccheroni, rigatoni, penne and tubetti, and long tubes such as candele, maccaronelli, ziti and zitoni. They are eaten with meat ragùs and tomato sauces. The tubes catch the sauce in their holes. Long pasta such as ziti, are also used to line dishes and make timbalo and pasticcio. These pastas tend to be dried and are made from durum wheat.

Soup pastas are called pastina and include shaped pastas like stelline (stars), alfabeto, ditalini (little tubes), orzo (barley), semi di melon (melon seeds) and anellini (little rings). Pastina are small and are added at the end of the cooking time. Pastina are sold dried and are made from durum wheat.

Filled pasta includes ravioli, raviolini and agnolotti (stuffed squares of pasta); tortelloni and tortellini (stuffed squares or rounds of pasta); capelletti (stuffed hat-like shapes of pasta); and agnolini (similar to capelletti). The fillings for these pastas vary.

Cannelloni was originally made with sheets of pasta but is now made into large short tubes, which can be stuffed using a spoon or piping bag. It is made from egg pasta.

Lasagne is the name of sheets of pasta that are baked in dishes such as lasagne al forno. Some sheets are flat; others have a ridged or curled edge, which helps give lightness to the pasta layer. Lasagne is usually made from egg pasta and may be coloured with spinach (lasagne verde).

Buckwheat pasta is made with buckwheat and 00 flour from the Valtellina valley in Lombardy. It is cut into flat noodles and is cooked with potato cubes, beans or cabbage and cheese to make pizzocheri.

Coloured pastas are made with added natural colours to give them different flavours and visual appeal. Cuttlefish or squid ink is often used to make black pasta (nero) and spinach for green (verdi). Red pasta (tomato), pink pasta (beetroot) and brown pasta (mushroom) are also available.

FRESH AND DRIED PASTA

A lot of information about the pasta contained in the packet can be gleaned from its name. A name ending in -ricce means the pasta has a wavy edge; -nidi indicates that the lengths are formed into nests; -rigate means ridged and -lisce, smooth surfaced. If the name of the pasta ends with -oni, this indicates a larger size· for example, conchiglioni are large conchiglie. Likewise, -ini and -ette means smaller versions, as in farfallini. However, names vary from manufacturer to manufacturer and book to book... one man's tortelloni can be another man's agnolotti.

Many people think that fresh pasta must be better than dried. This is not always the case — some sauces are better teamed with fresh pasta and some are best with dried. Fresh pasta works well with rich sauces made from cream, butter and cheese, because its soft texture absorbs the sauce. Alfredo is one of the nicest sauces to serve on fresh home-made pasta, as is a simple topping of butter and grated parmesan. Dried pasta is the one to choose if you're serving a heartier, tomato-based sauce. If your sauce has olives, anchovies, chilli, meat or seafood, you'll almost certainly need dried.

Pasta is a combination of flour, water and sometimes eggs and oil. Pasta made with wholewheat flour is darker. If dried pasta is made with durum wheat flour, it is considered to be of superior quality. Other dried pastas that are available include those made from different flours and cereals such as buckwheat, corn, rice and soya beans. Pastas are sometimes flavoured with a purée of herbs, tomato, spinach or other vegetables.

STORAGE

Dried pasta will last up to six months, stored in an airtight container in a cool dark place. However, dried wholewheat pasta will only last for one month before turning rancid.

Fresh pasta must be refrigerated and won't keep for very long, so buy it as you need it. It can also be wrapped in plastic and frozen for five days. If double wrapped, it will last up to four months. Don't thaw before cooking.

Filled pasta is best bought a day or so before you need it, but some vacuum-packed filled pastas can be kept for up to 3 weeks (check the use-by date). It can be frozen in a single layer between sheets of plastic wrap for up to 3 months but creamy fillings don't freeze well.

QUANTITY

As pasta varies so much in shape, size and type, it is hard to be specific about how much pasta you need per serve. Another highly charged subject as far as pasta aficionados are concerned, is how much pasta each person should be served and, even more controversially, how much sauce should be served on that pasta. As a general guide, use 60 g (2¼ oz) of fresh pasta per person for a starter, and 125 g (4½ oz) for a main dish. You should allow a little bit more if you are using dried (it contains less moisture, so is lighter), about 90 g (3¼ oz) each for a starter and 150 g (5½ oz) per person for a main course.

How much sauce is obviously a matter of personal taste, but the biggest mistake novice cooks make is to use too much sauce: the pasta should be lightly coated, not drenched. When the pasta and sauce are tossed, there shouldn't be extra sauce swimming around at the bottom.

COOKING TIPS

Pasta should be cooked in a large, deep saucepan of water to allow room for expansion and to prevent it sticking together. Allow about 6 litres (24 cups) of water for every 500 g (1 lb 2 oz) pasta, but never use less than 4 litres (16 cups). Filled pasta and large pasta, such as lasagne, will need more water (9–12 litres/36–48 cups), as they are more likely to stick. If you need to cook large amounts of pasta, cook up to 1 kg (2 lb 4 oz) of pasta per saucepan.

Always bring the water to the boil before stirring in the pasta. When the water comes back to the boil, begin timing, stirring often once the pasta softens a little. Test the pasta just prior to the final cooking time.

Adding oil to the pasta while cooking contributes very little, but seasoning the water with a little salt can add to the flavour. This is entirely a matter of personal preference. Unsalted water will come to the boil faster than salted water, so add the salt once the water is boiling. Use a large pan of water, enough so that the pasta has plenty of room to move around, and only add the pasta when the water has reached a rapid boil. Some people like to add a tablespoon of olive oil to help prevent the water boiling over or the pasta sticking together. After the pasta has been added, cover the pan to help bring the water back to the boil as quickly as possible, then remove the lid as soon as the water returns to the boil.

COOKING TIME

Cooking times for pasta vary enormously depending on the size, shape and freshness of the pasta. Generally, the fresher the pasta, the shorter the cooking time. Fresh pasta usually only needs 1–2 minutes. Vacuum-packed fresh pasta from the supermarket requires a little longer — about 6 minutes. Dried pasta varies depending on the size and shape but because it needs rehydrating as well as cooking, it usually takes longer than fresh pasta. For the most accurate times for all pasta, follow the packet instructions.

The best way to ensure pasta is cooked is to taste it. The pasta should be just tender, not at all raw or soft and gluggy.

PERFECT PASTA

Cooked pasta should be al dente, tender but still firm 'to the tooth'. It is important to drain the pasta and then turn it immediately into a heated dish, into the pan with the sauce, or back into its cooking pan. It should never be overdrained, as it needs to be slippery for the sauce to coat it well. Never leave it sitting in the colander or it will become a sticky mass.

Never rinse the pasta unless stated in the recipe: it is usually only rinsed if used in a baked meal or served cold in a salad because the starches released in cooking the pasta help it meld beautifully with the sauce.

A little oil or butter tossed through the drained pasta will stop it sticking together. Alternatively, lightly spray the pasta with some boiling water and toss it gently (it is always a good idea to keep a little of the cooking water for this, in case you overdrain the pasta).

Pasta that is to be used in cold pasta salads should be rinsed under cold water then tossed with a small amount of oil. Cover and refrigerate until ready to use.

Timing can make all the difference between a good pasta meal and a great one. Always read the recipe through first and then coordinate your cooking times. Try to have the sauce ready to dress the pasta as soon as it is cooked, especially if the pasta is fresh (it will continue to cook if it is left to sit around).

SERVING

Timing is essential when preparing a pasta meal. The sauce should be ready as soon as possible after the pasta is cooked because pasta continues to cook if left to sit around and can become soggy and unappetising.

Angel hair pasta

Bucatini

Fettucine

Linguine

Ziti

Spaghetti

onchiglie

Orecchiette

italini

Farfalle

Penne

Orzo

Pasta gnocchi

Cotelli

Cresti di gallo

Fricelli

Rotelle

Garganelli

Fusilli

Elbow macaroni

anolotti

Ravioli

onchiglione

Tortellini

_asagne

Lasagnette

Pappardelle

PENNE CARBONARA

Preparation time 10 minutes
Total cooking time 20 minutes
Serves 4–6

400 g (14 oz) penne
1 tablespoon olive oil
200 g (7 oz) piece pancetta or bacon, cut into
    long thin strips
6 egg yolks
185 ml (6 fl oz/¾ cup) pouring (whipping) cream
75 g (2½ oz/¾ cup) grated parmesan cheese

1 Cook the pasta in a large saucepan of
boiling salted water until al dente. Drain
well and return to the pan to keep warm.

2 Meanwhile, heat the oil in a frying pan
over high heat. Cook the pancetta for about
6 minutes, or until crisp and golden. Remove
with a slotted spoon and drain well on
paper towel.
3 Beat the egg yolks, cream and parmesan
together in a bowl and season well.
4 Pour the egg mixture over the pasta,
tossing gently. Add the pancetta and cook
over very low heat for 30–60 seconds, or
until the sauce thickens and coats the pasta.
Season and serve immediately.
Note Be careful not to cook the pasta over
high heat once you have added the egg
mixture, or the sauce risks being scrambled
by the heat.

PENNE WITH TOMATO AND BASIL SAUCE

Preparation time 15 minutes
Total cooking time 25 minutes
Serves 4

500 g (1 lb 2 oz) penne rigate
4 tablespoons extra virgin olive oil
4 garlic cloves, crushed
4 anchovy fillets, finely chopped
2 small red chillies, seeded and finely chopped
6 large vine-ripened tomatoes, peeled, seeded and diced
4 tablespoons white wine
1 tablespoon tomato paste (concentrated purée)
2 teaspoons sugar
2 tablespoons finely chopped flat-leaf (Italian) parsley

3 tablespoons shredded basil
grated parmesan cheese, to serve (optional)

1 Cook the pasta in a large saucepan of boiling salted water until al dente. Drain well and return the pasta to the pan to keep warm.
2 Meanwhile, heat the oil in a large frying pan over medium heat. Cook the garlic for about 30 seconds. Stir in the anchovy and chilli and cook for a further 30 seconds.
3 Increase the heat to high, add the tomato and cook for 2 minutes. Add the wine, tomato paste and sugar and simmer, covered, for 10 minutes, or until thickened.
4 Toss the tomato sauce and herbs through the pasta. Season and serve with grated parmesan, if desired.

RAVIOLI WITH ROASTED RED CAPSICUM SAUCE

Preparation time 15 minutes
Total cooking time 20 minutes
Serves 4

6 red capsicums (peppers)
625 g (1 lb 6 oz) ravioli
2 tablespoons olive oil
3 garlic cloves, crushed
2 leeks, thinly sliced
1 tablespoon chopped oregano
2 teaspoons soft brown sugar
250 ml (9 fl oz/1 cup) vegetable or chicken stock

1 Cut the capsicum into large flattish pieces and remove the membrane and seeds. Cook, skin side up, under a hot grill (broiler) until the skin blackens and blisters. Cool in a plastic bag, then peel the skin.
2 Cook the pasta in a large saucepan of boiling salted water until al dente. Drain well and return to the pan to keep warm.
3 Meanwhile, heat the olive oil in a frying pan over medium heat. Cook the garlic and leek for 3–4 minutes, or until softened. Add the oregano and brown sugar and stir for 1 minute.
4 Place the capsicum and leek mixture in a food processor or blender, season and process until combined. Add the stock and process until smooth. Gently toss the sauce through the pasta over low heat until warmed through.

PASTA GNOCCHI WITH GRILLED CAPSICUM

Preparation time 15 minutes
Total cooking time 30 minutes
Serves 4–6

6 large red capsicums (peppers), halved
400 g (14 oz) pasta gnocchi (see Note)
2 tablespoons olive oil
1 onion, thinly sliced
3 garlic cloves, finely chopped
2 tablespoons shredded basil leaves
whole basil leaves, to garnish
shaved parmesan cheese, to serve

1 Cut the capsicums into large flattish pieces. Cook, skin side up, under a hot grill (broiler) until the skin blackens and blisters. Cool in a plastic bag, then peel the skin.

2 Cook the pasta in a large saucepan of boiling salted water until al dente. Drain well and return to the pan to keep warm.

3 Meanwhile, heat the oil in a large frying pan, add the onion and garlic and cook over medium heat for 5 minutes, or until soft. Slice 1 capsicum into thin strips and add to the onion mixture.

4 Chop the remaining capsicum, then purée in a food processor until smooth. Add to the onion mixture and cook over low heat for 5 minutes, or until warmed through.

5 Toss together the sauce and pasta. Season, then stir in the shredded basil. Garnish with the basil leaves and serve with shaved parmesan cheese.

Note If pasta gnocchi is similar in shape to potato gnocchi. If unavailable, use conchiglie or orecchiette.

SPAGHETTI VONGOLE

Preparation time 15 minutes +
Total cooking time 30 minutes
Serves 4

1 kg (2 lb 4 oz) baby clams (vongole)
375 g (13 oz) spaghetti
125 ml (4 fl oz/½ cup) extra virgin olive oil
40 g (1½ oz) butter
1 small onion, very finely chopped
6 large garlic cloves, finely chopped
125 ml (4 fl oz/½ cup) dry white wine
1 small red chilli, seeded and finely chopped
15 g (½ oz) chopped flat-leaf (Italian)
    parsley

1 Scrub the clams with a small stiff brush to remove any grit, discarding any that are open or cracked. Soak and rinse the clams in several changes of water over 1 hour, or until the water is clean and free of grit. Drain and set aside.

2 Cook the pasta in a large saucepan of boiling salted water until al dente. Drain well and return to the pan to keep warm.

3 Heat the oil and 1 tablespoon of the butter in a large saucepan over medium heat. Add the onion and half the garlic and cook for 10 minutes, or until lightly golden.

4 Add the wine and cook for 2 minutes. Add the clams, chilli and the remaining butter and garlic. Cook, covered, for 8 minutes, shaking regularly, until the clams pop open. Discard any that are still closed.

5 Stir in the parsley and season. Add the pasta and toss together.

SPAGHETTI PUTTANESCA

Preparation time 10 minutes
Total cooking time 25 minutes
Serves 4

400 g (14 oz) spaghetti
2 tablespoons olive oil
1 onion, finely chopped
2 garlic cloves, finely sliced
1 small red chilli, cored, seeded and sliced
6 anchovy fillets, finely chopped
400 g (14 oz) tinned chopped tomatoes
1 tablespoon fresh oregano, finely chopped
16 black olives, halved and pitted
2 tablespoons baby capers
1 handful basil leaves

1 Cook the pasta in a large saucepan of boiling salted water until al dente. Drain well and return to the pan to keep warm.
2 Heat the olive oil in a large saucepan and add the onion, garlic and chilli. Gently fry for about 8 minutes, or until the onion is soft. Add the anchovies and cook for a further 1 minute.
3 Add the tomato, oregano, olive halves and capers and bring to the boil. Reduce the heat, season with salt and pepper, and leave the sauce to simmer for 3 minutes.
4 Add the spaghetti to the sauce. Toss together well so that the pasta is coated in the sauce. Scatter the basil over the top and serve.

RUOTE WITH LEMON, OLIVES AND BACON

Preparation time 10 minutes
Total cooking time 15 minutes
Serves 4

500 g (1 lb 2 oz) ruote (see Note)
6 bacon slices
125 g (4½ oz/1 cup) black olives, sliced
4 tablespoons lemon juice
2 teaspoons finely grated lemon zest
4 tablespoons olive oil
4 tablespoons chopped flat-leaf (Italian)
  parsley

1 Cook the pasta in a large saucepan of boiling salted water until al dente. Drain well and return to the pan to keep warm.
2 While the pasta is cooking, discard the bacon rind and cut the bacon into thin strips. Cook in a frying pan until lightly browned.
3 In a bowl, combine the black olives, lemon juice, lemon zest, olive oil, chopped parsley and the bacon. Gently toss the olive and bacon mixture through the pasta until it is evenly distributed.
Note Ruote is a pasta resembling wagon wheels. Small chunks of sauce are trapped between the spokes.

MEATBALLS WITH FUSILLI

Preparation time 35 minutes

Total cooking time 30 minutes

Serves 4

750 g (1 lb 10 oz) minced (ground) pork and veal
80 g (2¾ oz/1 cup) fresh breadcrumbs
3 tablespoons freshly grated parmesan cheese
1 onion, finely chopped
2 tablespoons chopped flat-leaf (Italian) parsley
1 egg, beaten
1 garlic clove, crushed
zest and juice of ½ lemon
30 g (1 oz/¼ cup) plain (all-purpose) flour, seasoned
2 tablespoons olive oil
500 g (1 lb 2 oz) fusilli

Sauce
425 g (15 oz) tinned tomato passata (puréed tomatoes)
125 ml (4 fl oz/½ cup) beef stock
125 ml (4 fl oz/½ cup) red wine
2 tablespoons chopped basil
1 garlic clove, crushed

1 Combine the meat, breadcrumbs, parmesan, onion, parsley, egg, garlic, lemon zest and juice in a large bowl and season to taste.
2 Roll tablespoons of the mixture into balls and roll the balls in the seasoned flour.
3 Heat the oil in a large frying pan and fry the meatballs until golden. Remove from the pan and drain well on paper towels. Remove the excess fat and meat juices from the pan.
4 To make the sauce, in the same pan, combine the tomato passata, stock, wine, basil, garlic, salt and pepper. Bring to the boil.
5 Reduce the heat and return the meatballs to the pan. Allow to simmer for 10–15 minutes.
6 Meanwhile, cook the pasta in a saucepan of boiling salted water until al dente. Drain well and serve with meatballs and sauce over the top.

PENNE WITH MUSHROOM AND HERB SAUCE

Preparation time 15 minutes
Total cooking time 25 minutes
Serves 4

2 tablespoons olive oil
500 g (1 lb 2 oz) button mushrooms, sliced
2 garlic cloves, crushed
2 teaspoons chopped marjoram
125 ml (4 fl oz/½ cup) dry white wine
4 tablespoons pouring (whipping) cream
375 g (13 oz) penne
1 tablespoon lemon juice
1 teaspoon finely grated lemon zest
2 tablespoons chopped flat-leaf (Italian) parsley
50 g (1¾ oz/½ cup) grated parmesan cheese

1 Heat the oil in a large heavy-based frying pan over high heat. Add the mushrooms and cook for 3 minutes, stirring constantly to prevent the mushrooms from burning.
2 Add the garlic and marjoram and cook for a further 2 minutes. Add the white wine to the pan, reduce the heat and simmer for 5 minutes or until nearly all the liquid has evaporated. Stir in the cream and cook over low heat for 5 minutes, or until thick.
3 Meanwhile, cook the pasta in a saucepan of boiling salted water until al dente. Drain well and return to the pan to keep warm.
4 Add the lemon juice, zest, parsley and half the parmesan to the sauce. Season to taste. Toss the pasta through the sauce and sprinkle with the remaining parmesan.

PENNE ALL'ARRABBIATA

Preparation time 10 minutes
Total cooking time 30 minutes
Serves 4

2 tablespoons olive oil
2 large garlic cloves, thinly sliced
1–2 dried chillies
800 g (1 lb 12 oz) tinned tomatoes
400 g (14 oz) penne
1 basil sprig, torn into pieces

1 Cook the pasta in a large saucepan of boiling salted water until al dente. Drain well and return to the pan to keep warm.
2 Meanwhile, heat the olive oil in a saucepan over low heat. Add the garlic and chillies, turning the chillies over during cooking. Add the tomatoes and season. Cook, breaking up the tomatoes with a wooden spoon, for about 20 minutes, or until thick.
3 Add the basil to the sauce and toss with the pasta. Season to taste.

LINGUINE PESTO

Preparation time 15 minutes
Total cooking time 15 minutes
Serves 4–6

Pesto
100 g (3½ oz) basil
2 garlic cloves, crushed
40 g (1½ oz/¼ cup) pine nuts, toasted
185 ml (6 fl oz/¾ cup) olive oil

50 g (1¾ oz/½ cup) freshly grated parmesan
    cheese, plus extra, to serve
500 g (1 lb 2 oz) linguine

1 To make the pesto, process the basil, garlic and pine nuts together in a food processor. With the motor running, add the oil in a steady stream until mixed to a smooth paste.
2 Transfer the mixture to a bowl, stir in the parmesan cheese and season to taste.
3 Cook the pasta in a large saucepan of boiling salted water until al dente. Drain well and return to the pan to keep warm.
4 Toss enough of the pesto through the pasta to coat well. Serve sprinkled with parmesan.
Note Refrigerate any leftover pesto in an airtight jar for up to a week. Cover the surface with a layer of oil. Freeze for up to 1 month.

SPAGHETTINI WITH GARLIC AND CHILLI

Preparation time 10 minutes
Total cooking time 20 minutes
Serves 4–6

500 g (1 lb 2 oz) spaghettini
125 ml (4 fl oz/½ cup) extra virgin olive oil
2–3 garlic cloves, finely chopped
1–2 red chillies, seeded and finely chopped
3 tablespoons chopped flat-leaf (Italian) parsley
freshly grated parmesan cheese, to serve

1 Cook the pasta in a large saucepan of boiling salted water until al dente. Drain well and return to the pan to keep warm.
2 Meanwhile, heat the extra virgin olive oil in a large frying pan. Add the garlic and chilli, and cook over very low heat for 2–3 minutes, or until the garlic is golden. Take care not to burn the garlic or chilli as this will make the sauce bitter.
3 Toss the parsley and the warmed oil, garlic and chilli mixture through the pasta. Season. Serve with the parmesan.

PENNE WITH BACON, RICOTTA CHEESE AND BASIL SAUCE

Preparation time 20 minutes
Total cooking time 15 minutes
Serves 4

2 teaspoons olive oil
4 slices low-fat back bacon, chopped
2–3 garlic cloves, crushed
1 onion, finely chopped
2 spring onions (scallions), finely chopped
250 g (9 oz/1 cup) low-fat ricotta cheese
3 handfuls basil, finely chopped, plus extra
   whole leaves, to garnish
325 g (11½ oz) penne
12 cherry tomatoes, halved

1 Heat the oil in a frying pan. Add the bacon, garlic, onion and spring onion and stir over medium heat for 5 minutes, or until cooked. Remove from the heat, stir in the ricotta and chopped basil and beat until smooth.

2 Cook the pasta in a large saucepan of boiling salted water for 10 minutes, or until al dente. Just prior to draining the pasta, add about 250 ml (9 fl oz/1 cup) of the pasta cooking water to the ricotta mixture to thin the sauce. Add more water if you prefer an even thinner sauce. Season with salt and freshly ground black pepper.

3 Drain the pasta and stir the ricotta sauce and tomato halves through the pasta. Garnish with extra basil.

FUSILLI WITH TUNA, CAPERS AND PARSLEY

Preparation time 10 minutes
Total cooking time 15 minutes
Serves 4

425 g (15 oz) tinned tuna in springwater,
    drained
2 tablespoons olive oil
2 garlic cloves, finely chopped
2 small red chillies, finely chopped
3 tablespoons capers, rinsed and squeezed dry
15 g (¾ oz) chopped flat-leaf (Italian)
    parsley
3 tablespoons lemon juice

375 g (13 oz) fusilli
125 ml (4 fl oz/½ cup) chicken stock

1 Put the tuna in a bowl and flake lightly with a fork. Combine the oil, garlic, chilli, capers, parsley and lemon juice in a small bowl. Pour the mixture over the tuna and mix. Season.
2 Meanwhile, cook the pasta in a large saucepan of boiling salted water until al dente. Drain well and return to the pan to keep warm.
3 Toss the tuna mixture through the pasta, adding enough of the hot chicken stock to make it moist.

TAGLIATELLE WITH VEAL, WINE AND CREAM

Preparation time 15 minutes
Total cooking time 20 minutes
Serves 4

500 g (1 lb 2 oz) veal scaloppine or escalopes,
    cut into thin strips
plain (all-purpose) flour, seasoned
60 g (2¼ oz) butter
1 onion, sliced
125 ml (4 fl oz/½ cup) dry white wine
3 tablespoons beef stock or chicken stock
170 ml (5½ fl oz/⅔ cup) pouring (whipping) cream
600 g (1 lb 5 oz) fresh tagliatelle
1 tablespoon freshly grated parmesan cheese
flat-leaf (Italian) parsley, to garnish

1 Coat the veal strips with the seasoned flour. Melt the butter in a frying pan. Add the veal strips and fry quickly until browned. Remove with a slotted spoon and set aside.
2 Add the onion slices to the pan and stir until soft and golden. Pour in the wine and cook rapidly to reduce the liquid. Add the stock and cream and season to taste. Reduce the sauce again, and add the veal towards the end.
3 Meanwhile, cook the pasta in a large saucepan of boiling salted water until al dente. Drain well and return to the pan to keep warm.
4 Stir the parmesan through the sauce and pour the sauce over the pasta. Garnish with the parsley.

CREAMY BOSCAIOLA

Preparation time 15 minutes
Total cooking time 25 minutes
Serves 4

500 g (1 lb 2 oz) pasta
1 tablespoon olive oil
6 bacon slices, chopped
200 g (7 oz) button mushrooms, sliced
625 ml (21½ fl oz/2½ cups) pouring (whipping)
   cream
2 spring onions (scallions), sliced
1 tablespoon chopped flat-leaf (Italian) parsley

1 Cook the pasta in a large saucepan of boiling salted water until al dente. Drain well and return to the pan to keep warm.

2 While the pasta is cooking, heat the oil in a large frying pan, add the bacon and mushroom and cook, stirring, for 5 minutes, or until golden brown.

3 Stir in a little of the cream and scrape the wooden spoon on the bottom of the pan to dislodge any bacon that has stuck.

4 Add the remaining cream, bring to the boil and cook over high heat for 15 minutes, or until the sauce is thick enough to coat the back of a spoon. Stir the spring onion through the mixture. Pour the sauce over the pasta and toss to combine. Serve sprinkled with the parsley.

Note This sauce is normally served with spaghetti, but you can use any pasta. We have shown it with pappardelle.

CREAMY PESTO CHICKEN PENNE

Preparation time 15 minutes
Total cooking time 30 minutes
Serves 4

1 tablespoon oil
40 g (1½ oz) butter
400 g (14 oz) boneless, skinless chicken breast
170 g (6 oz) thin asparagus, cut into 4 cm
   (1½ in) lengths
3 spring onions (scallions), chopped
4 garlic cloves, crushed
300 g (10½ oz) sour cream
125 ml (4 fl oz/½ cup) pouring (whipping)
   cream
185 ml (6 fl oz/¾ cup) chicken stock
100 g (3½ oz/1 cup) grated parmesan cheese
30 g (1 oz) basil, finely chopped
2 tablespoons toasted pine nuts
400 g (14 oz) penne
basil leaves, to garnish

1 Heat the oil and half the butter in a large frying pan over high heat. Add the chicken and cook for 5 minutes on each side, or until just cooked. Remove, cover and cool, then cut into 1 cm (½ in) slices.
2 Add the asparagus and spring onion to the pan and cook for 2 minutes, or until the asparagus is tender. Remove and set aside. Wipe the pan clean using paper towels.
3 Reduce the heat to medium and add the remaining butter and the garlic. Cook for 2 minutes. Add the sour cream, cream and stock, and simmer for 10 minutes. Add the parmesan and basil and stir for 2 minutes.
4 Return the chicken and asparagus to the pan. Add the pine nuts and cook for 2 minutes to heat through. Season.
5 Meanwhile, cook the pasta in a saucepan of boiling salted water until al dente. Drain well and return to the pan to keep warm.
6 Combine the sauce and the pasta. Garnish with basil leaves.

ORECCHIETTE WITH BROCCOLI

Preparation time 10 minutes
Total cooking time 20 minutes
Serves 6

750 g (1 lb 10 oz) broccoli, cut into
    florets
450 g (1 lb) orecchiette
3 tablespoons extra virgin olive oil
½ teaspoon dried chilli flakes
30 g (1 oz/⅓ cup) grated pecorino or
    parmesan cheese

1 Blanch the broccoli in a large saucepan of boiling salted water for 5 minutes, or until just tender. Remove with a slotted spoon, drain well and return the water to the boil.
2 Cook the pasta in the boiling water until al dente. Drain well and return to the pan to keep warm.
3 Meanwhile, heat the oil in a heavy-based frying pan over medium heat. Add the chilli flakes and broccoli and cook, stirring, for 5 minutes, or until the broccoli is well coated and beginning to break apart. Season. Add to the pasta, stir through the cheese and serve.

TAGLIATELLE WITH GREEN OLIVES AND EGGPLANT

Preparation time 20 minutes

Total cooking time 20 minutes

Serves 4

500 g (1 lb 2 oz) tagliatelle
175 g (6 oz/1 cup) green olives
1 large eggplant (aubergine)
2 tablespoons olive oil
2 garlic cloves, crushed
125 ml (4 fl oz/½ cup) lemon juice
2 tablespoons chopped flat-leaf (Italian) parsley
50 g (1¾ oz/½ cup) grated parmesan cheese

1 Cook the pasta in a large saucepan of boiling salted water until al dente. Drain well and return to the pan to keep warm.

2 Meanwhile, chop the olives, removing the stones, and cut the eggplant into small cubes.

2 Heat the oil in a heavy-based frying pan. Add the garlic and stir for 30 seconds. Add the eggplant and cook over medium heat, stirring frequently, for 6 minutes or until tender.

3 Add the olives, lemon juice and salt and pepper to the pan. Add the sauce to the pasta and toss. Serve in bowls, sprinkled with parsley and parmesan cheese.

Note If you prefer, the eggplant can be salted to draw out any bitter juices. Sprinkle the cut eggplant liberally with salt and leave to stand for 30 minutes. Make sure you rinse the eggplant well before using.

TAGLIATELLE WITH CHICKEN LIVERS AND CREAM

Preparation time 20 minutes

Total cooking time 15 minutes

Serves 4

375 g (13 oz) tagliatelle

300 g (10½ oz) chicken livers

2 tablespoons olive oil

1 onion, finely chopped

1 garlic clove, crushed

250 ml (9 fl oz/1 cup) pouring (whipping) cream

1 tablespoon snipped chives

1 teaspoon wholegrain mustard

2 eggs, beaten

freshly grated parmesan cheese, to serve

snipped chives, to serve

1 Cook the pasta in a large saucepan of boiling salted water until al dente. Drain well and return to the pan to keep warm.

2 While the pasta is cooking, trim any green or discoloured parts from the chicken livers, then slice them. Heat the olive oil in a large frying pan. Add the onion and garlic and stir over low heat until the onion is tender.

3 Add the chicken liver to the pan and cook gently for 2–3 minutes. Remove from the heat and stir in the cream, chives and mustard and season to taste. Return to the heat and bring to the boil. Add the beaten eggs and stir quickly to combine. Remove from the heat.

4 Add the sauce to the hot pasta and toss well to combine. Serve sprinkled with parmesan and snipped chives.

ORECCHIETTE WITH CAULIFLOWER, BACON AND PECORINO

Preparation time 20 minutes

Total cooking time 20 minutes

Serves 4

750 g (1 lb 10 oz) cauliflower, cut into florets

500 g (1 lb 2 oz) orecchiette (see Note)

125 ml (4 fl oz/½ cup) olive oil, plus extra, to drizzle

150 g (5½ oz) bacon, diced

2 garlic cloves, finely chopped

80 g (2¾ oz/½ cup) pine nuts, toasted

45 g (1½ oz/½ cup) grated pecorino cheese

15 g (½ oz) chopped flat-leaf (Italian) parsley

60 g (2¼ oz/¾ cup) fresh breadcrumbs, toasted

1 Bring a large saucepan of salted water to the boil and cook the cauliflower for 5–6 minutes, or until tender. Drain.

2 Cook the pasta in a large saucepan of boiling salted water until al dente. Drain well and return to the pan to keep warm.

3 Heat the oil in a frying pan over medium heat. Cook the bacon for 4–5 minutes, or until just crisp. Add the garlic and cook for 1 minute, or until just golden. Add the cauliflower and toss well.

4 Add the pasta to the pan with the pine nuts, pecorino cheese, parsley and 40 g (1½ oz/½ cup) of the breadcrumbs and stir. Season, sprinkle with the remaining breadcrumbs and drizzle with extra oil.

Note If orecchiette is unavailable, you can use conchiglie or cavatelli.

SPAGHETTINI WITH ANCHOVIES, CAPERS AND CHILLI

Preparation time 15 minutes
Total cooking time 20 minutes
Serves 4

400 g (14 oz) spaghettini
125 ml (4 fl oz/½ cup) olive oil
4 garlic cloves, finely chopped
10 anchovy fillets, chopped
1 tablespoon baby capers, rinsed and squeezed dry
1 teaspoon chilli flakes
2 tablespoons lemon juice
2 teaspoons finely grated lemon zest
3 tablespoons chopped flat-leaf (Italian) parsley
3 tablespoons chopped basil leaves
3 tablespoons chopped mint
50 g (1¾ oz/½ cup) coarsely grated parmesan cheese, plus extra, to serve
extra virgin olive oil, to drizzle

1 Cook the pasta in a large saucepan of boiling salted water until al dente. Drain well and return to the pan to keep warm.
2 Heat the oil in a frying pan over medium heat. Cook the garlic for 2–3 minutes, or until starting to brown. Add the anchovies, capers and chilli and cook for 1 minute.
3 Add the pasta to the pan with the lemon juice, zest, parsley, basil, mint and parmesan. Season and toss together.
4 To serve, drizzle with a little extra oil and sprinkle with the parmesan.

CHILLI LINGUINE WITH CHERMOULA CHICKEN

Preparation time 15 minutes
Total cooking time 30 minutes
Serves 4

600 g (1 lb 5 oz) chicken breast fillets
500 g (1 lb 2 oz) chilli linguine

Chermoula
100 g (3½ oz) coriander (cilantro) leaves, chopped
60 g (2¼ oz) flat-leaf (Italian) parsley leaves, chopped
4 garlic cloves, crushed
2 teaspoons ground cumin
2 teaspoons ground paprika
125 ml (4 fl oz/½ cup) lemon juice
2 teaspoons lemon zest
100 ml (3½ fl oz) olive oil

1 Heat a large non-stick frying pan over medium heat. Add the chicken breasts and cook until tender. Remove from the pan and leave for 5 minutes before cutting into thin slices.
2 Cook the pasta in a large saucepan of boiling salted water until al dente. Drain well and return to the pan to keep warm.
3 Meanwhile, combine the chermoula ingredients in a bowl and add the sliced chicken. Serve the pasta topped with the chermoula chicken.

CREAMY TOMATO AND PRAWN TAGLIATELLE

Preparation time 20 minutes

Total cooking time 30 minutes

Serves 4

400 g (14 oz) dried egg tagliatelle

1 tablespoon olive oil

3 garlic cloves, finely chopped

20 medium raw prawns (shrimp), peeled and deveined, with tails intact

550 g (1 lb 4 oz) roma (plum) tomatoes, diced

2 tablespoons thinly sliced basil

125 ml (4 fl oz/½ cup) white wine

4 tablespoons pouring (whipping) cream

basil leaves, to garnish

1 Cook the pasta in a large saucepan of boiling salted water until al dente. Drain well, reserving 2 tablespoons of the cooking water. Return the pasta to the saucepan to keep warm.

2 Meanwhile, heat the oil and garlic in a large frying pan over low heat for about 1–2 minutes. Increase the heat to medium, add the prawns and cook for 3–5 minutes, stirring frequently until cooked. Remove the prawns and keep warm.

3 Add the tomato and sliced basil and stir for 3 minutes, or until the tomato is soft. Pour in the wine and cream, bring to the boil and simmer for 2 minutes.

4 Purée the sauce in a blender. Return to the pan, then add the reserved pasta water and bring to a simmer. Stir in the prawns until heated through. Toss through the pasta. Serve immediately, garnished with the basil leaves.

SPICY EGGPLANT SPAGHETTI

Preparation time 15 minutes
Total cooking time 30 minutes
Serves 4

300 g (10½ oz) spaghetti
125 ml (4 fl oz/½ cup) extra virgin olive oil
2 red chillies, finely sliced
1 onion, finely chopped
3 garlic cloves, crushed
4 bacon slices, chopped
400 g (14 oz) eggplant (aubergine), diced
2 tablespoons balsamic vinegar
2 tomatoes, chopped
3 tablespoons shredded basil

1 Cook the pasta in a large saucepan of boiling salted water until al dente. Drain well and return to the pan to keep warm.
2 Heat 1 tablespoon of the oil in a large, deep frying pan over medium heat. Cook the chilli, onion, garlic and bacon for about 5 minutes, or until the onion is golden and the bacon browned. Remove from the pan and set aside.
3 Add half the remaining oil to the pan and cook half the eggplant over high heat, tossing to brown on all sides. Remove from the pan and set aside to keep warm. Repeat with the remaining oil and eggplant.
4 Return the bacon mixture and all the eggplant to the pan. Add the vinegar, tomato and basil and cook until heated through. Season well.
5 Serve the spaghetti topped with the eggplant mixture.

SUMMER SEAFOOD MARINARA

Preparation time 15 minutes
Total cooking time 30 minutes
Serves 4

300 g (10½ oz) fresh saffron angel hair pasta
1 tablespoon extra virgin olive oil
30 g (1 oz) butter
2 garlic cloves, finely chopped
1 large onion, finely chopped
1 small red chilli, finely chopped
600 g (1 lb 5 oz) tinned peeled tomatoes, chopped
250 ml (9 fl oz/1 cup) white wine
zest of 1 lemon
½ tablespoon sugar
200 g (7 oz) scallops without roe
500 g (1 lb 2 oz) raw prawns (shrimp), peeled and deveined
300 g (10½ oz) clams (vongole)

1 Cook the pasta in a large saucepan of boiling salted water until al dente. Drain well and return to the pan to keep warm.
2 Meanwhile, heat the oil and butter in a frying pan over medium heat. Add the garlic, onion and chilli and cook for 5 minutes, or until soft. Add the tomatoes and wine and bring to the boil. Cook for 10 minutes, or until the sauce has thickened slightly.
3 Add the lemon zest, sugar, scallops, prawns and clams. Cook, covered, for 5 minutes, or until the seafood is tender. Discard any clams that do not open. Season and serve the pasta topped with the sauce.

BUCKWHEAT PASTA WITH CABBAGE, POTATO AND CHEESE SAUCE

Preparation time 10 minutes

Total cooking time 10 minutes

Serves 6

350 g (12 oz) savoy cabbage, roughly chopped

175 g (6 oz) potatoes, cut into 2 cm (¾ in) cubes

500 g (1 lb 2 oz) buckwheat pasta (see Note)

4 tablespoons extra virgin olive oil

30 g (1 oz) sage, finely chopped

2 garlic cloves, finely chopped

350 g (12 oz) mixed cheeses (such as mascarpone, fontina, taleggio and gorgonzola)

grated parmesan cheese, to serve

1 Bring a large saucepan of salted water to the boil. Add the cabbage, potato and the pasta and cook for 3–5 minutes, or until the pasta is al dente and the vegetables are cooked. Drain well, reserving about 250 ml (9 fl oz/1 cup) of the cooking water.

2 Add the olive oil to the saucepan and gently cook the sage and garlic for about 1 minute. Add the mixed cheeses to the pan. Stir, then add the pasta, cabbage and potatoes. Season.

3 Remove the saucepan from the heat and gently stir the mixture together, adding some of the reserved pasta water to loosen it up a little if necessary. Serve with parmesan.

Note Buckwheat pasta is called pizzoccheri in Italy.

SPAGHETTINI WITH ASPARAGUS AND ROCKET

Preparation time 10 minutes

Total cooking time 25 minutes

Serves 4

100 ml (3½ fl oz) extra virgin olive oil

16 thin asparagus spears, cut into 5 cm (2 in) lengths

375 g (13 oz) spaghettini

120 g (4¼ oz) rocket, shredded

2 small red chillies, finely chopped

2 teaspoons finely grated lemon zest

1 garlic clove, finely chopped

100 g (3½ oz/1 cup) grated parmesan cheese

2 tablespoons lemon juice

1 Bring a large saucepan of water to the boil over medium heat. Add 1 tablespoon of the oil and a pinch of salt to the water and blanch the asparagus for 3–4 minutes. Remove the asparagus with a slotted spoon, refresh under cold water, drain and place in a bowl.

2 Return the water to a rapid boil and add the spaghettini. Cook the pasta until al dente. Drain well and return to the pan to keep warm.

3 Meanwhile, add the rocket, chilli, lemon zest, garlic and 65 g (2¼ oz/⅔ cup) of the parmesan to the asparagus and mix well. Add to the pasta, pour on the lemon juice and remaining olive oil and season. Stir to combine. Top with the remaining parmesan.

FUSILLI WITH ROASTED TOMATOES, TAPENADE AND BOCCONCINI

Preparation time 15 minutes
Total cooking time 20 minutes
Serves 4–6

800 g (1 lb 12 oz) cherry or teardrop tomatoes (or a mixture of both), halved if they are large
500 g (1 lb 2 oz) fusilli
300 g (10½ oz) baby bocconcini (fresh baby mozzarella cheese), sliced
1 tablespoon chopped thyme

Tapenade
1½ tablespoons capers
2 small garlic cloves
185 g (6½ oz/1½ cups) sliced black olives
3 tablespoons lemon juice
4–5 tablespoons extra virgin olive oil

1 Preheat the oven to 200°C (400°F/Gas 6). Place the tomatoes on a baking tray. Season well and roast for 10 minutes, or until slightly dried.
2 To make the tapenade, put the capers, garlic, olives and lemon juice in a food processor and mix together. With the motor running, gradually add the oil until the mixture forms a smooth paste.
3 Cook the pasta in a large saucepan of boiling salted water until al dente. Drain well and return to the pan to keep warm.
4 Toss the tapenade and bocconcini through the pasta. Serve topped with the tomatoes and thyme.

FUSILLI WITH BROCCOLINI, CHILLI AND OLIVES

Preparation time 15 minutes
Total cooking time 25 minutes
Serves 4

3 tablespoons olive oil
1 onion, finely chopped
3 garlic cloves
1 teaspoon chilli flakes
700 g (1 lb 9 oz) broccolini, cut into 1 cm
  (½ in) pieces
125 ml (4 fl oz/½ cup) vegetable stock
400 g (14 oz) fusilli
90 g (3¼ oz/½ cup) black olives, pitted and
  chopped
1 handful flat-leaf (Italian) parsley, finely chopped

25 g (1 oz/¼ cup) grated pecorino cheese
2 tablespoons basil leaves, shredded

1 Heat the olive oil in a large non-stick frying pan over medium heat. Cook the onion, garlic and chilli until softened. Add the broccolini and cook for 5 minutes. Pour in the stock and cook, covered, for 5 minutes.
2 Meanwhile, cook the pasta in a large saucepan of boiling salted water until al dente. Drain well and return to the pan to keep warm.
3 When the broccolini is tender, remove from the heat. Add to the pasta with the olives, parsley, pecorino and basil, and season. Toss together to combine.

PASTA GNOCCHI WITH SAUSAGE AND TOMATO

Preparation time 15 minutes
Total cooking time 20 minutes
Serves 4–6

500 g (1 lb 2 oz) pasta gnocchi
2 tablespoons olive oil
400 g (14 oz) thin Italian sausages
1 red onion, finely chopped
2 garlic cloves, finely chopped
800 g (1 lb 12 oz) tinned chopped tomatoes
1 teaspoon caster (superfine) sugar
35 g (1½ oz) basil, torn
45 g (1½ oz/½ cup) grated pecorino cheese

1 Cook the pasta in a large saucepan of boiling salted water until al dente. Drain well and return to the pan to keep warm.
2 Meanwhile, heat 2 teaspoons of the oil in a large frying pan. Add the sausages and cook, turning, for 5 minutes, or until well browned and cooked through. Drain on paper towels, then slice when they have cooled enough to touch. Keep warm.
3 Wipe clean the frying pan and heat the remaining oil. Add the onion and garlic and cook over medium heat for 2 minutes, or until the onion has softened. Add the tomato, sugar and 250 ml (9 fl oz/1 cup) water and season with ground black pepper. Reduce the heat and simmer for 12 minutes, or until thickened and reduced a little.
4 Pour the sauce over the pasta and stir through the sausage, then the basil and half of the cheese. Serve with the extra cheese.

ORECCHIETTE WITH SPICED PUMPKIN AND YOGHURT

Preparation time 15 minutes

Total cooking time 35 minutes

Serves 6

1 kg (2 lb 4 oz) pumpkin, cut into 2 cm (¾ in) cubes

4 tablespoons olive oil

500 g (1 lb 2 oz) orecchiette

2 garlic cloves, crushed

1 teaspoon dried chilli flakes

1 teaspoon coriander (cilantro) seeds, crushed

1 tablespoon cumin seeds, crushed

200 g (7 oz) Greek-style yoghurt

3 tablespoons chopped coriander (cilantro) leaves

1 Preheat the oven to 200°C (400°F/Gas 6). Toss the pumpkin in 2 tablespoons of the oil, place in a roasting tin. Cook for 25 minutes, or until golden, tossing halfway through.

2 Meanwhile, cook the pasta in a saucepan of boiling salted water until al dente. Drain well and return to the pan to keep warm.

3 Heat the remaining oil in a saucepan. Add the garlic, chilli, coriander and cumin and cook for 30 seconds, or until fragrant.

4 Toss the spice mix and pumpkin through the pasta, then stir in the yoghurt and coriander and season to taste.

FARFALLE WITH SPINACH AND BACON

Preparation time 10 minutes
Total cooking time 15 minutes
Serves 4

400 g (14 oz) farfalle
2 tablespoons extra virgin olive oil
250 g (9 oz) bacon, chopped
1 red onion, finely chopped
250 g (9 oz) baby English spinach leaves
1–2 tablespoons sweet chilli sauce (optional)
35 g (1½ oz/¼ cup) crumbled goat's feta cheese

1 Cook the pasta in a large saucepan of boiling salted water until al dente. Drain well and return to the pan to keep warm.
2 Meanwhile, heat the oil in a large frying pan over high heat. Add the bacon and reduce the heat to medium. Cook for about 3 minutes, or until lightly browned. Add the onion and cook for a further 4 minutes, or until softened.
3 Toss the spinach leaves through the onion and bacon mixture for 30 seconds, or until just wilted.
4 Add the bacon and spinach mixture to the drained pasta, then stir in the sweet chilli sauce. Season to taste with salt and ground black pepper and toss well.
5 Scatter with the crumbled feta cheese and serve immediately.

PENNE WITH PUMPKIN, BAKED RICOTTA AND PROSCIUTTO

Preparation time 15 minutes
Total cooking time 15 minutes
Serves 4

500 g (1 lb 2 oz) penne
460 g (1 lb) butternut pumpkin (squash), cut into
    1 cm (½ in) cubes
3 tablespoons extra virgin olive oil
2 garlic cloves, crushed
100 g (3½ oz) semi-dried (sun-blushed) tomatoes,
    chopped
4 slices prosciutto, chopped
3 tablespoons shredded basil

250 g (9 oz) baked ricotta cheese, cut into
    1 cm (½ in) cubes

1 Cook the pasta in a large saucepan of boiling salted water until al dente. Drain well and return to the pan to keep warm.
2 Meanwhile, cook the pumpkin in a large saucepan of boiling water for 10–12 minutes, or until just tender, then drain well.
3 Heat the oil in a large saucepan, add the garlic and cook over medium heat for 30 seconds. Add the tomato, prosciutto, pumpkin and penne and toss over low heat for 1–2 minutes, or until heated through.
4 Add the basil and baked ricotta, season and serve immediately.

PASTA DI STALLA

(Pasta from the barn)

Preparation time 10 minutes

Total cooking time 15 minutes

Serves 4

375 g (13 oz) orecchiette

1 large potato, cut into 1.5 cm (⅝ in) cubes

400 g (14 oz) broccoli

4 tablespoons olive oil

3 garlic cloves, crushed

1 small red chilli, finely chopped

800 g (1 lb 12 oz) tinned chopped tomatoes

25 g (1 oz/¼ cup) grated pecorino cheese

1 Bring a large saucepan of salted water to the boil and cook the pasta and potato for 8–10 minutes, or until the pasta is al dente. Drain and return to the pan.

2 Meanwhile, trim the broccoli into florets and discard the stems. Place in a saucepan of boiling water and cook for 1–2 minutes, then drain and plunge into iced water. Drain the broccoli and add to the pasta and potato.

3 Heat the oil in a large saucepan over medium heat. Add the garlic and chilli and cook for 30 seconds. Add the tomato and simmer for 5 minutes, or until slightly reduced and thickened. Season to taste with salt and pepper.

4 Pour the tomato mixture over the pasta, potato and broccoli. Toss well and stir over low heat until warmed through. Serve sprinkled with grated pecorino cheese.

CREAMY PASTA GNOCCHI WITH PEAS AND PROSCIUTTO

Preparation time 15 minutes

Total cooking time 20 minutes

Serves 4

100 g (3½ oz) thinly sliced prosciutto

3 teaspoons oil

2 eggs

250 ml (9 fl oz/1 cup) cream

35 g (1½ oz/⅓ cup) grated parmesan cheese

2 tablespoons chopped flat-leaf (Italian) parsley

1 tablespoon chopped chives

250 g (9 oz) fresh or frozen peas

500 g (1 lb 2 oz) pasta gnocchi

1 Cut the prosciutto into 5 mm (¼ in) wide strips. Heat the oil in a large frying pan over medium heat. Cook the prosciutto for about 2 minutes, or until crisp. Drain on paper towels.

2 Put the eggs, cream, parmesan and herbs in a bowl and whisk well.

3 Bring a large saucepan of salted water to the boil. Add the peas and cook for about 5 minutes, or until just tender. Leaving the pan on the heat, use a slotted spoon and transfer the peas to the bowl of cream mixture, and then add 3 tablespoons of the cooking liquid to the same bowl. Using a potato masher or the back of a fork, roughly mash the peas.

4 Add the gnocchi to the boiling water and cook until al dente. Drain well, then return to the pan.

5 Add the cream mixture, then warm through over low heat, gently stirring for about 30 seconds until the gnocchi is coated in the sauce. Season and serve topped with the prosciutto.

Note Be careful not to overheat or cook for too long as the egg will begin to set and the result will look like a scrambled egg sauce.

SPAGHETTI WITH HERB, GARLIC AND CHILLI OIL

Preparation time 15 minutes

Total cooking time 15 minutes

Serves 4–6

250 ml (9 fl oz/1 cup) olive oil

2 bird's eye chillies, seeded and thinly sliced

5–6 large garlic cloves, crushed

500 g (1 lb 2 oz) spaghetti

100 g (3½ oz) thinly sliced prosciutto

30 g (1 oz) chopped flat-leaf (Italian) parsley

2 tablespoons chopped basil

2 tablespoons chopped oregano

75 g (2½ oz/¾ cup) grated parmesan cheese

1 Pour the oil into a small saucepan with the chilli and garlic. Slowly heat the oil over low heat for about 12 minutes to infuse the oil with the garlic and chilli. Don't allow the oil to reach smoking point or the garlic will burn and taste bitter.

2 Meanwhile, cook the pasta in a saucepan of boiling salted water until al dente. Drain well and return to the pan to keep warm.

3 Lay the prosciutto on a baking tray and cook under a hot grill (broiler) for 2 minutes each side, or until crispy. Cool and break into pieces.

4 Pour the hot oil mixture over the spaghetti and toss well with the prosciutto, fresh herbs and parmesan. Season to taste.

LINGUINE WITH BROCCOLI, PINE NUTS AND LEMON

Preparation time 15 minutes
Total cooking time 15 minutes
Serves 4–6

500 g (1 lb 2 oz) linguine
600 g (1 lb 5 oz) broccoli, cut into small
    florets
80 g (2¾ oz/½ cup) pine nuts
125 ml (4 fl oz/½ cup) extra virgin olive oil
2 teaspoons finely grated lemon zest
3 tablespoons lemon juice
1 teaspoon dried chilli flakes
50 g (1¾ oz/½ cup) finely grated parmesan
    cheese

1 Cook the pasta in a large saucepan of boiling salted water until al dente. Drain well and return to the pan to keep warm.
2 Meanwhile, bring a saucepan of water to the boil and cook the broccoli for 2 minutes, or until just tender. Drain and set aside.
3 Heat a large non-stick frying pan and toast the pine nuts for 2–3 minutes, or until just golden, shaking the pan to prevent them burning. Remove from the pan and chop.
4 Reduce the heat to low, add the oil and lemon zest to the frying pan and gently heat until fragrant. Add the broccoli, chopped nuts, lemon juice and chilli and stir until warmed through. Season. Add to the pasta with the parmesan cheese.

TAGLIATELLE WITH FETA, TOMATO AND ROCKET

Preparation time 15 minutes

Total cooking time 15 minutes

Serves 4

4 vine-ripened tomatoes

1 small red onion, finely chopped

4 tablespoons shredded basil

2 tablespoons olive oil

375 g (13 oz) tagliatelle

2 garlic cloves, finely chopped

150 g (5½ oz) baby rocket (arugula) leaves

150 g (5½ oz) soft feta cheese, crumbled

15 g (½ oz) small whole basil leaves

1 Score a cross in the base of each tomato, then place in a bowl of boiling water for 1 minute. Plunge into cold water and peel the skin away from the cross. Cut in half and remove the seeds with a teaspoon. Chop, then transfer to a bowl.

2 Add the onion and basil, stir in 1 tablespoon of the oil and set aside.

3 Cook the pasta in a large saucepan of boiling water until al dente. Drain, reserving 125 ml (4 fl oz/½ cup) pasta water. Return the pasta to the pan, add the remaining oil, the garlic and reserved pasta water, tossing over medium heat for 1–2 minutes until warm. Stir in the tomato mixture, rocket and feta. Season and garnish with basil leaves.

TAGLIATELLE WITH SALMON AND CREAMY DILL DRESSING

Preparation time 10 minutes

Total cooking time 15 minutes

Serves 4

350 g (12 oz) fresh tagliatelle

3 tablespoons olive oil

3 x 200 g (7 oz) salmon fillets, skinned and boned (ask your fishmonger to do this for you)

3 garlic cloves, crushed

375 ml (13 fl oz/1½ cups) cream

1½ tablespoons chopped dill

1 teaspoon mustard powder

1 tablespoon lemon juice

40 g (1½ oz) shaved parmesan cheese

1 Cook the pasta in a large saucepan of boiling water until al dente. Drain, then toss with 1 tablespoon oil.

2 Meanwhile, heat the remaining oil in a deep frying pan; cook the salmon for 2 minutes each side, or until crisp on the outside but still pink inside. Remove from the pan, cut into 2 cm (¾ in) cubes.

3 In the same pan, add the garlic and cook for 30 seconds, or until fragrant. Add the cream, dill and mustard powder, bring to the boil, then reduce the heat and simmer, stirring, for 4–5 minutes, or until thickened. Season.

4 Add the salmon and any juices plus the lemon juice to the dill sauce and stir until warm. Gently toss the salmon sauce through the pasta and divide among four serving bowls. Sprinkle with parmesan and serve.

PASTA PRONTO

Preparation time 10 minutes
Total cooking time 15 minutes
Serves 4

2 tablespoons extra virgin olive oil
4 garlic cloves, finely chopped
1 small red chilli, finely chopped
1.2 kg (2 lb 10 oz) tinned crushed
   tomatoes
1 teaspoon sugar
4 tablespoons dry white wine
3 tablespoons chopped herbs (such as basil
   or parsley)

400 g (14 oz) vermicelli
30 g (1 oz) shaved parmesan cheese

1 Heat the oil in a large deep frying pan and
cook the garlic and chilli for 1 minute. Add
the tomato, sugar, wine, herbs and 440 ml
(15¼ fl oz/1¾ cups) water. Bring to the boil.
2 Reduce the heat to medium and add the
pasta, breaking the strands if they are too
long. Cook for 10 minutes, or until al dente,
stirring often to stop the pasta from sticking.
The pasta will thicken the sauce as it cooks.
3 Season to taste and serve in bowls with
shaved parmesan.

SPAGHETTINI WITH HERBS, BABY SPINACH AND GARLIC CRUMBS

Preparation time 15 minutes

Total cooking time 15 minutes

Serves 4

375 g (13 oz) spaghettini

125 g (4½ oz) day-old crusty Italian bread, crusts removed

100 ml (3½ fl oz) extra virgin olive oil, plus extra for drizzling

4 garlic cloves, finely chopped

400 g (14 oz) baby English spinach leaves

25 g (1 oz) chopped flat-leaf (Italian) parsley

4 tablespoons chopped basil

1 tablespoon thyme leaves

30 g (1 oz) shaved parmesan cheese

1 Cook the pasta in a saucepan of boiling water until al dente. Drain, reserving 125 ml (4 fl oz/½ cup) of the pasta water. Return the pasta to the saucepan and keep warm.

2 To make the garlic breadcrumbs, place the crustless bread in a food processor or blender and pulse until coarse breadcrumbs form.

3 Heat 1 tablespoon of the oil in a saucepan. Add the breadcrumbs and half the garlic and toss for 2–3 minutes, or until lightly golden. Remove, then wipe the pan clean with paper towels.

4 Heat 2 tablespoons of the oil in the same pan. Add the spinach and remaining garlic, toss together for 1 minute, then add the herbs. Cook, tossing frequently, for a further 1 minute to wilt the herbs a little and to heat through.

5 Toss the spinach mixture through the pasta with the remaining oil and reserved pasta water. Scatter with the garlic crumbs. Serve hot sprinkled with the parmesan and drizzled with extra virgin olive oil.

VEAL AGNOLOTTI WITH ALFREDO SAUCE

Preparation time 10 minutes
Total cooking time 10 minutes
Serves 4–6

625 g (1 lb 6 oz) veal agnolotti
90 g (3¼ oz) butter
150 g (5½ oz/1½ cups) grated parmesan cheese
300 ml (10½ fl oz) cream
2 tablespoons chopped marjoram

1 Cook the pasta in a large saucepan of boiling salted water until al dente. Drain well and return to the pan to keep warm.

2 Just before the pasta is cooked, melt the butter in a saucepan over low heat. Add the parmesan and cream and bring to the boil. Reduce the heat and simmer, stirring constantly, for 2 minutes, or until the sauce has thickened slightly.

3 Stir in the marjoram and season with well salt and ground black pepper. Toss the sauce through the pasta until well coated and serve immediately.

Variation Marjoram can be replaced with any other fresh herb you prefer — for example, try parsley, thyme, chervil or dill.

LASAGNETTE WITH SPICY CHICKEN MEATBALLS

Preparation time 10 minutes

Total cooking time 15 minutes

Serves 4

750 g (1 lb 10 oz) minced (ground) chicken
2 tablespoons chopped coriander (cilantro) leaves
1½ tablespoons red curry paste
2 tablespoons oil
1 red onion, finely chopped
3 garlic cloves, crushed
875 g (1 lb 15 oz/3½ cups) tomato pasta sauce
2 teaspoons soft brown sugar
350 g (12 oz) lasagnette

1 Line a tray with baking paper. Combine the meat, coriander and 1 tablespoon of the curry paste. Roll heaped tablespoons of the mixture into balls and put on the tray (the mixture should make about 20 balls). Refrigerate until ready.

2 Heat the oil in a large deep frying pan and cook the onion and garlic over medium heat for 2–3 minutes, or until softened. Add the remaining curry paste and cook, stirring, for 1 minute, or until fragrant. Add the pasta sauce and sugar and stir well. Reduce the heat, add the meatballs and cook, turning halfway through, for 10 minutes, or until the meatballs are cooked through.

3 Meanwhile, cook the pasta in a large saucepan of boiling salted water until al dente. Drain well. To serve, top with the sauce and meatballs and sprinkle with coriander, if desired.

CHICKEN RAVIOLI WITH PESTO

Preparation time 10 minutes
Total cooking time 10 minutes
Serves 4

625 g (1 lb 6 oz) chicken ravioli
50 g (1¾ oz) basil
2 garlic cloves
40 g (1½ oz/¼ cup) pine nuts, toasted
125 ml (4 fl oz/½ cup) extra virgin olive oil
50 g (1¾ oz/½ cup) grated parmesan cheese
50 g (1¾ oz) pecorino cheese, grated
15 g (¼ oz) basil, extra, torn
30 g (1 oz) shaved parmesan cheese, to serve

1 Cook the pasta in a large saucepan of boiling salted water until al dente. Drain well and return to the pan to keep warm.
2 Meanwhile, blend the basil, garlic, pine nuts and olive oil in a food processor or blender until smooth.
3 Stir in the grated parmesan and pecorino and season to taste with salt and pepper.
4 Drain the pasta, reserving 1 tablespoon of the cooking water to add to the pesto. Carefully toss the ravioli in the pesto and reserved water.
5 To serve, drizzle with the extra virgin olive oil and top with a little torn basil and the parmesan cheeses.

PASTA WITH CREAMY SEMI-DRIED TOMATO SAUCE AND BACON

Preparation time 10 minutes

Total cooking time 20 minutes

Serves 4

4 bacon slices

625 g (1 lb 6 oz) veal or chicken agnolotti

1 tablespoon olive oil

2 garlic cloves, finely chopped

110 g (3¾ oz/⅔ cup) thinly sliced semi-dried (sun-blushed) tomatoes

1 tablespoon chopped thyme

375 ml (13 fl oz/1½ cups) cream

1 teaspoon finely grated lemon zest

35 g (1¼ oz/⅓ cup) finely grated parmesan cheese

1 Grill (broil) the bacon for 5 minutes each side, or until crisp and golden. Remove, drain well on paper towel, then break into pieces.

2 Cook the pasta in a large saucepan of boiling salted water until al dente. Drain well and return to the pan to keep warm.

3 Heat the oil in a frying pan and cook the garlic over medium heat for 1 minute, or until just golden. Add the tomato and thyme and cook for 1 minute.

4 Add the cream, bring to the boil, then reduce the heat and simmer for 6–8 minutes, or until the cream has thickened and reduced by one third. Season, add the lemon zest, and 2 tablespoons of the parmesan.

5 Add the pasta to the sauce and stir gently to combine. Sprinkle with the remaining parmesan and the bacon pieces.

CREAMY CHICKEN AND PEPPERCORN PAPPARDELLE

Preparation time 15 minutes

Total cooking time 15 minutes

Serves 4

2 chicken breast fillets (420 g/15 oz in total)

30 g (1 oz) butter

1 onion, halved and thinly sliced

2 tablespoons drained green peppercorns, slightly crushed

125 ml (4 fl oz/½ cup) white wine

300 ml (10½ fl oz) cream

400 g (14 oz) fresh pappardelle

80 g (2¾ oz/⅓ cup) sour cream (optional)

2 tablespoons chopped chives

1 Cut the chicken in half so that you have four flat fillets and season.

2 Melt the butter in a frying pan, add the chicken and cook for 3 minutes each side, or until browned and cooked through. Remove from the pan, cut into slices and keep warm.

3 Add the onion and peppercorns to the same pan and cook over medium heat for 3 minutes, or until the onion has softened slightly. Add the wine and cook for 1 minute, or until reduced by half. Stir in the cream and cook for 4–5 minutes, or until thickened slightly, then season.

4 Meanwhile, cook the pasta in a large saucepan of boiling salted water until al dente. Drain well and return to the pan to keep warm.

5 Mix together the pasta, chicken and any juices and cream sauce. To serve, top with a dollop of sour cream and sprinkle with the chives.

VEAL TORTELLINI WITH CREAMY MUSHROOM SAUCE

Preparation time 15 minutes
Total cooking time 20 minutes
Serves 4

500 g (1 lb 2 oz) veal tortellini
3 tablespoons olive oil
600 g (1 lb 5 oz) Swiss brown mushrooms, thinly sliced
2 garlic cloves, crushed
125 ml (4 fl oz/½ cup) dry white wine
300 ml (10½ fl oz) thick (double/heavy) cream
pinch of ground nutmeg
3 tablespoons finely chopped flat-leaf (Italian) parsley
30 g (1 oz) grated parmesan cheese

1 Cook the pasta in a large saucepan of boiling salted water until al dente. Drain well and return to the pan to keep warm.
2 Meanwhile, heat the oil in a large frying pan over medium heat. Add the mushrooms and cook, stirring occasionally, for 5 minutes, or until softened.
3 Add the garlic and cook for about 1 minute, then stir in the wine and cook for 5 minutes, or until the liquid has reduced by half.
2 Add the cream, nutmeg and parsley and stir well to combine. Cook for about 3–5 minutes, or until the sauce thickens slightly. Season with well salt and ground black pepper. To serve, spoon the sauce over the tortellini and sprinkle with the parmesan cheese.

FRESH VEGETABLE LASAGNE WITH ROCKET

Preparation time 15 minutes
Total cooking time 25 minutes
Serves 4

Balsamic syrup
4 tablespoons balsamic vinegar
1½ tablespoons brown sugar

16 asparagus spears, trimmed and cut into 5 cm
   (2 in) lengths
150 g (5½ oz/1 cup) peas
2 large zucchini (courgettes), cut into thin ribbons
2 fresh lasagne sheets
100 g (3½ oz) rocket (arugula) leaves
1 large handful basil, torn
2 tablespoons olive oil
250 g (9 oz) ricotta cheese
150 g (5½ oz) semi-dried tomatoes
shaved parmesan cheese, to serve

1 Stir the vinegar and brown sugar in a saucepan over medium heat until the sugar dissolves. Reduce the heat and simmer for 3–4 minutes. Remove from the heat.

2 Bring a saucepan of salted water to the boil. Blanch the asparagus, peas and zucchini in separate batches until just tender. Remove with a slotted spoon and refresh each batch in cold water. Drain well. Return the cooking liquid to the boil. Cook the lasagne sheets in the water for 1–2 minutes, or until al dente. Drain. Cut each sheet in half lengthways.

3 Toss the vegetables and the rocket with the basil and olive oil. Season. Place one strip of pasta on a plate — one-third on the centre of the plate and two-thirds overhanging one side. Place some salad on the centre one-third, topped with some ricotta and tomato. Season and fold over one-third of the lasagne sheet. Top with another layer of salad, ricotta and tomato. Fold back the final layer of pasta and garnish with salad and tomato. Repeat with the remaining pasta, salad, ricotta and tomato.

4 Drizzle with the balsamic syrup and serve with the parmesan.

PUMPKIN, SPINACH AND RICOTTA LASAGNE

Preparation time 15 minutes
Total cooking time 15 minutes
Serves 4

3 tablespoons olive oil
1.5 kg (3 lb 5 oz) butternut pumpkin (squash), cut into 1.5 cm (⅝ in) dice
500 g (1 lb 2 oz) baby English spinach leaves
4 fresh lasagne sheets
500 g (1 lb 2 oz/2 cups) ricotta cheese
2 tablespoons pouring (whipping) cream
25 g (1 oz/¼ cup) grated parmesan cheese
pinch of ground nutmeg

1 Heat the oil in a non-stick frying pan over medium heat. Add the pumpkin and cook, stirring occasionally, for 15 minutes, or until tender. Season and keep warm.
2 Cook the spinach in a large saucepan of boiling water for 30 seconds, or until wilted. Using a slotted spoon, transfer to a bowl of cold water. Drain well and squeeze out as much excess water as possible. Finely chop the spinach.
3 Meanwhile, add the lasagne sheets to the saucepan of boiling water and cook, stirring occasionally, until al dente. Drain. Cut each lasagne sheet widthways into thirds.
3 Combine the ricotta, cream, parmesan, spinach and nutmeg in a small saucepan over low heat. Stir for 2–3 minutes, or until warmed through.
4 Place a piece of lasagne on the base of each plate. Using half the pumpkin, top each of the sheets, then cover with another piece of lasagne. Use half the ricotta mixture to spread over the lasagne sheets, then add another lasagne piece. Top with the remaining pumpkin, then remaining ricotta mixture. Season well and serve immediately.

RICE & NOODLES

Known as 'the grain of life', rice is the staple food for almost half the world's population, and it is grown on every continent except Antarctica. Rice has shaped the cuisines and cultures of billions of people, easily becoming a household favourite thanks to its versatility and the variety of types available. Noodles have a similar appeal — flavour, texture, shape and thickness vary enormously. Noodles are easy to prepare and can be used in anything from soups and salads to stir-fries and hotpots.

RICE BASICS

A staple grain eaten daily by over 300 billion people. Rice comes in many colours (black, white, brown, red), sizes (short-grain, long-grain, round), consistencies (sticky, glutinous), and forms (whole, milled, popped, flaked and ground).

BUYING RICE

Supermarkets stock enough varieties of rice to cover most of the basic uses. They will generally have arborio, jasmine and basmati, as well as short-grain, long-grain and brown rice. Most will also include some wild rice, but you may have to venture to a health food store if your supermarket doesn't stock it.

STORAGE

If you eat a lot of rice, buy it in large quantities — it has a long shelf life. Once you have opened a fresh packet of rice, store it in a cool, dark, dry place in an airtight container. Rice bought in large sacks should be stores in a dry, clean container with a lid.

Brown rice is the exception — it goes rancid if left in a warm place for too long. Store in an airtight container in the fridge.

You also need to take extra care with cooked rice. If it is not consumed immediately, cover, then chill it quickly as harmful bacteria can grow rapidly. Cooked rice will store in the fridge for up to 2 days.

COOKING RICE

One of the best things about rice is that it needs very little attention. Give it a quick rinse and then put it on to cook while you focus on the rest of the meal.

Rice can be cooked in many ways, including the absorption method, boiling the rice in water, cooking it in a microwave, in a rice cooker or in the oven. Rice can also be steamed, first by boiling it, then finishing it in a steamer. Some rices will lend themselves to being cooked using more than one method, but others suit just one method. Rice varies in cooking time, so refer to the packet instructions.

If reheating cooked rice, make sure all the rice is piping hot to destroy any bacteria that may be present.

Absorption method Probably the most familiar method of cooking rice, the absorption method is an efficient and nutritious way to cook rice, as nutrients are not discarded with the cooking water. Generally, long-grain rices suit this method. To cook, put the rice in cold water, then bring to the boil, cover with a tight-fitting lid, then reduce the heat to a simmer so that the rice at the bottom of the pan doesn't burn. Once cooked, simply fluff up with a fork and serve immediately.

The electric rice cooker is designed to cook rice the absorption way. Sold in Asian stores, many kitchen stores and some department stores, they have markings on the inside to show the amount of water needed for the amount of rice. It automatically switches off when the grains are cooked, so the rice is then steam-dried. The rice cooker then keeps the rice warm until you're ready to eat it.

When cooking by the absorption method is to make sure that the depth of uncooked rice in the pan, pot or electric rice cooker is no more than 5 cm (2 in) high, or the rice will cook unevenly.

Rapid boiling Like pasta, many rices, from arborio to parboiled rices, cook well in plenty of water. Bring a large saucepan of water to the boil, uncovered. Sprinkle in the rice and keep an eye on it, so it does not stick or overcook. Drain the rice in a sieve.

Steaming rice This method is preferred for sticky rice. Soak the rice overnight, then drain. Spread out the grains in a steamer, and put the steamer over a wok or pan of boiling water. The rice does not touch the water — it is cooked only by the steam.

TYPES OF RICE

Basmati This is a long-grained, needle-shaped rice used predominantly in Indian cooking. It has a light, dry texture and is lightly perfumed. The grains are very fluffy and stay separate when cooked, as well as elongating.

Brown rice The grains of brown rice have had their husk (hull) removed, but the outer bran layer left intact, not milled and polished like white rice. The result is a more nutritious rice. With a pronounced nutty flavour and chewy texture, brown rice requires a longer cooking time than other varieties. It is available both as a short- and medium-grain rice. Also known as wholegrain rice.

Camargue red Also sold as Griotto rice. It has a distinctive nutty flavour and chewy texture. It is good with duck and game. The rice is grown in the Camargue region of southern France.

Easy-cook This rice may be either white or brown, short or long grained. The rice is parboiled before milling and it is a non-sticky all-purpose rice.

Japanese short-grain rice This is the style of rice that the Japanese prefer. It is short-grain, relatively sticky rice. The raw grains are slightly glassy with a light powder on them to keep them separate. When properly cooked, the rice is slightly sticky, but with firm grains.

Jasmine This is a fragrant rice, usually long-grained. It is named after the sweet-smelling jasmine flower of Southeast Asia because, on cooking, it releases a similar floral aroma. Jasmine rice cooks to a soft, slightly sticky grain and its taste enhances the traditional spices of Thai dishes. It is also served plain as it needs no seasoning.

Long-grain Long-grain rice is a descriptive term for the size of the rice grains — the grains are three to five times as long as they are wide. The long and slender grains usually stay separate and fluffy after cooking, so it is a good rice to choose when you want a dry, fluffy texture in your dish with every grain separate. There are several types of long-grain rice. Long-grain is an absorbent, fine long-grained rice mainly used for savoury dishes; a good all-purpose rice.

Paella rice Varieties of short- to medium-grained Spanish paella rices include Bahia, Calasparra, sequia and the firm-grained bomba. Paella rices can absorb a lot of water and they soak up a lot of the delicious flavours from the paella; they are also suitable for puddings. Valencia is the most prized Spanish grain for paella as it cooks up tender, moist and clingy due to its high starch content.

Risotto rice Risotto rices are short-grain rices high in starch, which give risottos their creaminess. There are several types of risotto rice. Arborio is a large, plump grain. Vialone nano is a stubby small grain that gives a looser consistency but keeps more of a bite. Carnaroli is the best of all risotto rices. The outer skin has enough of the soft starch to dissolve and make the risotto creamy but it also keeps a firm consistency.

Short-grain Though short-grain rices vary in total length, they are classified as such because the grains are less than twice as long as they are wide. The grains looks almost round, with moist grains that stick together. When cooked, the grains swell without disintegrating and the high starch content makes it sticky and good for puddings, moulds and stuffings.

Thai black sticky rice This attractive dark rice has had its husk removed, but not the black bran layer, hence, its colour. Typically used in desserts, it is often mixed with white sticky rice to combine the best qualities of each — colour and stickiness.

Wild rice blend Natural wild rice can be very expensive, so it is often extended with brown or white rice — usually brown because the cooking times are similar. Sometimes the rices are precooked. By combining wild rice with 'real' rice, texture, colour and taste are added, and the wild rice has the effect of enhancing the nutritional value of plain rice.

Jasmine rice

Brown rice

Camargue red rice

Thai black sticky rice

ong-grain rice

Japanese short-grain rice

Wild rice blend

Wild rice

Risotto rice

Paella rice

NOODLE BASICS

A type of pasta made from flour, water and sometimes egg, the word noodle can be used to describe hundreds of different types used in cuisines around the world. They can also be made from many different ingredients, from rice and wheat to vegetable starches.

Noodles are important to Asian cuisine, especially to China and Japan, and long egg noodles are eaten with stews in Eastern Europe. In Asia, noodles may be served at main meals along with other dishes or eaten as a snack, especially served in soupy broths. Short lengths of noodle may be cooked in soup or the pasta may be filled to make wontons (this was probably the original form that noodles took).

In Asia, noodles are not only a staple but a symbol of longevity. Chinese e-fu noodles are eaten on special occasions such as birthdays and at New Year. Chinese noodles, unlike pasta and Japanese noodles, are very long and are never cut — this would only bring bad luck. There is also some symbolism attached to the noodle in Japan, especially soba, which are eaten on New Year's Eve and special occasions. Japanese noodles are not made from rice, as it is too precious a commodity. Instead they are made from buckwheat and/or wheat.

Choose noodles that are appropriate to the recipe if they are not specified exactly. Thin, delicate rice vermicelli will soak up Vietnamese flavours well but thick egg noodles won't. Noodles for use in soups must be robust enough to pick up without breaking and falling back into the soup. Noodles can now be bought pre-cooked to various stages.

COOKING NOODLES

Some noodles need to be softened in boiling water; others are cooked in water or fried, so always refer to the instructions on the packet. Cook noodles in plenty of boiling water and drain well.

If cooking small or individual portions of fresh noodles, put them in a sieve and dunk them in a saucepan of boiling water. This is a good method for quick-cooking noodles, such as egg noodles or rice noodles, and keeps them separated for individual servings.

Cold noodles can be tossed in a little oil to keep them from sticking and then reheated in boiling water.

TYPES OF NOODLES

Arrowroot noodles Sold in bundles, these need to be softened in hot water before use and are used in soups and desserts.

Bean curd noodles Also called **soya noodles**, these are made from pressed bean curd cut into ribbons. They are thin and brown and are usually used in cold dishes. Bean curd noodles are available both plain and with flavourings such as soy sauce added.

Buckwheat noodles These include **Japanese soba noodles**, which are sold fresh and dried and are made from buckwheat or a mixture of buckwheat and wheat flour. They are eaten cold or in soups. **Chasoba** are made from buckwheat and green tea. Buckwheat noodles are also eaten cold in soups.

Egg noodles These are made of wheat flour and eggs, and are widely available both fresh and dried. Fresh egg noodles are sold in a range of widths. The thin round variety are used in soups, stir-fries and for deep-frying, while the flatter, wider noodles are used in soups.

Harusame noodles Harusame, meaning 'spring rain', are noodles made from potato and corn starches and sometimes mung bean or soy bean starch. These are very fine, white, almost transparent Japanese noodles. They are very similar to dried mung bean vermicelli. Sold dried in small packets, these are also called **salad noodles**.

Hiyamugi These are thin noodles eaten cold with a dipping sauce.

Hokkien (egg) noodles They are thick,

yellow, rubbery-textured fresh egg noodles, which have been cooked and lightly oiled before packaging. They are perfect for stir-frying, as they absorb the flavour of the sauce and are also used in soups and noodle salads.

Mung bean vermicelli Also known as **cellophane, glass** or **bean thread noodles.** These are made with a mixture of mung bean and tapioca starches, and water. They are sold dried in tight opaque bundles. They are difficult to cut or separate, so try to buy in smaller bundles. They can be deep-fried straight from the packet, eaten as a soft noodle, and are ideal for soups and hotpots. They have a soft gelatinous texture, and become almost transparent.

Pancit canton (Chinese e-fu noodles) Referred to as 'birthday' or 'long-life' noodles, the longer the noodle, the longer the eater's life, so don't cut them.

Potato starch noodles These are also known as Korean vermicelli. They are long, fine, green-brown, translucent dried noodles.

Reshteh These are a Middle Eastern egg noodle, hand cut into either ribbons or fine noodles like vermicelli.

Rice noodles Dried noodles such as rice stick and vermicelli are made from rice powder. These are softened in hot water, then used in soups, stir-fries or deep-fried until crispy. Thicker rice sticks are used for pad Thai. Fresh rice noodles may be shaped in sheets, ribbons or long, round strands, such as laksa noodles.

Rice stick noodles These are short, translucent flat noodles and are available dried and may be a little thicker than rice vermicelli, or a flat medium-width noodle. They are used in both stir-fries and soups, and also sometimes in salads.

Rice vermicelli These are thread-like white noodles made with rice flour and are used in soups, stir-fries and spring rolls. .

Shanghai noodles These thick, round egg noodles are similar to Hokkien noodles but are not cooked, or oiled. They are sold fresh and will keep refrigerated for up to

4 days. Use these noodles as an alternative to Hokkien noodles, particularly in dishes where the sauce tends to be oily, or in traditional Shanghai noodle dishes.

Shirataki noodles Thin, translucent and jelly-like, they are made from the starchy root of a plant known in Japan as devil's tongue. They have a crunchy texture, but little flavour. They are available fresh or dried.

Soba noodles These are Japanese noodles made from buckwheat flour, or a combination of buckwheat and wheat flour. They are available fresh, though more easily found dried. They are beige-coloured noodles and some are lightly flavoured with green tea or beetroot. Usually eaten in a simple broth, or served cold with a dipping sauce.

Somen noodles These thin, delicate Japanese noodles made from wheat flour are commonly available dried. Somen are traditionally eaten cold with a dipping sauce, but may also be served in broth. Some varieties have added green tea powder, egg yolk, or plum with shiso oil, which create different coloured and flavoured noodles.

Sweet potato noodles These are thin, wiry grey noodles when raw and need to be soaked to soften them. They have a fairly chewy texture when cooked.

Udon noodles These are thick, white Japanese noodles made from wheat flour. They are most often eaten in soups, but also in hotpots and braised dishes.

Wheat flour noodles Chinese wheat noodles, mian, can be dried in flat, long thin strands, wrapped in skeins or fresh, as in wheat Shanghai noodles. They are used in soups and stir-fries. Japanese wheat noodles include **udon**, which are round or square plump noodles used in soups.

Wheat noodles These are thin, round noodles made simply with wheat flour and water. They are available both fresh and dried. Wheat noodles are fabulous for stir-frying as they are quite strong, and will absorb the delicious flavours of their sauce.

Hokkien noodles

Shanghai noodles

Somen noodles

Ramen noodles

Pancit canton

Dried rice noodles

Wheat noodles

Mung bean vermicelli

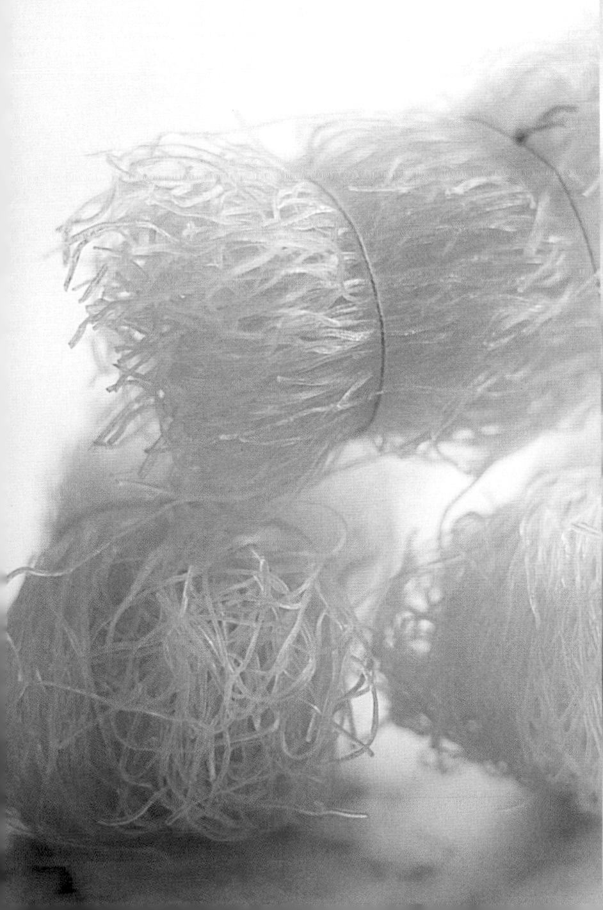

Udon noodles

SPICED BASMATI AND NUT RICE

Preparation time 15 minutes
Total cooking time 25 minutes
Serves 4

small pinch saffron threads
250 g (9 oz/1¼ cups) basmati rice
2 tablespoons vegetable oil
2 cinnamon sticks
6 green cardamom pods, crushed
6 cloves
75 g (2½ oz/½ cup) blanched almonds, toasted
75 g (2½ oz/⅔ cup) raisins
1 teaspoon salt
2 tablespoons chopped coriander (cilantro) leaves

1 Soak the saffron threads in 3 tablespoons of boiling water until required. Put the rice in a sieve and wash under cold running water until the water runs clear.

2 Heat the oil in a saucepan, add the spices and fry gently over medium heat for about 1–2 minutes, or until they start to release their aroma.

3 Add the rice, nuts and raisins and stir well until all the grains are glossy. Add 500 ml (17 fl oz/2 cups) of cold water and the salt and bring to the boil. Cover and simmer gently over low heat for 15 minutes.

4 Remove the pan from the heat, remove the lid, and drizzle over the saffron water. Cover and leave to stand for a further 10 minutes. Stir through the coriander and serve.

THAI BASIL FRIED RICE

Preparation time 15 minutes
Total cooking time 16 minutes
Serves 4

2 tablespoons oil
3 Asian shallots, sliced
1 garlic clove, finely chopped
1 small red chilli, finely chopped
100 g (3½ oz) snake or green beans, cut into
   short pieces
1 small red capsicum (pepper), cut into batons
90 g (3¼ oz) button mushrooms, halved
470 g (1 lb/2½ cups) cooked jasmine rice
1 teaspoon grated palm sugar
3 tablespoons light soy sauce

10 g (¼ oz) Thai basil, shredded
1 tablespoon chopped coriander (cilantro) leaves
fried red Asian shallot flakes, to garnish
Thai basil leaves, to garnish

1 Heat a wok over high heat, add the oil
and swirl. Stir-fry the shallots, garlic and
chilli for 3 minutes, or until the shallots start
to brown.
2 Add the beans, capsicum and mushrooms,
stir-fry for 3 minutes, or until cooked,
then stir in the cooked jasmine rice and
heat through.
3 Dissolve the palm sugar in the soy sauce,
then pour over the rice. Stir in the herbs.
Garnish with the shallot flakes and basil.

NASI GORENG

Preparation time 35 minutes

Total cooking time 30 minutes

Serves 4

2 eggs

4 tablespoons oil

3 garlic cloves, finely chopped

1 onion, finely chopped

2 red chillies, seeded and very finely chopped

1 teaspoon shrimp paste

1 teaspoon coriander seeds

½ teaspoon sugar

400 g (14 oz) raw prawns (shrimp), peeled
   and deveined

200 g (7 oz) rump steak, thinly sliced

200 g (7 oz/1 cup) long-grain rice, cooked
   and cooled

2 teaspoons kecap manis

1 tablespoon soy sauce

4 spring onions (scallions), finely chopped

½ lettuce, finely shredded

1 cucumber, thinly sliced

3 tablespoons crisp fried onion

1 Beat the eggs and ¼ teaspoon salt together. Heat a frying pan over medium heat.

2 Pour about one-quarter of the egg into the pan and cook for 1–2 minutes, or until the omelette sets. Turn the omelette over and cook the other side for about 30 seconds. Remove from the pan and repeat with the remaining egg mixture, working with one-quarter of the egg mixture at a time. Allow to cool, then roll up and cut into strips.

3 Combine the garlic, onion, chilli, shrimp paste, coriander and sugar in a food processor or mortar and pestle, and process or pound to form a smooth paste.

4 Heat 1–2 tablespoons of the oil in a wok or large, deep frying pan. Add the paste and cook over high heat for 1 minute, or until fragrant. Add the prawns and steak and stir-fry for 2–3 minutes, or until they change colour.

5 Add the remaining oil and the cold rice to the wok and stir-fry, breaking up any lumps, until the rice is heated through. Add the kecap manis, soy sauce and spring onion and stir-fry for another minute.

6 Arrange the lettuce around the outside of a large platter. Put the rice in the centre and garnish with the omelette strips, cucumber slices and fried onion. Serve immediately.

CHINESE FRIED RICE

Preparation time 20 minutes +
Total cooking time 20 minutes
Serves 4

350 g (12 oz/1¾ cups) long-grain rice
1 tablespoon vegetable or peanut oil
2 eggs, beaten
3 Chinese sausages (lap cheong), thinly sliced
   on diagonal (see note)
100 g (3½ oz) snake beans, cut into 2 cm
   (¾ in) lengths
6 spring onions (scallions), finely chopped
2 garlic cloves, crushed
2 teaspoons grated fresh ginger
160 g (5½ oz) small green prawns (shrimp),
   peeled and deveined
100 g (3½ oz/⅔ cup) frozen peas, thawed
2 tablespoons soy sauce
2 spring onions (scallions), extra, thinly sliced
   on diagonal, to serve

1 Wash the rice under cold running water until the water runs clear. Bring a large saucepan of water to the boil, add the rice and cook for 10–12 minutes, or until tender. Drain and rinse under cold water to remove any excess starch. Spread out on a flat tray and refrigerate for 2 hours or overnight.

2 Heat a wok over high heat, add half the oil and swirl to coat. Add the egg, swirling to coat the side of the wok. When the egg is almost set, roll it up in the wok, turn the heat off, then remove. Roughly chop and set aside.

3 Reheat the wok over high heat, add the remaining oil and swirl to coat. Add the Chinese sausage and snake beans and stir-fry for 2–3 minutes. Add the spring onion, garlic and ginger and stir-fry for 1 minute. Add the prawns and stir-fry for 1–2 minutes, or until cooked. Stir in the rice and peas and toss until well combined and heated through. Stir in the soy sauce and serve garnished with the chopped egg and extra spring onion.

Note Lap cheong sausage is a Chinese dried pork sausage and can be found in Asian food stores.

CHICKEN PILAF

Preparation time 15 minutes

Total cooking time 20 minutes

Serves 6

½ large barbecued chicken

50 g (1¾ oz) margarine

1 onion, finely chopped

2 garlic cloves, crushed

300 g (10½ oz/1½ cups) basmati rice

1 tablespoon currants

2 tablespoons finely chopped dried apricots

1 teaspoon ground cinnamon

pinch of ground cardamom

750 ml (26 fl oz/3 cups) chicken stock

1 handful coriander (cilantro) leaves, chopped

1 Remove the skin and any fat from the chicken and shred the meat into bite-sized pieces.

2 Melt the margarine in a large, deep frying pan over medium heat. Add the onion and garlic and cook for 2 minutes, stirring often. Add the rice, currants, apricots and spices and stir until well coated.

3 Pour in the stock and bring to the boil. Reduce the heat to low and simmer, covered, for about 15 minutes. Add a little water if the pilaf starts to dry out.

4 Add the shredded chicken and stir for about 1–2 minutes, or until thoroughly heated through. Stir in the coriander and serve immediately.

PAELLA

Preparation time 20 minutes
Total cooking time 26 minutes
Serves 4

500 g (1 lb 2 oz) black mussels
3 tablespoons olive oil
600 g (1 lb 5 oz) chicken drumettes or
    thigh fillets, halved
1 onion, chopped
2 large garlic cloves, chopped
3 vine-ripened tomatoes, peeled, seeded and
    finely chopped
1 small red capsicum (pepper), diced
1 small green capsicum (pepper), diced
¼ teaspoon chilli flakes
1 teaspoon paprika
¼ teaspoon saffron threads soaked in
    3 tablespoons of warm water
290 g (10¼ oz/1⅓ cups) short-grain rice
1 litre (35 fl oz/4 cups) vegetable stock
12 raw prawns (shrimp), peeled, deveined,
    tails intact
155 g (5½ oz/1 cup) peas
3 tablespoons dry sherry

30 g (1 oz) parsley, chopped
1 lemon, cut into wedges

1 Scrub the mussels and remove the beards. Discard any open mussels that don't close when tapped.
2 Heat 2 tablespoons oil in a large frying pan, add the chicken and cook over medium heat for 5–7 minutes, or until browned. Remove from the pan and keep warm.
3 Add the remaining oil to the pan, then add the onion, garlic and tomato, and cook over low heat for 5 minutes, or until soft.
4 Add the capsicum and cook for 1 minute, then stir in the chilli flakes, paprika and saffron and its soaking liquid. Pour in the rice and return the chicken to the pan. Add the stock, bring to the boil, then reduce the heat and simmer for 10 minutes.
5 Stir in the prawns, peas, sherry and mussels. Cover for 2 minutes, or until the mussels open. Discard any that do not open. Stir for 2 minutes, or until the prawns are pink and cooked through. Stir in the parsley. Serve immediately with the lemon wedges.

BIRYANI-STYLE RICE

Preparation time 20 minutes
Total cooking time 25 minutes
Serves 4

200 g (7 oz/1 cup) basmati rice
pinch of saffron threads
1 cinnamon stick
4 cardamom pods, smashed
1 large potato, cut into 2 cm (¾ in) cubes
1 teaspoon sea salt
3 tablespoons vegetable or peanut oil
1 eggplant (aubergine), cut into 2 cm (¾ in) cubes
1 red onion, cut into thin wedges
3 garlic cloves, crushed
1 tablespoon grated fresh ginger
1 teaspoon dried chilli flakes
1 teaspoon ground cinnamon
1 teaspoon ground coriander
2 teaspoons ground cumin
1 teaspoon ground cardamom
1 teaspoon fennel seeds, ground
155 g (5½ oz/1¼ cups) green beans, trimmed and cut into 2 cm (¾ in) lengths, blanched
100 g (3½ oz/⅔ cup) frozen peas, thawed
50 g (1¾ oz/⅓ cup) currants

1 small handful coriander (cilantro) leaves
2 tablespoons chopped toasted pistachio kernels

1 Wash the rice under cold water until it runs clear. Put the rice, saffron, cinnamon, cardamom pods, potato cubes and salt in a large saucepan. Fill with cold water to 2 cm (¾ in) above the rice and bring to a simmer over low heat. When the rice starts to pocket (after about 5 minutes), cover and cook for 10 minutes, or until the rice is tender. Fluff the rice with a fork and turn out onto a flat tray to cool slightly. Discard the cinnamon stick and cardamom pods.
2 Heat a wok over high heat, add about 2 tablespoons of the oil and swirl to coat. Add the eggplant and stir-fry for 3–4 minutes, or until softened and golden. Remove from the wok.
3 Heat the remaining oil in the wok, add the onion and cook for 1 minute, or until softened. Add the garlic, ginger, chilli, spices and beans and cook for 1 minute. Stir in the rice mixture, eggplant, peas, currants and coriander leaves and gently toss until combined. Serve sprinkled with the pistachios.

YANGZHOU-STYLE FRIED RICE

Preparation time 20 minutes +
Total cooking time 10 minutes
Serves 4

2 tablespoons dried shrimp
3 tablespoons vegetable oil
3 eggs, lightly beaten
250 g (9 oz) Chinese barbecue pork (char siu),
    finely diced
100 g (3½ oz/½ cup) tinned straw mushrooms,
    drained, rinsed and finely diced
740 g (1 lb 10 oz/4 cups) cooked long-grain rice,
    cold
2½ tablespoons light soy sauce
3 spring onions (scallions), finely chopped
2 tablespoons finely chopped garlic chives
white pepper, to taste
sesame oil, to taste

1 Put the dried shrimp in a heatproof bowl and cover with boiling water. Leave to soak for 15 minutes, then drain and finely chop.

2 Heat a wok until hot, add 1 tablespoon of oil and swirl to coat. Add the egg and leave it until it just starts to set. When the egg is almost cooked, break it into small strips with the edge of a spatula, then remove from the wok.

3 Heat another tablespoon of oil in the wok, add the barbecue pork and stir-fry over high heat for 1 minute, or until heated through. Add the straw mushrooms and soaked shrimp, and continue to stir-fry with the pork for an additional 1–2 minutes.

4 Add the remaining oil, then gradually add the cooked rice, tossing and stirring for 2 minutes, or until heated through. Reduce the heat to medium, add the soy sauce, spring onion and garlic chives, then continue to stir-fry until all the ingredients are thoroughly combined and the soy sauce evenly coats the rice. Season to taste with white pepper and a drizzle of sesame oil, and serve, topped with the omelette strips.

CAPSICUM, SNOWPEA AND HOKKIEN NOODLE STIR-FRY

Preparation time 10 minutes
Total cooking time 10 minutes
Serves 4

500 g (1 lb 2 oz) hokkien (egg) noodles
1 tablespoon vegetable or peanut oil
1 red onion, cut into thin wedges
2 garlic cloves, crushed
3 cm (1¼ in) piece fresh ginger, julienned
150 g (5½ oz) snowpeas (mangetout), topped
  and tailed, large ones halved on the diagonal
1 carrot, halved lengthways, sliced on the
  diagonal
1 red capsicum (pepper), julienned
4 tablespoons Chinese barbecue sauce
  (char siu sauce)
1 handful coriander (cilantro) leaves

1 Soak the noodles in boiling water for
5 minutes to soften and separate. Drain well.
2 Heat a wok over high heat, add the oil
and swirl to coat. Add the onion, garlic and
ginger and stir-fry for 1 minute. Add the
snowpeas, carrot and capsicum and cook
for 2–3 minutes.
3 Stir in the noodles and barbecue sauce
and cook for a further 2 minutes. Toss in the
coriander leaves and serve.

SICHUAN RICE NOODLES

Preparation time 10 minutes
Total cooking time 10 minutes
Serves 4

6 dried shiitake mushrooms
1 tablespoon Chinese rice wine
3 tablespoons kecap manis
1 tablespoon peanut oil
6 spring onions (scallions), cut into 3 cm
   (1¼ in) lengths
2 garlic cloves, crushed
1 teaspoon Chinese five-spice
2 tablespoons chopped coriander (cilantro) stems
   and roots
1 teaspoon sichuan pepper, pounded
1 large long red chilli, thinly sliced on the diagonal
375 g (13 oz) baby bok choy (pak choy),
   quartered lengthways
500 g (1 lb 2 oz) fresh rice noodles, 2 cm
   (¾ in) wide

1 small handful coriander (cilantro) leaves
2 spring onions (scallions), extra, finely sliced on
   the diagonal

1 Soak the mushrooms in boiling water for 5 minutes to soften. Drain, reserving 3 tablespoons of the liquid. Discard the woody stems and finely slice the caps. Combine the reserved liquid, rice wine and kecap manis.
2 Heat a wok over high heat, add the oil and swirl to coat. Stir-fry the spring onion, garlic, five-spice powder, coriander stems, pepper and chilli for 1–2 minutes.
3 Add the bok choy, mushrooms and the mushroom sauce mixture and stir-fry for a further 2 minutes, or until the bok choy has wilted. Add the noodles and gently toss until well combined and coated in the sauce. Serve sprinkled with the coriander leaves and extra spring onion.

DUCK RICE NOODLE ROLLS

Preparation time 20 minutes +
Total cooking time 15 minutes
Serves 4

700 g (1 lb 9 oz) barbecued or roast duck
8 fresh rice noodle rolls, at room temperature
2 spring onions (scallions), thinly sliced
2 thick slices fresh ginger, thinly sliced
1 handful coriander (cilantro) leaves
oyster sauce, for drizzling
chilli sauce, to serve

1 Cut the duck into bite-sized pieces. You may have to strip the flesh off the bones first, depending on how you bought it — leave the skin on but trim off any fatty bits.

2 Carefully unroll the rice noodle rolls. Put a pile of duck (an eighth of the whole amount) at one edge of the narrower end of one noodle roll and arrange some spring onion, ginger and coriander over it. Drizzle with about a teaspoon of oyster sauce and roll the sheet up. Repeat this with the remaining sheets. Put the sheets on a heatproof plate.

3 Put the plate in a bamboo or metal steamer and set the steamer above a wok filled with simmering water. Cover and steam for about 5 minutes.

4 Serve the rolls cut into lengths with some more oyster sauce drizzled over them and some chilli sauce on the side.

RICE NOODLES WITH BEEF, BLACK BEANS AND CAPSICUMS

Preparation time 15 minutes
Total cooking time 15 minutes
Serves 4

300 g (10½ oz) rump steak
1 garlic clove, crushed
3 tablespoons oyster sauce
2 teaspoons sugar
2 tablespoons soy sauce
5 tablespoons black bean sauce
2 teaspoons cornflour (cornstarch)
¾ teaspoon sesame oil
1.2 kg (2 lb 11 oz) fresh or 600 g (1 lb 5 oz) dried flat rice noodles
1½ tablespoons oil
2 red capsicums (peppers), sliced
1 green capsicum (pepper), sliced
1 handful coriander (cilantro) leaves

1 Cut the steak across the grain into thin slices. Combine the garlic, oyster sauce, sugar, soy sauce, black bean sauce, cornflour and sesame oil in a bowl. Add the steak, making sure the slices are all well coated.
2 If you are using dried rice noodles, soak them in boiling water for 10 minutes, or until they are opaque and soft. Drain well.
3 Heat the oil in a wok or frying pan and add the capsicum. Stir-fry for 1–2 minutes or until they start to soften, then add the meat mixture and cook for a minute.
4 Add the noodles and gently toss to combine. Cook until the meat is cooked through, then toss in the coriander leaves and stir. Serve immediately.

FRIED NOODLES WITH CHICKEN, PORK AND PRAWN

Preparation time 20 minutes

Total cooking time 10 minutes

Serves 4

900 g (2 lb) fresh flat rice noodle sheets, cut into 2 cm (¾ in) thick slices

100 ml (3½ fl oz) oil

2 garlic cloves, finely chopped

1 tablespoon grated fresh ginger

70 g (2½ oz) garlic chives, cut into 5 cm (2 in) lengths

½ barbecue chicken, cut into 1 cm (½ in) slices

300 g (10½ oz) Chinese barbecue pork fillet (char siu), cut into 1 cm (½ in) slices

1 small fresh red chilli, chopped

12 large cooked prawns (shrimp), peeled and deveined

180 g (6 oz) bean sprouts, trimmed

100 g (3½ oz) baby English spinach leaves

2 eggs, beaten

2 teaspoons caster (superfine) sugar

125 ml (4 fl oz/½ cup) light soy sauce

2 tablespoons dark soy sauce

2 tablespoons fish sauce

1 Rinse the rice noodles under warm running water and carefully separate. Drain.

2 Heat a wok over high heat, add about 3 tablespoons of the oil and swirl to coat. Add the garlic and ginger, and cook, stirring, for 30 seconds. Then add the chives and cook, stirring, for 10 seconds.

3 Add the barbecue chicken, barbecue pork, chilli and prawns, and cook, stirring, for 2 minutes, then add the bean sprouts and spinach, and cook, stirring, for 1 minute.

4 Make a well in the centre of the mixture, add the egg and scramble for 1 minute, or until firm but not hard. Stir in the remaining oil, then add the rice noodles. Stir to combine. Add the combined caster sugar, light and dark soy sauce, and fish sauce, and stir-fry for 2–3 minutes, or until heated through. Season with pepper.

SPICY CELLOPHANE NOODLES WITH MINCED PORK

Preparation time 15 minutes +
Total cooking time 25 minutes
Serves 4

200 g (7 oz) minced (ground) pork
1 teaspoon cornflour (cornstarch)
1½ tablespoons light soy sauce
2 tablespoons Chinese rice wine
1 teaspoon sesame oil
150 g (5½ oz) cellophane noodles (mung bean vermicelli)
2 tablespoons oil
4 spring onions (scallions), finely chopped
1 garlic clove, crushed
1 tablespoon finely chopped ginger
2 teaspoons chilli bean sauce
185 ml (6 fl oz/¾ cup) chicken stock
½ teaspoon sugar
2 spring onions (scallions), green part only, extra, thinly sliced on the diagonal

1 Combine the pork, cornflour, 1 tablespoon of the soy sauce, 1 tablespoon of the rice wine and ½ teaspoon of the sesame oil in a bowl. Cover with plastic wrap and marinate for about 10–15 minutes.

2 Meanwhile, place the noodles in a heatproof bowl. Cover with boiling water and soak for 3–4 minutes, or until softened. Drain well.

3 Heat the oil in a wok over high heat. Cook the spring onion, garlic, ginger and chilli bean sauce for 10 seconds, then add the mince mixture and cook for about 2 minutes, stirring to break up any lumps. Stir in the stock, sugar, ½ teaspoon salt, and the remaining soy sauce, rice wine and sesame oil.

4 Add the noodles to the wok and toss to combine. Bring to the boil, then reduce the heat to low and simmer, stirring occasionally, for 7–8 minutes, or until the liquid is almost completely absorbed. Garnish with the extra spring onion and serve.

MANY MUSHROOM NOODLES

Preparation time 30 minutes +
Total cooking time 15 minutes
Serves 4–6

25 g (1 oz) dried shiitake mushrooms
375 ml (13 fl oz/1½ cups) boiling water
500 g (1 lb 2 oz) thin hokkien (egg) noodles
1 tablespoon vegetable oil
½ teaspoon sesame oil
1 tablespoon finely chopped fresh ginger
4 garlic cloves, crushed
100 g (3½ oz) fresh shiitake mushrooms,
   trimmed, sliced
150 g (5½ oz) oyster mushrooms, sliced
150 g (5½ oz) shimeji mushrooms, trimmed
1½ teaspoons dashi granules dissolved in 185 ml
   (6 fl oz/¾ cup) water
3 tablespoons soy sauce
3 tablespoons mirin
¼ teaspoon white pepper
25 g (1 oz) butter
2 tablespoons lemon juice
100 g (3½ oz) enoki mushrooms, trimmed
1 tablespoon chopped chives

1 Put the dried shiitake mushrooms in a heatproof bowl, cover with the boiling water and soak for 20 minutes, or until soft. Drain, reserving the soaking water. Squeeze the mushrooms dry, discard the stems and slice the caps.
2 Cover the noodles with boiling water for 1 minute, then drain and rinse. Set aside.
3 Heat a wok over high heat, add the oils and swirl to coat the base and side. Add the ginger, garlic, fresh shiitake, oyster and shimeji mushrooms and stir-fry for 1–2 minutes, or until the mushrooms have wilted. Remove from the wok. Set aside.
4 Combine the dashi, soy sauce, mirin, white pepper and 185 ml (6 fl oz/¾ cup) of the reserved liquid, add to the wok and cook for 3 minutes.
5 Add the butter, lemon juice and 1 teaspoon salt and cook for 1 minute, or until the sauce thickens. Return the mushrooms to the wok, cook for a further 2 minutes, then stir in the enoki and sliced shiitake mushroom caps. Add the noodles and stir for 3 minutes, or until heated through. Sprinkle with the chives and serve immediately.

INDONESIAN-STYLE FRIED NOODLES

Preparation time 20 minutes

Total cooking time 18 minutes

Serves 4

400 g (14 oz) fresh flat egg noodles (5 mm/
    ¼ in wide)

2 tablespoons peanut oil

4 red Asian shallots, thinly sliced

2 garlic cloves, chopped

1 small red chilli, finely diced

200 g (7 oz) pork fillet, thinly sliced across the
    grain

200 g (7 oz) chicken breast fillet, thinly sliced

200 g (7 oz) small raw prawns (shrimp), peeled
    and deveined, with tails intact

2 Chinese cabbage leaves, shredded

2 carrots, cut in half lengthways and thinly sliced

100 g (3½ oz) snake beans, cut into 3 cm (1¼ in)
    lengths

3 tablespoons kecap manis

1 tablespoon light soy sauce

2 tomatoes, peeled, seeded and chopped

4 spring onions (scallions), sliced on the diagonal

1 tablespoon crisp fried onion flakes

flat-leaf (Italian) parsley, to garnish

1 Cook the noodles in a large saucepan of boiling water for 1 minute, or until tender. Drain and rinse them under cold water.

2 Heat a wok over high heat, add the oil and swirl to coat. Stir-fry the Asian shallots for 30 seconds. Add the garlic, chilli and pork and stir-fry for 2 minutes. Add the chicken and cook a further 2 minutes, or until the meat is golden and tender.

3 Add the prawns and stir-fry for a further 2 minutes, or until pink and just cooked. Stir in the cabbage, carrot and beans and cook for 3 minutes.

4 Add the noodles and gently stir-fry for about 4 minutes, or until heated through — taking care not to break up the noodles. Stir in the kecap manis, soy sauce, chopped tomato and spring onion and stir-fry for 1–2 minutes.

4 Season with salt and freshly ground black pepper. Garnish with the fried onion flakes and parsley.

Note This dish, called bahmi goreng in Indonesian, is traditionally eaten with chopped roasted peanuts and sambal oelek on the side. It is also delicious with satay sauce.

GINGER CHICKEN STIR-FRY WITH HOKKIEN NOODLES

Preparation time 20 minutes

Total cooking time 15 minutes

Serves 4

2½ tablespoons finely shredded fresh ginger

3 tablespoons mirin

2 tablespoons soy sauce

600 g (1 lb 5 oz) chicken tenderloins or chicken breast fillets, cut diagonally into thin strips

180 g (6 oz) fresh baby corn

350 g (12 oz) choy sum

150 g (5½ oz) fresh oyster mushrooms

500 g (1 lb 2 oz) hokkien (egg) noodles

2 tablespoons oil

2 tablespoons oyster sauce

1 Combine the ginger, mirin and soy sauce in a non-metallic bowl. Add the chicken, coat well, then marinate.

2 Cut the corn in half lengthways; trim the ends off the choy sum and cut into 6 cm (2½ in) lengths.

3 Soak the noodles in a large heatproof bowl in boiling water for 5 minutes. Drain and refresh under cold running water.

4 Heat 1 tablespoon of the oil in a wok until very hot. Remove the chicken from the marinade with a slotted spoon. Cook in two batches over very high heat for 2 minutes, or until brown and just cooked. Remove from the wok.

5 Add the remaining oil to the wok and stir-fry the mushrooms and corn for 1–2 minutes, or until just softened. Add the remaining marinade and bring to the boil.

6 Add the chicken, choy sum and noodles. Stir in the oyster sauce and cook, tossing well, for 1–2 minutes, or until the choy sum has wilted slightly and the noodles are warmed through.

SINGAPORE NOODLES

Preparation time 10 minutes +
Total cooking time 10 minutes
Serves 4

2 tablespoons dried shrimp
300 g (10½ oz) rice vermicelli
100 g (3½ oz) Chinese barbecue pork (char siu)
100 g (3½ oz) bean sprouts, trimmed
4 tablespoons oil
2 eggs, beaten
1 onion, thinly sliced
1 teaspoon salt
1 tablespoon Chinese curry powder
2 tablespoons light soy sauce
2 spring onions, shredded
2 red chillies, shredded

1 Soak the dried shrimp in boiling water for 1 hour, then drain. Soak the noodles in hot water for 10 minutes, then drain. Thinly slice the pork. Wash the bean sprouts and drain thoroughly.
2 Heat 1 tablespoon of the oil in a wok over high heat until very hot. Pour in the egg and make an omelette. Remove from the wok and cut into pieces.
3 Reheat the wok over high heat, add the remaining oil and heat until very hot. Stir-fry the onion and bean sprouts with the pork and shrimp for 1 minute.
4 Add the noodles, salt, curry powder and soy sauce, blend well and stir for 1 minute. Add the omelette, spring onion and chilli and toss to combine.

YAKISOBA

Preparation time: 30 minutes +
Total cooking time: 10 minutes
Serves 4

4 dried shiitake mushrooms
600 g (1 lb 5 oz) hokkien (egg) noodles
3 teaspoons finely chopped fresh ginger
2 large garlic cloves, finely chopped
300 g (10½ oz) beef fillet, sliced across the grain
6 bacon slices, cut into 3 cm (1¼ in) pieces
2 tablespoons peanut oil
½ teaspoon sesame oil
6 spring onions (scallions), cut into 3 cm (1¼ in) lengths
1 carrot, thinly sliced on the diagonal
1 small green pepper (capsicum), thinly sliced
220 g (7 oz) Chinese cabbage, shredded

Sauce
3 tablespoons Japanese soy sauce
2 tablespoons Worcestershire sauce
1½ tablespoons Japanese rice vinegar
1 tablespoon sake
1 tablespoon mirin
1 tablespoon tomato sauce
1 tablespoon oyster sauce
2 teaspoons soft brown sugar

1 Soak the mushrooms in boiling water for 20 minutes, or until soft. Squeeze dry, reserving 2 tablespoons of the soaking liquid. Discard the stalks and thinly slice the caps.
2 Put the noodles in a heatproof bowl, cover with boiling water and soak for 1 minute. Drain and separate.
3 Combine half the ginger and half the garlic in a small bowl, then add the beef. Set aside.
4 To make the sauce, combine all the ingredients with the reserved mushroom liquid and the remaining ginger and garlic.
5 Heat a wok over medium–high heat, add the bacon and cook for 2–3 minutes, or until softened. Transfer to a bowl. Combine the peanut and sesame oils. Increase the wok to high, add a little of the oil mixture and stir-fry the beef for 1 minute. Add to the bacon.
6 Heat a little more of the oil mixture in the wok, add the spring onion, carrot and pepper and stir-fry for 1 minute. Add the cabbage and mushrooms and cook for 30 seconds, then add to the bowl with the bacon.
7 Heat the remaining oil in the wok, add the noodles and stir-fry for 1 minute. Return the bacon, beef and vegetables to the wok, pour on the sauce and stir-fry for about 2–3 minutes.

CHICKEN SATAY NOODLES

Preparation time 20 minutes +
Total cooking time 25 minutes
Serves 4

Peanut sauce
1 tablespoon peanut oil
8 red Asian shallots, finely chopped
8 garlic cloves, crushed
1 tablespoon finely chopped ginger
4 small red chillies, finely chopped
250 g (9 oz/1 cup) crunchy peanut butter
1½ tablespoons light soy sauce
3 tablespoons fish sauce
400 ml (14 fl oz) coconut milk
4 tablespoons grated palm sugar
2 kaffir lime leaves
4 tablespoons lime juice

400 g (14 oz) hokkien (egg) noodles
2 tablespoons peanut oil
1 small white onion, finely chopped
2 garlic cloves, finely chopped
1 small red chilli, finely chopped
400 g (14 oz) chicken tenderloins, tendon
    removed, halved
200 g (7 oz) bean sprouts, trimmed
150 g (5½ oz) spring onions (scallions), chopped
1 small Lebanese (short) cucumber, cut in half
    lengthways and sliced
lime wedges, to serve

1 To make the peanut sauce, heat a wok over medium heat, add the oil and swirl to coat. Add the shallots, garlic, ginger and chilli and cook for 5 minutes. Reduce the heat to low, add the remaining sauce ingredients and simmer for 10 minutes, or until thickened. Remove and keep warm. Discard the lime leaves before serving. If the sauce is too thick, stir in 2 tablespoons water.
2 Place the noodles in a heatproof bowl, cover with boiling water and soak for 1 minute, or until tender and separated. Drain well.
3 Heat a clean wok over high heat, add the oil and swirl to coat. Stir-fry the onion, garlic and chilli for 30 seconds. Add the chicken and cook for 3–4 minutes, or until brown.
4 Stir in the bean sprouts and spring onion and cook for 30 seconds, then add the noodles and toss together for 1–2 minutes.
4 Divide the noodle mixture among the serving bowls and dollop with the peanut sauce. Garnish with the cucumber slices and serve with the lime wedges.

YAKIUDON

Preparation time 25 minutes

Total cooking time 25 minutes

Serves 4

5 dried shiitake mushrooms

1 garlic clove, crushed

2 teaspoons grated fresh ginger

125 ml (4 fl oz/½ cup) Japanese soy sauce

2 tablespoons rice wine vinegar

2 tablespoons sugar

1 tablespoon lemon juice

500 g (1 lb 2 oz) fresh udon noodles

2 tablespoons oil

500 g (1 lb 2 oz) chicken thigh fillets, thinly sliced

1 garlic clove, extra, finely chopped

1 small red capsicum (pepper), thinly sliced

150 g (5½ oz/2 cups) shredded cabbage

4 spring onions (scallions), thinly sliced

1 tablespoon sesame oil

2 tablespoons drained shredded pickled ginger

1 Place the mushrooms in a heatproof bowl and soak in boiling water for 10 minutes, or until tender. Drain, reserving 3 tablespoons of the liquid. Discard the stems, squeeze the caps dry and thinly slice.

2 Combine the crushed garlic, ginger, soy sauce, vinegar, sugar, lemon juice and reserved soaking liquid.

3 Place the noodles in a heatproof bowl, cover with boiling water and leave for 2 minutes, or until soft and tender. Drain.

4 Heat a wok over high heat, add half the oil and swirl to coat. Add the chicken in batches and stir-fry for 5 minutes, or until browned. Remove from the wok.

5 Add the remaining oil and swirl to coat. Add the extra chopped garlic, mushrooms, capsicum and cabbage, and stir-fry for 2–3 minutes, or until softened.

6 Add the noodles and stir-fry for another minute. Return the chicken to the wok and add the spring onion, sesame oil and soy sauce mixture, stirring until well combined and heated through. Season with white pepper and scatter with the pickled ginger.

STIR-FRIED LAMB WITH MINT, CHILLI AND SHANGHAI NOODLES

Preparation time 15 minutes

Total cooking time 10 minutes

Serves 4–6

400 g (14 oz) Shanghai noodles

1 teaspoon sesame oil

2 tablespoons peanut oil

220 g (7¾ oz) lamb fillet, cut into thin strips

2 garlic cloves, crushed

2 fresh red chillies, seeded and finely sliced

1 tablespoon oyster sauce

2 teaspoons palm sugar

2 tablespoons fish sauce

2 tablespoons lime juice

10 g (¼ oz) mint, chopped

lime wedges, to garnish

1 Cook the noodles in a large saucepan of boiling water for 4–5 minutes. Drain, then rinse in cold water. Add the sesame oil and toss through.

2 Heat the peanut oil in a wok over high heat. Add the lamb and cook in batches for 1–2 minutes, or until just browned. Return all the meat to the wok and add the garlic and chilli. Cook for 30 seconds.

3 Add the oyster sauce, palm sugar, fish sauce, lime juice and noodles. Cook for a further 2–3 minutes, or until the noodles are warm. Stir in the mint and serve immediately with the lime wedges.

SPICY CHILLI PRAWNS WITH HOKKIEN NOODLES

Preparation time 15 minutes

Total cooking time 10 minutes

Serves 4

400 g (14 oz) hokkien (egg) noodles

1 tablespoon peanut oil

1 tablespoon red curry paste

2 garlic cloves, crushed

1 lemongrass stem (white part only), finely
   chopped

2 tablespoons finely sliced coriander (cilantro) root

125 ml (4½ fl oz/½ cup) lime juice

60 g (2¼ oz/⅓ cup) grated palm sugar

2 tablespoons tomato sauce

2½ tablespoons fish sauce

185 ml (6 fl oz/¾ cup) chicken stock

16 prawns (shrimp), peeled and deveined

350 g (12 oz) choy sum, cut into 2 cm (¾ in)
   lengths

100 g (3½ oz) snake beans, cut into 1.5 cm
   (⅝ in) lengths

4 spring onions (scallions), finely chopped

115 g (4 oz/¾ cup) roasted cashew nuts, roughly
   chopped

15 g (½ oz) coriander (cilantro) leaves

Thai basil, to garnish

lime wedges, to serve (optional)

1 Place the noodles in a heatproof bowl, cover with boiling water and soak for 1 minute, or until tender. Drain, rinse under cold water and drain again.

2 Heat a wok over high heat, add the oil and swirl to coat. Add the curry paste and fry for 5 seconds, then add the garlic, lemongrass and coriander root and stir-fry for 30 seconds, or until well combined.

3 Whisk the lime juice, palm sugar, tomato sauce, fish sauce and stock together, then add to the wok. Cook over high heat for 2 minutes, or until slightly reduced.

4 Add the prawns and cook for 2–3 minutes, or until almost cooked. Add the noodles and stir-fry for 2 minutes. Add the choy sum and beans and continue to stir-fry for 2 minutes, or until the leaves have wilted and the beans are tender but not soft.

5 Stir in the spring onion, cashews and coriander leaves until combined. Garnish with the basil and serve with lime wedges.

SHANGHAI PORK NOODLES

Preparation time 25 minutes +
Total cooking time 20 minutes
Serves 4

½ teaspoon sesame oil
3 tablespoons soy sauce
2 tablespoons oyster sauce
250 g (9 oz) pork loin fillet, cut into very thin strips
2 tablespoons dried shrimp
8 dried shiitake mushrooms
1 teaspoon sugar
250 ml (9 fl oz/1 cup) chicken stock
300 g (10½ oz) fresh Shanghai noodles
2 tablespoons peanut oil
1 garlic clove, thinly sliced
2 teaspoons grated fresh ginger
1 celery stalk, cut into matchsticks
1 leek, white part only, cut into matchsticks
150 g (5½ oz) Chinese cabbage (wong bok), shredded
50 g (1¾ oz) tinned bamboo shoots, cut into matchsticks
8 spring onions (scallions), thinly sliced

1 Combine the sesame oil and 1 tablespoon each of the soy sauce and oyster sauce. Add the pork strips. Marinate for 30 minutes.
2 Meanwhile, put the dried shrimp in a bowl, cover with boiling water and soak for about 20 minutes. Drain and finely chop.
3 Meanwhile, put the shiitake mushrooms in a heatproof bowl, cover with boiling water and soak for 20 minutes. Drain, squeeze dry, discard the stems and thinly slice the caps.
4 To make the stir-fry sauce, combine the sugar, stock, remaining soy and oyster sauces and 1 teaspoon salt in a bowl. Set aside.
5 Cook the noodles in a saucepan of boiling water for 4–5 minutes, or until tender. Drain and refresh under cold water. Toss with 1 teaspoon of the peanut oil.
6 Heat 1 tablespoon of the peanut oil in a wok over high heat. Add the pork and stir-fry for 1–2 minutes, or until cooked. Remove.
7 Heat the remaining peanut oil, add the garlic, ginger, celery, leek and cabbage and stir-fry for 1 minute, or until softened. Add the bamboo shoots, spring onion, shrimp and mushrooms and stir-fry for 1 minute.
8 Add the noodles and the stir-fry sauce and toss together for 3–5 minutes.
9 Return the pork to the wok, with any juices, and toss for 1–2 minutes.

TERIYAKI BEEF WITH GREENS AND CRISPY NOODLES

Preparation time 20 minutes +
Total cooking time 20 minutes
Serves 4

450 g (1 lb) sirloin steak, cut into thin strips
125 ml (4 fl oz/½ cup) teriyaki marinade
vegetable oil, for deep-frying
100 g (3½ oz) dried rice vermicelli
2 tablespoons peanut oil
1 onion, sliced
3 garlic cloves, crushed
1 red chilli, seeded and finely chopped
200 g (7 oz) carrots, julienned
600 g (1 lb 5 oz) choy sum, cut into 3 cm
    (1¼ in) lengths
1 tablespoon lime juice

1 Combine the beef and teriyaki marinade in a non-metallic bowl and marinate for 2 hours.

2 Fill a wok one-third full of oil and heat to 190°C (375°F), or until a cube of bread browns in 10 seconds. Separate the vermicelli noodles into small bundles and deep-fry until they sizzle and puff up. Drain well on paper towels. Drain the oil and carefully pour it into a heatproof bowl to cool before discarding.

3 Heat 1 tablespoon of the peanut oil in the wok. When the oil is nearly smoking, add the beef (reserving the marinade) and cook in batches over high heat for 1–2 minutes. Remove to a plate. Heat the remaining oil. Add the onion and stir-fry for 3–4 minutes. Add the garlic and chilli and cook for 30 seconds. Add the carrot and choy sum and stir-fry for 3–4 minutes, or until tender.

4 Return the beef to the wok with the lime juice and reserved marinade and cook over high heat for 3 minutes. Add the noodles, toss well briefly, and serve immediately.

IDIYAPPAM

Preparation time 15 minutes +
Total cooking time 20 minutes
Serves 4

225 g (8 oz) rice sticks or vermicelli
4 tablespoons oil
50 g (1¾ oz/⅓ cup) cashew nuts
½ onion, chopped
3 eggs
150 g (5½ oz/1 cup) fresh or frozen peas
10 curry leaves
2 carrots, grated
2 leeks, finely shredded
1 red capsicum (pepper), diced
2 tablespoons tomato sauce (ketchup)
1 tablespoon soy sauce
1 teaspoon salt

1 Soak the rice sticks in cold water for 30 minutes, then drain and put them in a saucepan of boiling water. Remove from the heat and leave in the pan for 3 minutes. Drain and refresh in cold water.

2 Heat 1 tablespoon of the oil in a frying pan and fry the cashews until golden. Remove. Add the onion to the pan, fry until dark golden, then drain.

3 Cook the eggs in boiling water for about 10 minutes to hard-boil, then cool in cold water. When cold, peel and cut into wedges. Cook the peas in boiling water until tender.

3 Heat the oil in a pan and fry the curry leaves. Add the carrot, leek and capsicum and stir for 1 minute. Add the tomato sauce, soy sauce, salt and rice sticks. Serve with the peas, cashews, fried onion and egg.

RICE NOODLES WITH BEEF

Preparation time 1 hour +
Total cooking time 30 minutes
Serves 4

500 g (1 lb 2 oz) fresh rice noodle sheets
2 tablespoons peanut oil
2 eggs, lightly beaten
500 g (1 lb 2 oz) rump steak, thinly sliced across
    the grain
3 tablespoons kecap manis
1½ tablespoons soy sauce
1½ tablespoons fish sauce
300 g (10½ oz) Chinese broccoli (gai larn), cut into
    5 cm (2 in) lengths
¼ teaspoon ground white pepper
lemon wedges, to serve

1 Put the mushrooms in a small heatproof
bowl, cover with boiling water and soak for
10 minutes. Squeeze the mushrooms dry,
discard the stems and finely chop the caps.
2 Combine the mushrooms, pork, pork fat,
prawn meat, spring onion, bamboo shoots
and celery in a bowl.
3 Combine the cornflour, soy sauce, and
sugar in another bowl and stir to make a
smooth paste. Season and then stir into
the pork mixture. Cover and refrigerate
for 1 hour.
4 Working with one won ton wrapper at
a time, place 1 tablespoon of filling in the
centre of each wrapper. Moisten the edges
with water and gather the edges into the
centre, pressing together to seal. Set aside
on a lightly floured surface.
5 Line a bamboo steamer with baking paper.
Arrange the dim sims in the steamer, leaving
a gap between each one. Cover and steam
each batch over a wok of simmering water
for 8 minutes, or until the filling is cooked.
Serve with chilli sauce or soy sauce.

NOODLES WITH FISH AND BLACK BEANS

Preparation time 10 minutes

Cooking time 20 minutes

Serves 4

270 g (9½ oz) fresh rice noodles

200 g (7 oz) Chinese broccoli (gai larn), cut into 5 cm (2 in) lengths

550 g (1 lb 4 oz) skinless firm white fish fillets, cut into bite-sized pieces

2 tablespoons light soy sauce

1½ tablespoons Chinese rice wine

1 teaspoon sugar

½ teaspoon sesame oil

2 teaspoons cornflour (cornstarch)

1 tablespoon vegetable oil

5 garlic cloves, crushed

2 teaspoons finely chopped fresh ginger

2 spring onions (scallions), finely chopped

2 small red chillies, finely chopped

2 tablespoons salted black beans, rinsed and roughly chopped

155 ml (5 fl oz) fish stock

spring onions (scallions), sliced, extra, to garnish

1 Cover the noodles with boiling water and soak for 1–2 minutes, or until tender.

Separate gently and drain. Keep warm.
2 Put the Chinese broccoli in a steamer, cover and steam over a wok of simmering water for 3–4 minutes, or until slightly wilted. Remove from the heat. Keep warm.
3 Place the fish pieces in a bowl. Combine the soy sauce, rice wine, sugar, sesame oil and cornflour, then pour the mixture over the fish and toss to coat well.
4 Heat a wok over high heat until very hot, add the vegetable oil and swirl to coat the base and side. Add the garlic, ginger, spring onion, chilli and black beans and stir-fry for 1 minute. Add the fish and the marinade and cook for 2 minutes, or until the fish is almost cooked through. Remove the fish with a slotted spoon and keep warm.
5 Pour the fish stock into the wok and bring to the boil. Reduce the heat to low and bring to a slow simmer. Cook for 5 minutes, or until the sauce has slightly thickened. Return the fish to the wok, cover with a lid and continue to simmer gently for 2–3 minutes, or until just cooked.
6 To serve, divide the noodles among serving dishes, top with the Chinese broccoli and spoon the fish and black bean sauce on top. Garnish with the extra spring onion.

UDON NOODLE SOUP

Preparation time 20 minutes
Total cooking time 16 minutes
Serves 4

400 g (14 oz) dried udon noodles
1 litre (35 fl oz/4 cups) water
3 teaspoons dashi granules
2 leeks, white part only, finely sliced
200 g (7 oz) pork loin, cut into thin strips
125 ml (4 fl oz/½ cup) Japanese soy sauce
2 tablespoons mirin
4 spring onions (scallions), finely chopped
shichimi togarashi (see Note), to serve

1 Cook the noodles in a large saucepan of rapidly boiling water for 5 minutes, or until tender. Drain and cover to keep warm.
2 Combine the water and dashi in a large saucepan and bring to the boil. Add the leek, reduce the heat and simmer for 5 minutes. Add the pork, soy sauce, mirin and spring onion and simmer for 2 minutes, or until the pork is cooked. Divide the noodles among four serving bowls and ladle the soup over the top. Garnish with the spring onion and sprinkle the shichimi togarashi over the top.
Note Shichimi togarashi is a Japanese spice mix. It is available in Asian grocery stores.

CHILLI AND TOFU NOODLES

Preparation time 15 minutes
Total cooking time 12 minutes
Serves 6

3 tablespoons peanut oil
1 teaspoon bottled crushed chilli
2 teaspoons grated fresh ginger
2 garlic cloves, crushed
250 g (9 oz) hard tofu, cut into 1.5 cm (⅝ in)
  cubes
8 spring onions (scallions), sliced on the diagonal
150 g (5½ oz) fresh baby corn, halved lengthways
150 g (5½ oz) snowpeas (mangetout), topped
  and tailed
500 g (1 lb 2 oz) hokkien (egg) noodles
40 g (1½ oz/¼ cup) cashew nuts
2 tablespoons soy sauce
125 ml (4 fl oz/½ cup) vegetable stock
1 handful coriander (cilantro) leaves

1 Heat the oil in a wok over medium heat and swirl to coat. Add the chilli, ginger and garlic and stir-fry for about 2–3 minutes, or until aromatic. Add the tofu cubes, spring onion and baby corn and stir-fry for 2–3 minutes.

2 Add the snowpeas, noodles and cashews and cook, stirring, for 3–5 minutes, or until the vegetables are almost tender. Stir in the soy sauce and stock, then bring to the boil and simmer for 2 minutes, or until slightly reduced. Stir in the coriander and serve immediately.

BUDDHIST VEGETARIAN NOODLES

Preparation time 25 minutes +
Total cooking time 15 minutes
Serves 4

15 g (½ oz) dried Chinese mushrooms
400 g (14 oz) fresh flat egg noodles
2–3 tablespoons peanut oil
1 small carrot, julienned
150 g (5½ oz) baby corn, cut into quarters
   lengthways
230 g (8 oz) tinned julienned bamboo shoots,
   drained
150 g (5½ oz) snowpeas (mangetout), julienned
½ small red capsicum (pepper), julienned
1 small green capsicum (pepper), julienned
90 g (3¼ oz) bean sprouts, trimmed
40 g (1¼ oz) Chinese cabbage (wong bok), finely
   shredded
2 cm x 2 cm (¾ in x ¾ in) piece ginger,
   julienned
1 tablespoon mushroom soy sauce
1 tablespoon light soy sauce
1 tablespoon Chinese rice wine
2 tablespoons vegetarian oyster sauce
1 teaspoon sesame oil
ground white pepper, to taste
2 tablespoons coriander (cilantro) leaves

1 Place the Chinese mushrooms in a heatproof bowl, cover with boiling water and soak for 20 minutes. Drain. Discard the woody stems and thinly slice the caps.
2 Meanwhile, cook the noodles in a large saucepan of boiling water for 1 minute. Drain. Rinse under cold water. Drain.
3 Heat 1 tablespoon of the oil in a wok over high heat. Stir-fry the carrot and corn for 1–2 minutes, then add the bamboo shoots and stir-fry for 1–2 minutes, or until just cooked. Remove and set aside.
4 Add the snowpeas and red and green capsicum to the wok. Stir-fry for 2 minutes, or until just cooked. Add to the carrot and corn mixture.
5 Add the bean sprouts, cabbage and mushrooms to the wok and stir-fry for 30 seconds, or until wilted. Add the ginger and stir-fry for another 1–2 minutes. Remove and add to the other vegetables.
6 Heat the remaining oil in the wok, and stir-fry the noodles for 1–2 minutes, or until heated through. Stir in the mushroom soy sauce, light soy sauce, rice wine and oyster sauce. Return all the vegetables to the wok and stir for 1–2 minutes. Drizzle with the sesame oil, season and garnish with the coriander leaves.

CHAR KWAY TEOW WITH CRAB

Preparation time 20 minutes

Total cooking time 7 minutes

Serves 4

150 g (5½ oz) dried thin rice noodles

3 tablespoons vegetable or peanut oil

2 red Asian or French shallots, thinly sliced

1 garlic clove, finely chopped

2 small red chillies, finely chopped

180 g (6 oz/2 cups) bean sprouts, tails trimmed

175 g (6 oz) Chinese barbecue pork or other cooked pork, cut into small pieces

3 tablespoons light soy sauce

2 tablespoons oyster sauce

700 g (1 lb 9 oz) fresh or thawed frozen crab meat

2 tablespoons chopped coriander (cilantro) leaves

1 Put the rice noodles in a bowl and cover with boiling water. Leave to soak for about 10 minutes, then drain.

2 Heat the oil in a wok and swirl to coat. When hot, add the shallots, garlic and chilli. Cook over high heat, stirring, for 2–3 minutes. Add the bean sprouts and pork pieces and cook for 2 minutes.

3 Add the soy sauce, oyster sauce, noodles, crab meat and coriander and stir for about 2 minutes, or until heated through.

HOKKIEN NOODLES WITH ASIAN GREENS AND GLAZED TOFU

Preparation time 20 minutes
Total cooking time 10 minutes
Serves 4

300 g (10½ oz) firm tofu
3 tablespoons kecap manis
1 tablespoon mushroom soy sauce
1 tablespoon vegetarian oyster sauce
1 teaspoon sesame oil
1 tablespoon peanut oil
2 garlic cloves, crushed
1 tablespoon grated fresh ginger
1 onion, cut into wedges
450 g (1 lb) choy sum, roughly chopped
500 g (1 lb 2 oz) baby bok choy (pak choy),
    roughly chopped

450 g (1 lb) hokkien (egg) noodles, separated
2 tablespoons peanut oil, extra

1 Cut the tofu into 1 cm (½ in) thick slices and place in a shallow, non-metallic dish. Combine the kecap manis, soy and oyster sauces and pour over the tofu. Leave to marinate for about 15 minutes, then drain and reserve the marinade.
2 Heat the oils in a wok over medium heat, add the garlic, ginger and onion and stir-fry until the onion is soft. Remove from the wok.
3 Add the green vegetables to the wok and stir-fry until just wilted. Remove.
4 Add the separated noodles and the marinade and stir-fry until heated. Remove.
3 Fry the tofu in the extra oil until browned. Serve the noodles topped with the tofu, green vegetables and onion mixture.

SWEET GINGER AND CHILLI VEGETABLES WITH RICE NOODLES

Preparation time 15 minutes

Total cooking time 8 minutes

Serves 4

500 g (1 lb 2 oz) fresh rice noodle sheets,
   at room temperature

2 tablespoons oil

1 teaspoon sesame oil

3 tablespoons grated fresh ginger

1 onion, thinly sliced

1 red capsicum (pepper), sliced

100 g (3½ oz) fresh shiitake mushrooms, sliced

200 g (7 oz) baby corn, halved

500 g (1 lb 2 oz) Chinese broccoli (gai larn), sliced

200 g (7 oz) snowpeas (mangetout)

3 tablespoons sweet chilli sauce

2 tablespoons light soy sauce

2 tablespoons dark soy sauce

1 tablespoon lime juice

16 Thai basil leaves

1 Cut the noodle sheets into 3 cm (1¼ in) wide strips, then cut each strip into three. Gently separate the noodles (you may need to run a little cold water over them to do this).

2 Heat the oils in a wok, add the ginger and onion and stir-fry until the onion is soft. Add the vegetables and stir-fry until brightly coloured and just tender.

3 Add the noodles to the vegetables and stir-fry until the noodles start to soften. Stir in the combined sauces and lime juice and cook until heated through. Remove from the heat, toss through the basil leaves and serve.

MA PO TOFU WITH NOODLES

Preparation time 20 minutes +

Total cooking time 10 minutes

Serves 4

450 g (1 lb) silken firm tofu, cut into 2 cm (¾ in)
    cubes
375 g (13 oz) hokkien (egg) noodles
2 teaspoons cornflour (cornstarch)
1 tablespoon peanut oil
2 teaspoons finely chopped ginger
2 spring onions (scallions), finely sliced on the
    diagonal
225 g (8 oz) minced (ground) pork
1½ tablespoons salted black beans, rinsed and
    roughly chopped
1 tablespoon chilli bean paste
1 tablespoon dark soy sauce
125 ml (4 fl oz/½ cup) chicken stock
1 tablespoon Chinese rice wine
2 garlic cloves, finely chopped
2 spring onions (scallions) (green part only), extra,
    finely sliced on the diagonal
½ teaspoon sesame oil

1 Place the tofu on paper towel to drain the excess moisture.

2 Place the noodles in a heatproof bowl, cover with boiling water and soak for 1 minute, or until tender and separated. Drain well, rinse under cold water and drain again. Divide among four serving bowls.

3 Combine the cornflour and 1 tablespoon water in a small bowl.

4 Heat the oil in a wok over high heat. Add the ginger and spring onion and cook for 30 seconds, then add the minced pork and stir-fry for 2 minutes, or until almost cooked.

5 Add the black beans, chilli bean paste and soy sauce and stir-fry for 1 minute. Stir in the chicken stock, rice wine and tofu and cook for 3 minutes, or until heated through.

6 Stir the cornflour mixture and garlic into the wok and cook for a further minute, or until thickened.

7 Spoon over the noodles and season with some ground white pepper. Garnish with the extra spring onion and drizzle with the sesame oil.

PANCIT CANTON

Preparation time 20 minutes

Total cooking time 15 minutes

Serves 4

1½ tablespoons peanut oil

1 large onion, finely chopped

2 garlic cloves, finely chopped

2 x 2 cm (¾ x ¾ in) piece ginger, shredded

500 g (1 lb 2 oz) chicken thigh fillets, trimmed and
   cut into 2 cm (¾ in) pieces

175 g (6 oz) Chinese cabbage, shredded

1 carrot, julienned

200 g (7 oz) Chinese barbecued pork (char sui),
   cut into 5 mm (¼ in) thick pieces

3 teaspoons Chinese rice wine

2 teaspoons sugar

150 g (5½ oz) snowpeas (mangetout), trimmed

375 ml (13 fl oz/1½ cups) chicken stock

1 tablespoon light soy sauce

225 g (8 oz) pancit canton (or Chinese e-fu)
   noodles (see Note)

1 lemon, cut into wedges

1 Heat a wok over high heat, add the oil and swirl to coat. Add the onion and cook for 2 minutes, then add the garlic and ginger and cook for 1 minute.

2 Add the chicken and cook for 2–3 minutes, or until browned. Stir in the cabbage, carrot, pork, rice wine and sugar and cook for a further 3–4 minutes, or until the pork is heated and the vegetables are soft. Add the snowpeas and cook for 1 minute. Remove the mixture from the wok.

3 Add the chicken stock and soy sauce to the wok and bring to the boil. Add the noodles and cook, stirring, for 3–4 minutes, or until soft and almost cooked through.

4 Return the stir-fry mixture to the wok and toss with the noodles for 1 minute, or until combined. Divide among four warmed serving dishes and garnish with lemon wedges.

Note Pancit canton noodles are also called 'birthday' or 'long-life' noodles. Their length denotes a long life for those who eat them. You can find them in Asian grocery stores.

SWEET AND SOUR FISH WITH HOKKIEN NOODLES

Preparation time 20 minutes
Total cooking time 20 minutes
Serves 4

425 g (15 oz) hokkien (egg) noodles
1 tablespoon peanut oil
1 garlic clove, crushed
2 teaspoons grated ginger
1 onion, cut into thin wedges
1 carrot, halved lengthways and thinly sliced
½ red capsicum (pepper), cut into thin strips
½ green capsicum (pepper), cut into thin strips
1 celery stick, thinly sliced
60 g (2¼ oz/½ cup) plain (all-purpose) flour
45 g (1½ oz/¼ cup) rice flour
1 teaspoon caster (superfine) sugar
½ teaspoon ground white pepper
500 g (1lb 2 oz) firm white fish fillets (ling, flake, snapper), cut into 3–4 cm (1¼ in–1½ in cubes
1 egg, beaten with 1 tablespoon water
oil, to deep-fry
2 spring onions (scallions), sliced diagonally

Sauce
3 tablespoons rice vinegar
1 tablespoon cornflour (cornstarch)
3 tablespoons tomato sauce
2 tablespoons sugar
2 teaspoons light soy sauce
1 tablespoon dry sherry
3 tablespoons pineapple juice
2 tablespoons vegetable stock

1 Soak the noodles in boiling water for 1 minute. Drain.
2 To make the sauce, combine the vinegar and cornflour. Stir in the rest of the ingredients and 185 ml (6 fl oz/¾ cup) water.
3 Heat a wok over medium heat, add the oil and swirl to coat the side. Cook the garlic and ginger for 30 seconds. Add the onion, carrot, red and green capsicum and celery and stir-fry for 3–4 minutes.
4 Add the sauce to the wok, increase the heat to high and stir-fry for 1–2 minutes, or until thickened. Remove from the heat and keep warm.
5 Combine the flours, sugar and white pepper in a bowl. Dip each piece of fish in egg, then coat in the flour mix, shaking off any excess. Fill a deep heavy-based saucepan one-third full of oil and heat to 180°C (350°F), or until a cube of bread browns in 15 seconds. Deep-fry the fish in batches for 3 minutes, or until golden. Drain on paper towels and keep warm.
6 Return the wok with the sauce to medium heat, add the noodles and toss together for 3–4 minutes, or until heated through. Gently toss the fish through, top with the spring onion and serve immediately.

SUKIYAKI

Preparation time 20 minutes +
Total cooking time 12 minutes
Serves 4

Sauce
½–1 teaspoon dashi granules
4 tablespoons soy sauce
2 tablespoons sake
2 tablespoons mirin
1 tablespoon caster (superfine) sugar

300 g (10½ oz) shirataki noodles (see Notes)
50 g (1¾ oz) lard
5 large spring onions (scallions), cut into 1 cm
   (½ in) slices on the diagonal
16 fresh shiitake mushrooms (180 g/6 oz),
   cut into smaller pieces if too large
800 g (1 lb 12 oz) rump steak, thinly sliced across
   the grain
100 g (3½ oz) watercress, trimmed
4 eggs (optional)

1 To make the sauce, dissolve the dashi
granules in 125 ml (4 fl oz/½ cup) water in a
bowl. Stir in the soy sauce, sake, mirin and
caster sugar.

2 Drain the noodles, place in a large
heatproof bowl, cover with boiling water and
soak for 2 minutes. Rinse in cold water and
drain well.

3 Melt the lard in a large frying pan over
medium heat. Cook the spring onion,
mushrooms and beef in batches, stirring
continuously, for 1–2 minutes each batch, or
until just brown. Return all the meat, spring
onion and mushrooms to the pan, then add
the sauce and watercress. Cook for 1 minute,
or until the watercress has wilted — the
sauce needs to just cover the ingredients.

4 To serve, divide the noodles among four
serving bowls and spoon the sauce evenly
over the top. If desired, crack an egg into
each bowl and break up through the soup
using chopsticks until it partially cooks.

Notes Shirataki noodles are sold in the
refrigerated section in Japanese supermarkets.
You can also use dried rice vermicelli
— soak in boiling water for 5 minutes
before use.

LEMONGRASS BEEF NOODLE

Preparation time 20 minutes +
Total cooking time 10 minutes
Serves 4

Dressing
125 ml (4 fl oz/½ cup) lime juice
4 tablespoons fish sauce
1 tablespoon caster (superfine) sugar
4 tablespoons warm water
1–2 small red chillies, finely chopped
1 small garlic clove, finely chopped

Marinade
3 lemongrass stems, white part only, chopped
2 garlic cloves, crushed
1 tablespoon fish sauce
1 tablespoon light soy sauce
2 teaspoons caster (superfine) sugar
1 teaspoon vegetable oil
500 g (1 lb 2 oz) beef fillet, thinly sliced
240 g (8½ oz) dried rice vermicelli
1–2 tablespoons peanut oil
1 small Lebanese (short) cucumber, julienned

1 small carrot, julienned
150 g (5½ oz) bean sprouts, tails trimmed
1 handful coriander (cilantro) leaves
1 handful Vietnamese mint leaves, plus extra
70 g (2½ oz) ground unsalted toasted peanuts

1 To make the dressing, combine all the ingredients, stirring until the sugar has completely dissolved. Cover and set aside.
2 To make the marinade, put all the ingredients in a food processor and pulse to form a smooth paste. Put the beef slices in a bowl, cover with the marinade and stir to coat. Cover with plastic wrap and refrigerate for at least 2 hours.
3 Soak the rice vermicelli in boiling water for 5 minutes. Drain, rinse and drain again.
4 Heat a wok to high, add 1 tablespoon of the oil and swirl to coat. Add the beef in batches and sear for 2–3 minutes.
5 Put the vermicelli in a bowl, then add the cucumber, carrot, bean sprouts, coriander and mint leaves. Add the dressing and toss. Top with beef, mint leaves and peanuts.

THAI-STYLE CHICKEN NOODLE SOUP

Preparation time 15 minutes
Total cooking time 10 minutes
Serves 4

425 g (15 oz) tinned corn kernels, undrained
2 chicken stock (bouillon) cubes, crumbled
8 spring onions (scallions), sliced
1 tablespoon finely chopped fresh ginger
500 g (1 lb 2 oz) skinless chicken breast, trimmed
    and thinly sliced
1 tablespoon sweet chilli sauce
1 tablespoon fish sauce
200 g (7 oz) fresh thin rice noodles
2 large handfuls coriander (cilantro) leaves,
    chopped

2 teaspoons grated lime zest
2 tablespoons lime juice

1 Bring 1 litre (35 fl oz/4 cups) water to the boil in a large saucepan over high heat. Add the corn kernels and their juice, the stock cubes, spring onion and ginger, then reduce the heat and simmer for 1 minute.
2 Add the chicken, sweet chilli sauce and fish sauce and simmer for 3 minutes, or until the chicken is cooked through.
3 Put the noodles in a large heatproof bowl, cover with boiling water and soak for 5 minutes, or until softened. Separate gently and drain.
4 Add the noodles, coriander, lime zest and lime juice to the soup and serve immediately.

GREEN CURRY CHICKEN NOODLE STIR-FRY

Preparation time 20 minutes
Total cooking time 15 minutes
Serves 4

400 g (14 oz) hokkien (egg) noodles
1 tablespoon peanut oil
1 onion, cut into thin wedges
1½ tablespoons good-quality green curry paste
150 g (5½ oz) baby corn, cut in half on the diagonal
125 g (4½ oz) snake beans, cut into 4 cm (1½ in) lengths
250 ml (9 fl oz/1 cup) coconut milk
125 ml (½ cup) chicken stock
500 g (1 lb 2 oz) chicken breast fillet, cut into 1 cm (½ in) strips
2 teaspoons grated palm sugar or soft brown sugar
1 tablespoon fish sauce
2 teaspoons lime juice

3 tablespoons chopped coriander (cilantro) leaves
coriander (cilantro) leaves, extra, to garnish

1 Place the noodles in a heatproof bowl, cover with boiling water and soak for 1 minute, or until tender and separated. Drain.
2 Heat a wok over high heat, add the oil and swirl to coat. Stir-fry the onion for 1–2 minutes, or until softened. Add the curry paste and cook for 1 minute, or until fragrant.
3 Add the baby corn, snake beans, coconut milk and stock to the wok and simmer for 3–4 minutes. Add the chicken, and continue to cook for another 3–4 minutes, or until the chicken is cooked.
4 Stir the palm sugar, fish sauce and lime juice into the wok. Add the noodles and chopped coriander and toss until well combined and the noodles are warmed through. Serve immediately, garnished with the extra coriander leaves.

HOKKIEN MEE

Preparation time 20 minutes
Total cooking time 10 minutes
Serves 4

400 g (14 oz) hokkien (egg) noodles
350 g (12 oz) prawns (shrimp)
2 tablespoons peanut oil
3 garlic cloves, finely chopped
200 g (7 oz) Chinese barbecued pork (char siu),
    thinly sliced
400 g (14 oz) baby bok choy (pak choy), trimmed
    and leaves separated
250 ml (9 fl oz/1 cup) hot chicken stock
2 tablespoons dark soy sauce
1 tablespoon oyster sauce
½ teaspoon sugar
90 g (3¼ oz) bean sprouts, trimmed

1 Place the noodles in a heatproof bowl, cover with boiling water and soak for 1 minute, or until tender. Drain and rinse.
2 To peel the prawns, remove the tails, and gently pull out the vein from the backs, starting at the head end. Remove the tails.
3 Heat 1 tablespoon of the peanut oil in a wok over high heat. Add the prawns and garlic and cook for 1–2 minutes, or until just cooked through. Remove from the wok.
4 Heat the remaining oil in the wok over high heat, add the noodles, pork and bok choy and cook for 3–4 minutes.
5 Add the chicken stock, soy and oyster sauces, and the sugar. Return the prawn and garlic mixture to the wok with the bean sprouts and stir for 1–2 minutes, or until heated through.

CHIANG MAI NOODLES

Preparation time 30 minutes
Total cooking time 15 minutes
Serves 4

250 g (9 oz) fresh thin egg noodles
2 tablespoons oil
6 red Asian shallots, finely chopped
3 garlic cloves, crushed
1–2 small red chillies, seeded and finely chopped
2–3 tablespoons red curry paste
375 g (13 oz) chicken breast fillet, cut into
    thin strips
2 tablespoons fish sauce
1 tablespoon grated palm sugar
750 ml (26 fl oz/3 cups) coconut milk
1 tablespoon lime juice
250 ml (9 fl oz/1 cup) chicken stock
4 spring onions (scallions), sliced, to garnish
10 g (¼ oz) coriander (cilantro) leaves
crisp fried shallots, to garnish
purchased fried noodles, to garnish
small red chilli, finely diced, to garnish

1 Cook the noodles in a saucepan of boiling water for 1 minute, or until tender. Drain, cover and set aside.
2 Heat a wok over high heat, add the oil and swirl to coat. Add the shallots, garlic and chilli, and stir-fry for 1–2 minutes, or until lightly golden. Stir in the curry paste and cook for 2 minutes, or until fragrant. Add the chicken and stir-fry for 3 minutes, or until almost cooked.
3 Stir in the fish sauce, palm sugar, coconut milk, lime juice and stock. Reduce the heat to low and simmer for 5 minutes—do not boil.
4 To serve, divide the noodles among four deep serving bowls and spoon the chicken mixture on top. Garnish with the spring onion, coriander leaves, crisp fried shallots, fried noodles and chilli.

DAN DAN NOODLES

Preparation time 15 minutes +
Total cooking time 25 minutes
Serves 4

1 tablespoon Chinese rice wine
½ teaspoon sesame oil
1 teaspoon chilli oil
3 tablespoons light soy sauce
500 g (1 lb 2 oz) minced (ground) chicken
1 tablespoon peanut oil
2 garlic cloves, finely chopped
1 teaspoon finely chopped ginger
2 teaspoons chilli bean paste
1 tablespoon Chinese sesame paste
185 ml (6 fl oz/¾ cup) chicken stock
1 tablespoon oyster sauce
375 g (13 oz) fresh flat egg noodles
3 spring onions (scallions), thinly sliced on the
    diagonal

1 Combine the rice wine, sesame oil, chilli oil and 2 tablespoons soy sauce in a bowl. Add the minced chicken and mix well. Cover with plastic wrap and marinate for 20 minutes.

2 Heat a wok over high heat, add the peanut oil and swirl to coat. Add the garlic, ginger and chilli bean paste and stir-fry for 1 minute, or until fragrant.

3 Add the chicken mixture and cook for 2–3 minutes, or until browned, stirring to break up any lumps. Stir in the sesame paste, chicken stock, oyster sauce and remaining soy sauce, then reduce the heat to medium–low and simmer for 20 minutes.

4 Meanwhile, cook the noodles in a saucepan of boiling water for 1 minute, or until tender. Drain, rinse, then drain again.

5 Stir the spring onion through the chicken mixture, then spoon over the noodles.

CURRY MEE NOODLES

Preparation time 30 minutes +
Total cooking time 20 minutes
Serves 4

2 large dried red chillies
1 teaspoon shrimp paste
400 g (14 oz) hokkien (egg) noodles
1 onion, chopped
4 garlic cloves, chopped
4 lemongrass stems, white part only, thinly sliced
1 teaspoon grated fresh ginger
500 ml (17 fl oz/2 cups) coconut cream
25 g (1 oz/¼ cup) Malaysian curry powder
400 g (14 oz) boneless, skinless chicken thighs,
    thinly sliced
120 g (4¼ oz) green beans, trimmed and
    cut into 5 cm (2 in) lengths
750 ml (26 fl oz/3 cups) chicken stock
10 fried tofu puffs, halved diagonally
2 tablespoons fish sauce
2 teaspoons sugar
180 g (6 oz) bean sprouts
2 hard-boiled eggs, quartered
2 tablespoons crisp fried shallots
lime wedges, to serve

1 Soak the chillies in boiling water for
20 minutes. Drain, then chop. Wrap the
shrimp paste in foil and put under a hot grill
(broiler) for 1–2 minutes. Unwrap.
2 Put the noodles in a bowl, cover with
boiling water and soak for 1 minute to
separate. Rinse under cold water and drain.
3 Put the onion, garlic, lemongrass, ginger,
chilli and shrimp paste in a food processor or
blender and process to a rough paste, adding
a little water if necessary.
4 Put 250 ml (9 fl oz/1 cup) of the coconut
cream in a wok and bring to the boil, then
simmer for 10 minutes, or until the oil starts
to separate from the cream. Stir in the paste
and curry powder and cook for 5 minutes.
Add the chicken and beans and cook for
3–4 minutes, or until the chicken is almost
cooked. Add the stock, tofu puffs, fish sauce,
sugar and the remaining coconut cream.
Simmer, covered, over low heat for
10 minutes, or until chicken is cooked.
5 Divide the noodles and bean sprouts
among four bowls, then ladle the curry over
the top. Garnish with the egg quarters and
crisp fried shallots. Serve with lime wedges.

PHAD THAI

Preparation time 30 minutes +
Total cooking time 10 minutes
Serves 4–6

250 g (9 oz) dried rice stick noodles
1 tablespoon tamarind purée
1 small red chilli, chopped
2 garlic cloves, chopped
2 spring onions (scallions), sliced
1½ tablespoons sugar
2 tablespoons fish sauce
2 tablespoons lime juice
2 tablespoons oil
2 eggs, beaten
8 large raw prawns (shrimp)
150 g (5½ oz) pork fillet, thinly sliced
100 g (3½ oz) fried tofu puffs, cut into thin strips
90 g (3¼ oz) bean sprouts
40 g (1½ oz/¼ cup) chopped roasted peanuts
3 tablespoons coriander (cilantro) leaves
1 lime, cut into wedges

1 Put the noodles in a heatproof bowl, cover with warm water and soak for 15–20 minutes, or until soft and pliable. Drain well.

2 Combine the tamarind purée with 1 tablespoon water. Put the chilli, garlic and spring onion in a spice grinder or mortar and pestle and grind to a smooth paste. Transfer the mixture to a bowl.

3 Stir in the tamarind mixture along with the sugar, fish sauce and lime juice, stirring until combined.

4 Heat a wok until hot. Add 1 tablespoon of the oil and swirl to coat the base and side. Add the egg, swirl to coat and cook for about 1–2 minutes, or until set. Remove, roll up and cut into thin slices.

5 Peel the prawns and gently pull out the dark vein from each prawn back, starting from the head end.

6 Heat the remaining oil in the wok, stir in the chilli mixture and stir-fry for 30 seconds. Add the pork and stir-fry for 2 minutes, or until tender. Add the prawns and stir-fry for a further minute, or until pink and curled.

7 Stir in the noodles, egg, tofu and bean sprouts and gently toss everything together until heated through. Serve immediately topped with the peanuts, coriander and lime wedges.

PORK AND PRAWN VERMICELLI

Preparation time 25 minutes +
Total cooking time 10 minutes
Serves 4

100 g (3½ oz) dried rice vermicelli
2 tablespoons peanut oil
200 g (7 oz) lean minced (ground) pork
100 g (3½ oz) red Asian shallots, finely
   chopped
2 garlic cloves, finely chopped
2 small red chillies, finely chopped
100 g (3½ oz) Chinese celery, finely chopped
12 prawns (shrimp), peeled and deveined
1 kaffir lime leaf, shredded
1½ tablespoons fish sauce
1 tablespoon sugar
2½ tablespoons lime juice
2 tablespoons mint
3 tablespoons Thai basil
4 tablespoons coriander (cilantro) leaves

1 Place the vermicelli in a large heatproof bowl, cover with boiling water and soak for 6–7 minutes, or until tender. Drain well and set aside.

2 Heat add 1 tablespoon of the oil in a wok until very hot and swirl to coat. Add the minced pork and stir-fry for 1–2 minutes, or until slightly brown, stirring to break up any lumps. Drain and transfer to a plate lined with paper towel.

3 Heat the remaining oil in the wok over high heat and stir-fry the shallots, garlic, chilli and celery for 1 minute. Add the prawns, lime leaf, fish sauce, sugar and lime juice and continue to stir-fry for 1 minute, or until the prawns start to turn pink.

4 Add the vermicelli and pork to the wok and stir-fry for 1–2 minutes, or until well combined and heated through. Divide among the four serving dishes, then toss in the mint, basil and coriander and serve immediately.

LAKSA

Preparation time 10 minutes
Total cooking time 12 minutes
Serves 4

200 g (7 oz) dried rice vermicelli
2 tablespoons peanut oil
2–3 tablespoons laksa paste
1 litre (35 fl oz/4 cups) vegetable stock
750 ml (26 fl oz/3 cups) coconut milk
250 g (9 oz) snowpeas (mangetout), halved
   diagonally
5 spring onions (scallions), cut into 3 cm
   (1¼ in) lengths
2 tablespoons lime juice
125 g (4½ oz) bean sprouts, trimmed

200 g (7 oz) fried tofu puffs, halved
3 tablespoons roughly chopped Vietnamese mint
20 g (¾ oz) coriander (cilantro) leaves

1 Put the vermicelli in a large bowl, cover with boiling water and soak for 5 minutes.
2 Heat the oil in a large saucepan, add the laksa paste and cook, stirring, over medium heat for 1 minute, or until fragrant.
3 Add the stock, coconut milk, snowpeas and spring onion and si

CHICKEN

Chicken has been a long-time family favourite. It's very versatile, lending itself to many different recipes, methods of cooking and styles of cuisine. Chicken is easy to buy, simple to cook, and adaptable to so many different flavours which is why it has become a staple in diets all over the world.

CHICKEN BASICS

Before intensive farming techniques took over in the 1970s, chicken meat had more flavour and texture, and was considered a luxury. For some time, most chicken meat sold has ranged from tasteless to just edible. However, more recently, consumer agitation has gradually changed the industry, and more humanely farmed chicken is finding its way onto the market.

A chicken that scratches around for its food is a happier, healthier animal than a battery bird, and yields more flavoursome and better textured meat. You can now buy free-range, open-range, corn-fed and organically farmed chickens in most outlets.

BUYING

When buying chicken, look for pieces with flesh that looks light pink and moist and is free of blemishes and bruises. Free-range and corn-fed chickens are available from speciality poultry shops and, while generally smaller and more expensive, tend to have a better flavour and texture than intensively farmed chickens.

Make sure the chicken looks and smells fresh. The limbs and skin should be undamaged and plump looking. Frozen chicken should not have ice within its packaging as this is a sign it may have defrosted slightly and then refrozen.

Whole chickens are sold by a number that relates to their weight. For example, a No. 14 chicken weighs 1.4 kg (3 lb 2 oz), a No. 15 chicken weighs 1.5 kg (3 lb 5 oz). As a general rule, a No. 15 chicken will serve 4 people.

Try to buy chicken last when you are out shopping to minimise the amount of time it is out of the refrigerator. If you are buying a frozen chicken, make sure it is frozen solid and tightly wrapped. If it has even slightly defrosted, do not try to refreeze it as this can promote the growth of harmful bacteria. Continue to defrost it on a tray on the bottom shelf of the refrigerator where it cannot drip onto any other foods. Thawed chicken should be cooked within 12 hours and must never be refrozen.

STORAGE

Before cooking, completely defrost frozen chicken in the fridge or a cool place—this can take hours so always check the central cavity for signs of ice. Dry thoroughly and cook as soon as it is defrosted. It is important to follow food safety instructions carefully to avoid harmful bacteria in your chicken.

Chicken wrapped in plastic should be unwrapped, wiped with paper towel, placed in a shallow dish and covered. If roasting the chicken, leave uncovered for an hour before cooking to dry out the skin (it will crisp better). If you buy a whole chicken with giblets, remove them before storing. Store on the bottom shelf of the fridge and eat within 2 days.

Fresh chicken should be taken out of its packaging, covered loosely with foil or plastic wrap and kept on a plate in the bottom of the refrigerator where it cannot drip onto any other food. Fresh chicken should be used within 2 days, or, alternatively, frozen for up to 8–12 months. When freezing, be sure to expel all the air from the freezer bag before sealing.

Whole chickens should be defrosted in the refrigerator. Chicken pieces can be defrosted in the microwave (with the thickest portions to the outside of the plate), but don't defrost whole chickens in the microwave, as they will defrost unevenly and some parts may start to cook while others remain frozen. Never defrost chicken at room temperature and never thaw under running water. Bacteria such as salmonella can be activated if a defrosting chicken gets too warm. And it must be fully thawed before cooking begins.

TYPES OF CHICKEN

Chicken The most common variety, these are sold drawn, plucked and ready to cook, and may be whole or jointed. Allow about 350–400 g (12–14 oz) per person.

Poussin Baby chickens sold in single or double portion sizes. They benefit from stuffing or marinating and are good grilled.

Bantam Miniature breed of hen. Usually bred for their eggs.

Boiling fowl Older birds that have stopped laying and can be used for slow cooking, stocks and soups.

Corn or grain These have been fed a diet of corn and have a yellow skin. Corn-fed does not mean free-range, but some are. This type may be confused with less common breeds of chicken that also have a yellowish skin.

Free-range Free-range can mean a life of complete freedom in a farm yard to statutory amounts of days the birds must roam free, or life in a barn. Laws vary locally.

Poulet de Bresse A particular breed of French chicken with a superior flavour and texture. Sold packaged under its name.

Cornish hens Have a prominent breast and a good covering of meat.

COOKING

Whole chickens These can be roasted, poached, pot-roasted, braised, stuffed or coated with a wet or dry marinade or salt crust. Whole birds can also be spatchcocked, which makes them easier to grill or barbecue.

Breast meat Tends to be dry and is best cooked in a way that will keep it moist such as poaching, grilling with the skin on, or roasting at a high heat. The breast can be slit open and stuffed, rolled around fillings, wrapped, or cut into strips and cubes. Breasts on the bone with the skin on retain their moisture better than those without skin. Remove any white sinew from the underside.

Thighs Moist, dark meat, perfect in curries, stews and casseroles. Can be marinated and barbecued or grilled. Thighs can be boned out and rolled around fillings or cut into

pieces. The skin can be quite fatty so either remove it or trim it very well.

Legs Best roasted, barbecued or grilled. Use in stews and casseroles or as finger food. They are excellent when marinated in robust flavours.

Wings Good for finger food, especially marinated and grilled or dusted with flour and deep-fried. In Chinese cuisine, wings are also boned and stuffed.

Chicken mince Use as you would minced (ground) beef, but as chicken flesh is drier with less fat, it benefits from being flavoured well and cooked in a less dry heat.

ROASTING

Trim the chicken of any extra fat, truss (tie) its legs together and tuck its wings back under the body. Trussing the chicken helps it to keep its shape and stops its legs springing out. For even roasting, start breast side down, then do each side and finish with it on its back. Baste as often as you can, brushing the bird with the juices. When the chicken is ready, the juices from the cavity will be clear, the flesh just pulling away from the drumstick and the skin crisp and golden. If in any doubt, push a skewer into the thigh — these juices should also be clear. There should be no pinkness when the flesh is carved. Roasting times and temperatures vary but generally a chicken to feed four (1.5–2 kg/2 lb 12 oz–4 lb 8 oz) will take 1 hour in a 200°C (400°F/Gas 6) oven.

STUFFING

To stuff under the skin, gently ease the skin from the chicken breast with your fingers and fill with the stuffing at the neck end only, smooth back the skin and massage the stuffing into place. Cavity stuffing is not recommended unless the stuffing is well cooked, but the breast may get too dry. If you do wish to stuff the cavity, dry it well and make sure the chicken is cooked straight away so the stuffing doesn't have time to soak up any raw juices.

JOINTING CHICKEN

1 Lay the bird on a board with the cavity end facing you. Pull both legs away from the carcass and twist the thigh bones out of their body sockets.

2 Cut through the flesh to remove the leg. Keep the small piece of meat, known as an oyster, that is found at the back of the body attached to the leg meat.

3 Cut between the drumstick and the thigh along the natural fat line, which is visible on the underside of the thigh. Your knife should slide easily through the joint.

4 Cut down either side of the backbone and lift it out. This is easier to do with a pair of poultry shears.

5 Turn the bird over, remove the wishbone and cut down the centre of the breastbone.

6 Cut through each piece of breast at an angle so it makes two equal pieces. Leave the wing attached to one piece and trim off the wing tips and any pieces of extra skin.

SPATCHCOCKING CHICKEN

1 Split the bird by cutting down each side of the backbone with a sharp knife or pair of poultry shears. Discard the backbone.

2 Put the bird cut side down on your chopping board and press firmly down on the rib cage, squashing it out flat.

3 You should end up with a bird that is flattened out. Trim off the wing tips and any excess fat or skin.

BONING CHICKEN

1 Pull the flap of skin from the neck down around the shoulder to expose the wishbone and the joint where the wing bone joins the shoulder. Carefully cut around the wishbone and snap it out.

2 Turn the bird over. Cut through the joints between the wings and backbone but leave the wing bones in.

3 Remove the shoulder bones by scraping away any flesh and cutting through the cartilage that joins them to the breastbone. Pull on the shoulder bones: they are attached together but both ends should now be loose.

4 Once the shoulder bones are out, use your knife to scrape down the bones of the carcass, making sure the flesh comes away in one piece. Angle the blade of the knife towards the bones so it doesn't slip and cut through the flesh.

5 When you reach the legs, pull the thigh bones out of their sockets. Leave the bones in the legs to give them more definition when they are cooked.

6 Carry on scraping down the carcass until you reach the bottom. Now sever the cartilage at the bottom of the breastbone on one side and cut through the bottom vertebrae on the other. You should now be able to lift out the carcass.

SPICY CHICKEN SCHNITZELS

Preparation time 15 minutes

Total cooking time 10 minutes

Serves 4

4 x 200 g (7 oz) boneless chicken breast
    fillets
1 tablespoon ground coriander
1 tablespoon ground cumin
½ teaspoon chilli powder, or to taste
2 garlic cloves, crushed
2 tablespoons lemon juice
2 tablespoons olive oil
250 g (9 oz/1 cup) thick plain yoghurt
½ teaspoon harissa paste, or to taste
½ teaspoon caster (superfine) sugar
2 tablespoons finely chopped mint leaves, plus
    extra sprigs, to serve

1 Place the chicken breasts between two sheets of plastic wrap and flatten them with a mallet or rolling pin until 1½ cm (⅝ in) thick.

2 In a small bowl, mix the ground coriander, cumin, chilli powder, garlic, lemon juice and oil together to form a paste. Thoroughly rub the paste all over the chicken fillets, then cover and leave to stand for 10 minutes.

3 Heat the grill (broiler) to high. Put the chicken on a lightly oiled grill tray and grill for 6–8 minutes, or until cooked through, turning once.

4 Meanwhile, blend 1 tablespoon of the yoghurt in a bowl with the harissa and sugar. Stir in the remaining yoghurt and mint, season to taste and serve with the warm chicken, garnished with extra mint sprigs.

SPICY CAYENNE CHICKEN PIECES

Preparation time 15 minutes +
Total cooking time 30 minutes
Serves 6

500 ml (17 fl oz/2 cups) buttermilk
3 garlic cloves, crushed
1 tablespoon finely chopped thyme
1 teaspoon salt
2 kg (4 lb 8 oz) chicken pieces, skin on (about
    12 assorted pieces)
peanut oil, for deep-frying
250 g (9 oz/2 cups) plain (all-purpose) flour
1 tablespoon Hungarian sweet paprika
1½ tablespoons cayenne pepper
1 tablespoon celery salt
2 tablespoons onion powder
lemon wedges, to serve (optional)

1 Combine the buttermilk, garlic, thyme and salt in a large bowl. Add the chicken pieces and stir to coat. Cover tightly with plastic wrap and refrigerate for a few hours, or overnight, stirring occasionally.
2 Fill a deep-fryer or large heavy-based saucepan one-third full with peanut oil and heat to 170°C (325°F), or until a cube of bread dropped in the oil browns in 20 seconds. Combine the flour, paprika, cayenne, celery salt and onion powder. Lift the chicken out of the buttermilk. Roll in the flour mixture until thickly coated.
3 Deep-fry the chicken pieces, a few at a time, for 10–12 minutes, or until golden and just cooked through. Drain on paper towel and rest in a warm oven while cooking the remaining chicken. Serve with lemon wedges, if desired.

CHARGRILLED MUSTARD-MARINATED CHICKEN

Preparation time 15 minutes +
Total cooking time 15 minutes
Serves 4

4 boneless, skinless chicken breasts, tenderloins
  removed

Marinade
5 cm (2 in) piece fresh ginger, finely diced
2 garlic cloves, crushed
3 tablespoons dijon mustard
1½ tablespoons soy sauce
1 tablespoon honey
1 tablespoon Chinese rice wine
1 teaspoon sesame oil
2 tablespoons chopped coriander (cilantro) leaves

1 tablespoon vegetable oil
green salad, to serve

1 Make incisions diagonally into the chicken with a knife, about 2.5 cm (1 in) apart.
2 Combine the marinade ingredients and rub liberally over the chicken breasts. Place in a bowl and cover. Refrigerate for at least 2 hours.
3 Heat a barbecue flat plate or grill plate to medium heat. Brush the flat plate or grill with the oil.
3 Cook the chicken for 7 minutes on each side, or until cooked through and a little charred. Brush the chicken with marinade as it cooks. The chicken is ready when firm to the touch. Serve immediately with a green salad.

FIVE-SPICE CHICKEN STIR-FRY WITH CELERY

Preparation time 15 minutes
Total cooking time 12 minutes
Serves 4

3 tablespoons cornflour (cornstarch)
3 teaspoons five-spice powder, plus ½ teaspoon extra
125 ml (4 fl oz/½ cup) chicken stock
2 tablespoons light soy sauce
1 tablespoon Chinese rice wine or sherry
2 teaspoons rice vinegar
2 teaspoons caster (superfine) sugar
½ teaspoon sesame oil
500 g (1 lb 2 oz) boneless, skinless chicken breasts, trimmed and cut into thin strips
3 tablespoons vegetable oil, for frying
4 spring onions (scallions), white part chopped, green part reserved
2 sticks celery, cut into 3 cm (1¼ in) slices diagonally
1 long red chilli, deseeded and finely chopped
2 garlic cloves, finely chopped
2 teaspoons grated fresh ginger
steamed jasmine rice, to serve

1 Combine the cornflour and five-spice powder on a plate. Take 1 teaspoon of the mixture and put in a small bowl with a little stock to form a paste, then add the remaining stock, soy sauce, rice wine, rice vinegar, caster sugar, sesame oil and extra five-spice powder and set aside.

2 Pat the chicken breast strips dry with paper towel and toss in the combined flour and five-spice powder. Shake off any excess.

3 Heat a wok until very hot and add about 1 tablespoon of the oil. Stir-fry half the chicken for 3 minutes, or until cooked.

4 Remove to a side plate and keep warm. Add another 1 tablespoon of oil and cook the remaining chicken. Remove to a side plate and keep warm.

5 Heat the remaining tablespoon of oil. Stir-fry the white spring onions, celery, chilli, garlic and ginger for 2–3 minutes, or until fragrant.

6 Return the chicken and combined sauce to the wok. Stir-fry for 2 minutes, or until the sauce has thickened a little and the chicken is hot. Shred the reserved spring onions and use to garnish. Serve immediately with steamed jasmine rice.

MOROCCAN-STYLE CHICKEN WITH COUSCOUS SALAD

Preparation time 15 minutes
Total cooking time 10 minutes
Serves 4

Couscous salad
500 ml (17 fl oz/2 cups) apple juice
370 g (13 oz/2 cups) couscous
½ small red onion, halved and finely sliced
   lengthways
50 g (1¾ oz/⅓ cup) pistachio nuts, toasted
8 dried apricots, chopped
60 g (2¼ oz/⅓ cup) green olives, pitted and
   chopped
¼ preserved lemon, pulp removed, rinsed and
   finely chopped
1 small handful mint, roughly chopped
1 small handful parsley, roughly chopped
2 tablespoons plain (all-purpose) flour
1 tablespoon ras el hanout
12 chicken tenderloins, trimmed
2–3 tablespoons olive oil

Yoghurt dressing
250 g (9 oz/1 cup) plain yoghurt
2 tablespoons chopped mint
2 teaspoons ras el hanout
1 teaspoon honey

1 Heat the apple juice in a pan until hot. Put the couscous in a bowl, pour over the apple juice, cover and set aside for 5 minutes. Fluff up with a fork. Toss the remaining salad ingredients through the couscous.

2 Meanwhile, combine the flour and ras el hanout on a flat plate. Coat the chicken tenderloins in the mixture and shake off the excess. Heat the oil in a large non-stick frying pan. Cook the chicken for 2–3 minutes on each side, or until cooked and golden. Add a little more oil as needed. Slice the chicken.

3 To make the yoghurt dressing, combine the ingredients in a bowl. To serve, pile the couscous onto plates, top with the chicken slices and spoon over the yoghurt dressing.

TURMERIC, GINGER AND LIME CHICKEN ON SKEWERS

Preparation time 20 minutes +
Total cooking time 15 minutes
Serves 4

8 boneless, skinless chicken thigh fillets
4 limes

Marinade
250 ml (9 fl oz/1 cup) coconut milk
2 teaspoons ground turmeric
2 tablespoons finely grated fresh ginger
1 tablespoon finely chopped lemongrass, white
    part only
2 garlic cloves, crushed
juice of 1 lime
1 tablespoon fish sauce

2 teaspoons grated palm sugar (jaggery)
cooked jasmine rice, to serve

1 Cut the chicken into 3 cm (1¼ in) cubes. Mix all the marinade ingredients in a non-metallic bowl and add the chicken pieces. Cover and refrigerate for 2 hours. Soak 8 bamboo skewers in cold water for 20 minutes.

2 Thread the chicken onto the skewers. Cut the limes in half crossways.

3 Cook the skewers on a barbecue flatplate over medium–high heat for 5 minutes, then turn and cook for a further 5 minutes, or until cooked through. Cook the limes, cut-side down, on the flatplate over medium–high heat for 4–5 minutes, or until caramelised.

4 Serve with jasmine rice, along with the limes for squeezing over the chicken.

BRAISED CHICKEN WITH VEGETABLES

Preparation time 15 minutes
Total cooking time 30 minutes
Serves 4

3 chicken thighs
3 chicken drumsticks
2 tablespoons vegetable oil
8 baby leeks, white part only, cut into 1 cm
  (½ in) slices
6 red Asian shallots, quartered
100 g (3½ oz) shiitake mushrooms, thickly sliced
juice of 1 mandarin or 4 tablespoons orange juice)
2 tablespoons soy sauce
2 tablespoons dry sherry
2 teaspoons soft brown sugar
2 teaspoons green peppercorns
1 teaspoon sesame oil

2 baby bok choy (pak choy), quartered
  lengthways

1 Chop the chicken thighs and legs into
bite-sized pieces through the bone. Heat
the oil in a large wok and brown the chicken
in batches over high heat for 1–2 minutes.
Remove from the wok.
2 Add the leeks and shallots and stir-fry for
1 minute. Add the mushrooms, stir-fry for
1 minute, then add the mandarin juice, soy
sauce, sherry, sugar, green peppercorns and
125 ml (4 fl oz/½ cup) of water.
3 Return the chicken pieces to the wok.
Reduce the heat and simmer, covered, for
20 minutes, or until the chicken is tender.
Add the sesame oil and bok choy and cook,
stirring, for 1 minute, or until wilted. Serve
with steamed rice.

TWICE-COOKED CHICKEN WITH BLACK VINEGAR DRESSING

Preparation time 20 minutes
Total cooking time 15 minutes
Serves 4

8 chicken pieces (use leg, breast, thigh), with
    bone in
1 small onion, quartered
1 carrot, quartered
5 whole black peppercorns
vegetable oil, for deep-frying
2 spring onions (scallions), thinly sliced

Dressing
3 tablespoons black vinegar
4 tablespoons vegetable oil
1 tablespoon soy sauce
1 small red chilli, seeded and finely chopped
2 tablespoons chopped coriander (cilantro)
    leaves

1 Put the chicken pieces in a large saucepan with the onion, carrot and peppercorns. Pour in enough water to cover the chicken by 2.5 cm (1 in) and bring slowly to the boil. Once boiling, reduce the heat and simmer for about 6 minutes. Remove from the heat and set aside to cool completely in the liquid (the chicken will continue to cook).

2 To make the dressing, whisk together the black vinegar, vegetable oil, soy sauce, red chilli and coriander.

3 Remove the chicken from the cooking liquid and pat dry with paper towels. Half fill a wok with oil and heat to 190°C (375°F), or until a cube of bread dropped in the oil browns in 10 seconds. Cook the chicken pieces for 4–5 minutes, or until golden and crisp. Drain well and transfer to serving plates. Pour the dressing over the chicken, scatter the spring onion over the top and leave for 5 minutes before serving. Serve with boiled rice or noodles.

CHICKEN THIGHS WITH PERSIAN SPICE MIX

Preparation time 20 minutes +
Total cooking time 16 minutes
Serves 4

8 chicken thigh fillets, trimmed
grated zest and juice of 2 limes
170 ml (5½ fl oz/⅔ cup) olive oil
1 tablespoon coarse black pepper
2½ handfuls basil leaves, shredded
lime wedges, to serve

Persian spice mix
½ teaspoon cumin seeds
½ teaspoon ground turmeric
1 teaspoon grated lemon zest
2 cardamom pods
4 black peppercorns

1 Place the chicken thighs between two sheets of plastic wrap and gently flatten with a rolling pin. Mix the lime zest, lime juice, oil, pepper and basil in a non-metallic bowl and season with salt. Add the chicken, toss well to coat all over, then cover and marinate in the refrigerator for 2 hours.

2 Put all the Persian spice mix ingredients in a spice grinder with a good pinch of salt and blend to a fine powder.

3 Heat the grill (broiler) to medium. Drain the chicken from the marinade and sprinkle with the spice mix. Spread the chicken on the grill tray and grill for 8 minutes on each side, or until cooked through. Serve hot with lime wedges.

Tip For an authentic Persian flavour, instead of the lemon zest use ½ teaspoon of green mango powder (this is also called amchoor).

MEXICAN-STYLE CHICKEN WITH AVOCADO SALSA AND CHEESE QUESADILLAS

Preparation time 20 minutes
Total cooking time 12 minutes
Serves 4

Avocado salsa
1 large avocado, diced
1 large tomato, seeded and diced
½ small red onion, diced
3 tablespoons finely chopped coriander (cilantro)
    leaves and stems
2 tablespoons extra virgin olive oil
1 tablespoon lime juice
3 teaspoons sweet chilli sauce
1 garlic clove, crushed

4 x 150 g (5½ oz) chicken breast fillets
2 x 35 g (1¼ oz) packets taco seasoning
oil, for brushing

Cheese quesadillas
200 g (7 oz) grated cheddar cheese
1½ tablespoons finely chopped coriander
    (cilantro) leaves and stems
1 small red chilli, seeded and finely chopped
1 teaspoon sea salt
4 flour tortillas

1 Preheat a barbecue grill plate or chargrill pan to medium. Meanwhile, put all the avocado salsa ingredients in a small bowl, mix well and set aside.

2 Place the chicken breasts between two sheets of plastic wrap and slightly flatten them with a rolling pin or mallet. Put them in a bowl with the taco seasoning and toss well to coat, pressing the mixture in with your hands. Lightly brush the barbecue hotplate with oil, then cook the chicken for about 5 minutes on each side, or until golden and cooked through. Take the chicken off the heat and keep warm. Turn the barbecue up high.

3 To make the quesadillas, put the cheese, coriander, chilli and salt in a bowl and mix well. Sprinkle the mixture over one half of each tortilla, then fold the other half over to form a little parcel, pressing the edges together to seal. Brush the grill plate again with oil and cook the quesadillas for about 1 minute on each side, or until grill marks appear. Drain on crumpled paper towels and slice in half.

4 Put a grilled chicken breast on each serving plate with 2 quesadilla halves. Top the chicken with a good dollop of salsa and serve immediately.

THREE MUSHROOM GINGER CHICKEN

Preparation time 30 minutes +
Total cooking time 10 minutes
Serves 4

500 g (1 lb 2 oz) boneless, skinless chicken breast
   fillet, thinly sliced
1 tablespoon scotch whisky
1 tablespoon light soy sauce
15 g (½ oz) dried black or wood ear fungus
3 tablespoons peanut oil
2 tablespoons finely julienned fresh ginger
2 spring onions (scallions), cut into 3 cm (1¼ in)
   lengths
1 small red capsicum (pepper), finely sliced
150 g (5½ oz) fresh shiitake mushrooms, stems
   removed, finely sliced
150 g (5½ oz) fresh oyster mushrooms, finely
   sliced
1 garlic clove, crushed
3 tablespoons mushroom oyster sauce or
   oyster sauce

1 tablespoon mushroom soy sauce
½ teaspoon ground white pepper

1 Put the chicken in a non-metallic bowl with the whisky and light soy sauce. Mix to coat, then cover and marinate in the refrigerator for 1 hour. Meanwhile, soak the fungus in boiling water for 20 minutes. Rinse, then finely slice.

2 Drain the chicken well. Heat a wok over high heat, add 1 tablespoon of the oil and swirl to coat. Stir-fry the chicken in batches for 2–3 minutes, or until golden brown and tender. Remove and keep warm.

3 Heat the remaining oil, then add the fungus, ginger, spring onion, capsicum and mushrooms and stir-fry for 1–2 minutes, or until the vegetables are soft. Return the chicken to the wok with the garlic and stir-fry for 1 minute. Add the mushroom oyster sauce, soy sauce and white pepper and stir to combine, cooking for 1 minute until the chicken is cooked through.

SALT AND PEPPER CHICKEN WITH ASIAN GREENS AND OYSTER SAUCE

Preparation time 10 minutes

Total cooking time 20 minutes

Serves 4

250 g (9 oz/1¼ cups) jasmine rice

40 g (1½ oz/⅓ cup) plain flour

¾ teaspoon five-spice powder

1½ teaspoons sea salt

1 teaspoon ground white pepper

750 g (1 lb 10 oz) chicken breast fillets, cut into thin strips

145 ml (4¾ fl oz) peanut oil

1.25 kg (2 lb 12 oz) mixed Asian greens (bok choy, choy sum or gai larn)

125 ml (4 fl oz/½ cup) oyster sauce

1 Bring a large saucepan of water to the boil. Add the rice and cook for 12 minutes, stirring occasionally. Drain well.

2 Meanwhile, combine the flour, five-spice powder, salt and pepper in a large bowl. Toss the chicken strips in the flour until well coated.

3 Heat 3 tablespoons of the oil in a large frying pan over medium–high heat. Add the chicken in three batches and cook, turning, for about 3 minutes, or until browned. Drain on crumpled paper towels and keep warm.

4 Heat the remaining oil and cook the mixed Asian greens over medium–high heat for 1–2 minutes. Add the oyster sauce and toss through. Serve on a bed of jasmine rice topped with the chicken strips.

STUFFED CHICKEN BREAST WITH TOMATO, GOAT'S CHEESE AND ASPARAGUS

Preparation time 20 minutes

Total cooking time 20 minutes

Serves 4

4 large chicken breast fillets

100 g (3½ oz) semi-dried tomatoes

100 g (3½ oz) goat's cheese, sliced

200 g (7 oz) asparagus spears, trimmed, halved
   and blanched

50 g (1¾ oz) butter

375 ml (13 fl oz/1½ cups) chicken stock

2 zucchini (courgettes), cut into 5 cm (2 in) batons

250 ml (9 fl oz/1 cup) cream

8 spring onions (scallions), thinly sliced

1 Pound each chicken breast between two sheets of plastic wrap with a mallet or rolling pin until 1 cm thick. Divide the tomato, goat's cheese and 155 g (5½ oz) of the asparagus pieces among the breasts. Roll up tightly lengthways, securing along the seam with toothpicks.

2 Heat the butter in a large frying pan over medium heat. Add the chicken, then brown on all sides. Pour in the stock, then reduce the heat to low. Cook, covered, for 10 minutes, or until the chicken is cooked through. Remove the chicken, set aside and keep warm.

3 Meanwhile, bring a saucepan of lightly salted water to the boil. Add the zucchini and remaining asparagus and cook for 2 minutes, or until just tender. Remove from the pan.

4 Whisk the cream into the frying pan. Add the spring onion and simmer over medium–low heat for 4 minutes, or until reduced and thickened. To serve, cut each chicken roll in half on the diagonal and place on serving plates. Spoon on the sauce and serve with the greens.

CHICKEN BREASTS WITH MUSTARD CREAM SAUCE

Preparation time 10 minutes

Total cooking time 20 minutes

Serves 4

4 chicken breasts (about 200 g/7 oz each)

2 tablespoons oil

1 garlic clove, crushed

3 tablespoons dry white wine

2 tablespoons wholegrain mustard

2 teaspoons chopped fresh thyme

300 ml (10½ fl oz) cream

250 g (9 oz) green beans, topped and tailed

320 g (11¼ oz) baby yellow squash, halved

1 Pound each chicken breast between sheets of plastic wrap with a mallet or rolling pin until about 1 cm (½ in) thick.

2 Heat the oil in a frying pan over high heat. Brown the chicken breasts for 4–5 minutes on each side, or until brown. Remove and cover with foil.

3 Add the garlic to the frying pan and cook for 1 minute over medium heat, then stir in the wine, mustard and thyme. Increase the heat to medium–high and pour in the cream. Simmer for about 5 minutes, or until the sauce has reduced and thickened slightly, then season to taste.

4 Meanwhile, bring a saucepan of lightly salted water to the boil, add the beans and squash and cook for 2–4 minutes, or until just tender. Season to taste. To serve, pour a little of the sauce over the chicken and serve with the vegetables on the side.

CAJUN CHICKEN WITH FRESH TOMATO AND CORN SALSA

Preparation time 10 minutes
Total cooking time 15 minutes
Serves 4

2 corn cobs
2 vine-ripened tomatoes, diced
1 Lebanese (short) cucumber, finely
    diced
2 tablespoons roughly chopped coriander
    (cilantro) leaves
4 x 200 g (7 oz) boneless, skinless chicken breast
    fillets
35 g (1¼ oz/¼ cup) Cajun seasoning
2 tablespoons lime juice
lime wedges, to serve

1 Cook the corn cobs in a saucepan of boiling water for 5 minutes, or until tender. Remove the kernels using a sharp knife and place in a bowl with the tomato, cucumber and coriander. Season and mix well.

2 Heat a chargrill pan or barbecue plate to medium heat and brush lightly with oil. Pound each chicken breast between two sheets of plastic wrap with a mallet or rolling pin until 2 cm (¾ in) thick. Lightly coat the chicken with the Cajun seasoning and shake off any excess. Cook for 5 minutes on each side, or until just cooked through.

3 Just before serving, stir the lime juice into the salsa. Place a chicken breast on each plate and spoon the salsa on the side. Serve with the lime wedges, a green salad and crusty bread.

PARMESAN CHICKEN WITH QUICK SALSA VERDE

Preparation time 15 minutes
Total cooking time 10 minutes
Serves 4

3 eggs
1 large handful basil
2 tablespoons capers, rinsed
1 tablespoon Dijon mustard
2 tablespoons freshly grated parmesan cheese
185 ml (6 fl oz/¾ cup) olive oil
100 g (3½ oz/1 cup) dry breadcrumbs
4 chicken breast fillets (about 120 g/4 oz each)
150 g (5½ oz) rocket (arugula) leaves
lemon wedges, to serve

1 Place 1 egg in a saucepan of cold water, bring to the boil and cook for 1 minute. Remove from the heat and refresh under cold water. Peel, then place in a food processor with the basil, capers, mustard and 1 tablespoon of the parmesan, until combined. Gradually add 3 tablespoons of the olive oil and process until you have a coarse sauce, taking care not to overprocess.

2 Beat the remaining eggs together with 1 tablespoon water. Combine the breadcrumbs with the remaining Parmesan on a plate. Pound each chicken breast between two sheets of plastic wrap with a mallet or rolling pin until 5 mm (¼ in) thick. Dip the chicken in the egg mixture, then coat in the breadcrumb mixture. Place on a paper-lined baking tray and refrigerate for 10 minutes, or until needed.

3 Heat the remaining oil in a large frying pan over high heat. Cook the chicken breasts in batches for 2–3 minutes each batch, or until golden on both sides and cooked through — keep each batch warm. Serve with the salsa verde, rocket leaves and lemon wedges.

MOROCCAN CHICKEN

Preparation time 15 minutes

Total cooking time 30 minutes

Serves 4

1 tablespoon Moroccan spice blend

800 g (1 lb 12 oz) chicken thigh fillets, trimmed
and halved

1 tablespoon oil

60 g (2¼ oz) butter

1 large onion, cut into wedges

1 cinnamon stick

2 garlic cloves, crushed

2 tablespoons lemon juice

250 ml (9 fl oz/1 cup) chicken stock

75 g (2½ oz/⅓ cup) pitted prunes, halved

225 g (8 oz/ 1½ cups) couscous

lemon wedges, to serve

1 Sprinkle half the spice blend over the chicken. Heat the oil and 20 g (¾ oz) of the butter in a large saucepan or deep-sided frying pan over medium heat. Cook the chicken in two batches for 5 minutes, or until evenly browned. Remove from the pan, then add the onion and cinnamon stick and cook for 2–3 minutes before adding the garlic. Return the chicken to the pan and add the lemon juice and the remaining spice blend. Season, then cook, covered, for 5 minutes.

2 Add the stock and prunes to the pan and bring to the boil. Reduce the heat to medium–low and cook, uncovered, for 15 minutes, or until the chicken is cooked and the liquid has reduced to a sauce. Before serving, stir 20 g (¾ oz) of the butter into the sauce.

3 About 10 minutes before the chicken is ready, place the couscous in a heatproof bowl, add 375 ml (13 fl oz/1½ cups) boiling water, and stand for 3–5 minutes. Stir in the remaining butter and fluff with a fork until the butter has melted and the grains separate. Serve with the chicken.

SATAY CHICKEN STIR-FRY

Preparation time 15 minutes
Total cooking time 15 minutes
Serves 4

300 g (10½ oz/1½ cups) jasmine rice
1½ tablespoons peanut oil
6 spring onions (scallions), cut into 3 cm lengths
800 g (1 lb 12 oz) chicken breast fillets, thinly
    sliced on the diagonal
1–1½ tablespoons Thai red curry paste
90 g (3¼ oz/⅓ cup) crunchy peanut butter
270 ml (9½ fl oz) coconut milk
2 teaspoons soft brown sugar
1½ tablespoons lime juice

1 Bring a large saucepan of water to the boil. Add the rice and cook for 12 minutes, stirring occasionally. Drain well.
2 Meanwhile, heat a wok until very hot, add 1 teaspoon of the peanut oil and swirl to coat. When hot, add the spring onion and stir-fry for 30 seconds, or until softened slightly. Remove from the wok. Add a little extra peanut oil to the wok as needed and stir-fry the chicken in three batches for about 1 minute per batch, or until the meat just changes colour. Remove from the wok.
3 Add a little more oil to the wok, add the curry paste and stir-fry for 1 minute, or until fragrant. Add the peanut butter, coconut milk, sugar and 250 ml (9 fl oz/1 cup) water and stir well. Bring to the boil and boil for 3–4 minutes, or until thickened and the oil starts to separate — reduce the heat slightly if the sauce spits at you. Return the chicken and the spring onion to the wok, stir well and cook for 2 minutes, or until heated through. Stir in the lime juice and season. Serve with the rice and a crisp green salad.

SICHUAN CHICKEN

Preparation time 15 minutes
Total cooking time 30 minutes
Serves 4

¼ teaspoon Chinese five-spice
750 g (1 lb 10 oz) chicken thigh fillets, halved
2 tablespoons peanut oil
1 tablespoon julienned fresh ginger
1 teaspoon sichuan peppercorns, crushed
1 teaspoon chilli bean paste (toban jian)
2 tablespoons light soy sauce
1 tablespoon Chinese rice wine
250 g (9 oz/1¼ cups) jasmine rice
600 g (1 lb 5 oz) baby bok choy (pak choy), leaves
    separated

1 Sprinkle the five-spice powder over the chicken. Heat a saucepan or wok until very hot, add half the oil and swirl to coat. Add the chicken and cook for 2 minutes each side, or until browned. Remove from the pan or wok.

2 Reduce the heat to medium and cook the ginger for 30 seconds. Add the peppercorns and chilli bean paste.

3 Return the chicken to the pan or wok, add the soy sauce, wine and 125 ml (4 fl oz/ ½ cup) water, then simmer for about 15–20 minutes, or until cooked.

4 Meanwhile, add the rice to a large saucepan of rapidly boiling water and cook for 12 minutes, stirring occasionally. Drain well.

5 Heat the remaining oil in a large saucepan. Add the bok choy and toss for 1 minute, or until the leaves wilt and the stems are tender. Serve with the chicken and rice.

CHICKEN WITH THAI BASIL, CHILLI AND CASHEWS

Preparation time 10 minutes
Total cooking time 15 minutes
Serves 4

3 tablespoons peanut oil
500 g (1 lb 2 oz) boneless, skinless chicken breast
    fillets, trimmed and cut into thin strips
1 garlic clove, crushed
4 spring onions (scallions), thinly sliced
150 g (5½ oz) snake beans, trimmed and cut into
    5 cm (2 in) lengths
2 small fresh red chillies, thinly sliced
35 g (1¼ oz) Thai basil
2 tablespoons chopped mint
1 tablespoon fish sauce
1 tablespoon oyster sauce
2 teaspoons lime juice
1 tablespoon grated palm sugar
Thai basil, extra, to garnish

1 Heat a wok over high heat, add about 1 tablespoon of the oil and swirl to coat. Cook the chicken in batches for about 3–5 minutes, or until lightly browned and almost cooked—add more oil if needed. Remove and keep warm.
2 Heat the remaining oil. Add the garlic, onion, snake beans and chilli, and stir-fry for 1 minute, or until the onion is tender. Add the chicken to the wok.
3 Toss in the basil and mint, then add the combined fish sauce, oyster sauce, lime juice, palm sugar and 2 tablespoons water and cook for 1 minute. Garnish with the extra basil and serve immediately with some steamed jasmine rice.

GREEN CHICKEN CURRY

Preparation time 10 minutes

Total cooking time 15 minutes

Serves 4

250 ml (9 fl oz/1 cup) coconut cream

4 tablespoons green curry paste

8 boneless, skinless chicken thighs or 4 chicken
   breasts, cut into pieces

250 ml (9 fl oz/1 cup) coconut milk

4 Thai eggplants (aubergines) or ½ of a purple
   eggplant, cut into chunks

2 tablespoons shaved palm sugar or
   brown sugar

2 tablespoons fish sauce

4 kaffir lime leaves, torn

a handful Thai basil leaves

1–2 large red chillies, sliced

coconut milk or cream, for drizzling

1 Put a wok over a low heat, add the coconut cream and let it come to the boil. Stir it for a while until the oil separates out. Don't let it burn.

2 Add the green curry paste, stir for a minute, then add the chicken. Cook the chicken until it turns opaque, then add the coconut milk and eggplant. Cook for about 1–2 minutes until the eggplant is tender. Add the sugar, fish sauce, lime leaves and half of the basil, then mix together.

3 Garnish with the rest of the basil, the chilli and a drizzle of coconut milk or cream. Serve with steamed rice.

STIR-FRIED CHICKEN WITH GINGER AND CASHEWS

Preparation time 10 minutes

Total cooking time 10 minutes

Serves 4

1½ tablespoons oil

8 spring onions (scallions), cut into pieces

3 garlic cloves, crushed

8 cm (3 in) piece ginger, finely shredded

2 skinless chicken breasts, cut into strips

2 red capsicums (peppers), cut into strips

150 g (5½ oz) snowpeas (mangetout)

100 g (3½ oz) cashews

2 tablespoons soy sauce

1½ teaspoons sesame oil

1 Heat the oil in a wok over high heat until it is smoking — this will only take a few seconds. Add the spring onion, garlic and ginger and stir for a few seconds.

2 Add the chicken and stir until lightly browned and cooked through. Add the red capsicum and continue stirring. Add the snowpeas and cashews and stir-fry for another 1–2 minutes.

3 When the red capsicum has started to soften a little, add the soy sauce and sesame oil. Toss everything together until well coated.

4 Serve immediately in bowls with your choice of steamed rice or noodles and extra soy sauce, to taste.

GRILLED CHICKEN WITH CAPSICUM COUSCOUS

Preparation time 15 minutes +
Total cooking time 25 minutes
Serves 4

200 g (7 oz/1 cup) instant couscous
1 tablespoon olive oil
1 onion, finely chopped
2 zucchini (courgettes), sliced
½ red or yellow chargrilled capsicum (pepper),
    chopped
12 semi-dried (sun-blushed) tomatoes, chopped
½ tablespoon grated orange zest
250 ml (9 fl oz/1 cup) orange juice
a large handful chopped mint
8 boneless, skinless chicken thighs or 4 chicken
    breasts, skin on
40 g (1½ oz) butter, softened

1 Heat the grill (broiler). Bring 500 ml (17 fl oz/2 cups) water to the boil in a saucepan, throw in the couscous, then take the pan off the heat and leave it to stand for 10 minutes.
2 Heat the oil in a frying pan and fry the onion and zucchini until lightly browned. Add the capsicum and semi-dried tomatoes, then stir in the couscous. Stir in the orange zest, one-third of the orange juice and the mint.
3 Put the chicken in a large shallow baking dish in a single layer and dot it with the butter. Sprinkle with the remaining orange juice and season well with salt and pepper. Grill the chicken for 8 to 10 minutes, turning it over halfway through.
4 Serve the chicken on the couscous with any juices poured over it.

HOT AND SWEET CHICKEN

Preparation time 20 minutes
Total cooking time 15 minutes
Serves 4

125 ml (4 fl oz/½ cup) rice vinegar
160 g (5¾ oz/⅔ cup) caster (superfine) sugar
6 garlic cloves, crushed
a large pinch of chilli flakes
1 teaspoon ground coriander
1 teaspoon ground white pepper
2 bunches coriander (cilantro), finely chopped
3 tablespoons olive oil
2 tablespoons lemon juice
8 boneless, skinless chicken thigh fillets, cut in half
2 tablespoons caster (superfine) sugar, extra
2 tablespoons fish sauce
1 small cucumber, peeled and sliced

1 Put the vinegar and sugar in a small saucepan, bring to the boil, then turn down the heat and simmer for a minute. Take the mixture off the heat and add two crushed garlic cloves, the chilli flakes and a pinch of salt. Leave the dressing to cool.

2 Heat a small frying pan for a minute, add the ground coriander and white pepper and stir it around for a minute. This will make the spices more fragrant.

Add the rest of the garlic, the fresh coriander and a pinch of salt. Add 2 tablespoons of the oil and all the lemon juice and mix to a paste. Rub this all over the chicken pieces.

3 Heat the rest of the oil in a wok, add the chicken and fry it on both sides for 8 minutes, or until it is cooked through. Sprinkle in the extra sugar and the fish sauce and cook for another minute or two until any excess liquid has evaporated and the chicken pieces are sticky.

4 Serve the chicken with the sliced cucumber and some steamed rice. Drizzle with the sauce and serve immediately.

CHICKEN WITH CHILLI JAM AND CASHEWS

Preparation time 20 minutes +
Total cooking time 30 minutes
Serves 4

Chilli jam
10 dried long red chillies
4 tablespoons peanut oil
1 red capsicum (pepper), chopped
1 head (50 g/1¾ oz) garlic, peeled and chopped
200 g (7 oz) red Asian shallots, chopped
100 g (3½ oz) palm sugar, grated, or soft brown
    sugar
2 tablespoons tamarind purée (see Note)

1 tablespoon peanut oil
6 spring onions (scallions), cut into 3 cm (1¼ in)
    lengths
500 g (1 lb 2 oz) boneless, skinless chicken breast
    fillet, cut into slices
50 g (1¾ oz/⅓ cup) roasted unsalted cashews
1 tablespoon fish sauce
1 small handful Thai basil

1 To make the chilli jam, soak the chillies in a bowl of boiling water for 15 minutes. Drain, remove the seeds and chop. Put in a food processor, then add the oil, capsicum, garlic and shallots and blend until smooth.
2 Heat a wok over medium heat and add the chilli mixture. Cook, stirring occasionally, for 10 minutes. Add the sugar and tamarind and simmer for 8 minutes, or until it darkens and reaches a jam-like consistency. Remove from the wok.
3 Clean and reheat the wok over high heat, add the oil and swirl to coat. Stir-fry the spring onion for 1 minute, then add the chicken and stir-fry for 3 minutes, or until golden brown and tender.
4 Stir in the cashews, fish sauce and about 4 tablespoons of the chilli jam. Stir-fry for a further 1 minute, then stir in the basil and serve.
Note Use a non-stick or stainless steel wok to cook this recipe because the tamarind purée will react with the metal in a regular wok and will taint the dish.

EASY CHICKEN STIR-FRY

Preparation time 10 minutes

Total cooking time 18 minutes

Serves 4

1 tablespoon cornflour (cornstarch)
2 teaspoons finely chopped ginger
2 garlic cloves, crushed
1 small red chilli, finely chopped
1 teaspoon sesame oil
3 tablespoons light soy sauce
500 g (1 lb 2 oz) boneless, skinless chicken breast
   fillet, thinly sliced
1 tablespoon peanut oil
1 onion, halved and thinly sliced
115 g (4 oz) baby corn, halved on the diagonal
425 g (15 oz) baby bok choy (pak choy), trimmed
   and quartered lengthwise
2 tablespoons oyster sauce
3 tablespoons chicken stock

1 Combine half the cornflour with the ginger, crushed garlic, chilli, sesame oil and 2 tablespoons soy sauce in a large bowl. Add the chicken, toss until well coated and marinate for 10 minutes.

2 Heat a wok over high heat, add the peanut oil and swirl to coat. Stir-fry the onion for 2 minutes, or until soft and golden. Add the chicken in two batches and stir-fry for 5 minutes, or until almost cooked through. Add the baby corn and stir-fry for a further 2 minutes, then add the bok choy and cook for 2 minutes, or until wilted.

3 Mix the remaining soy sauce and cornflour with the oyster sauce and chicken stock in a small bowl, add to the wok and stir-fry for 1–2 minutes, or until the sauce has thickened to coating consistency and the chicken is cooked. Serve immediately with steamed rice or noodles.

BACON-WRAPPED CHICKEN

Preparation time 10 minutes
Total cooking time 10 minutes
Serves 6

2 tablespoons olive oil
2 tablespoons lime juice
¼ teaspoon ground coriander
6 chicken breast fillets
4 tablespoons fruit chutney
3 tablespoons chopped pecan nuts
6 bacon slices

1 Mix together the olive oil, lime juice, coriander and salt and pepper. Using a sharp knife, cut a pocket in the thickest section of each fillet. Mix together the chutney and nuts. Spoon 1 tablespoon of the chutney mixture into each chicken breast pocket.
2 Turn the tapered ends of the fillets to the underside. Wrap a slice of bacon around each fillet and secure with a toothpick.
3 Put the chicken parcels on a hot, lightly oiled barbecue grill or flat plate and cook for 5 minutes on each side, or until cooked through, turning once. Brush with the lime juice mixture several times during cooking and drizzle with any leftover lime juice mixture to serve.
Note This recipe also works well with prosciutto, which is an Italian equivalent of bacon.

MARGARITA CHICKEN

Preparation time 10 minutes +
Total cooking time 16 minutes
Serves 4

4 boneless chicken breasts, skin on
3 tablespoons tequila
3 tablespoons lime juice
2 small chillies, finely chopped
3 garlic cloves, crushed
1 small handful finely chopped coriander (cilantro)
   leaves
1 tablespoon olive oil
lime wedges, to serve

1 Put the chicken, tequila, lime juice, chilli, garlic, coriander and olive oil in a non-metallic bowl and mix it all together so that the chicken is coated in the marinade. Cover the bowl and refrigerate for at least 2 hours, or overnight.

2 Preheat a barbecue chargrill to medium–high direct heat. Remove the chicken breasts from the marinade, season them with salt and pepper, and grill for 7–8 minutes on each side or until they are cooked through.

3 Slice the chicken breasts on the diagonal and serve with lime wedges and a green salad, if desired.

LIME AND CORIANDER CHARGRILLED CHICKEN

Preparation time 10 minutes +
Total cooking time 25 minutes
Serves 4

3 teaspoons finely grated fresh ginger
25 g (1 oz) chopped coriander (cilantro) leaves
1½ teaspoons grated lime zest
4 tablespoons lime juice
4 skinless chicken breast fillets (about 750 g/1lb 10 oz), trimmed
250 g (9 oz/1¼ cups) jasmine rice
2 tablespoons oil
3 zucchini (courgettes), cut into wedges
4 large flat mushrooms, stalks trimmed

1 Combine the ginger, coriander, lime zest and 2 tablespoons of the lime juice. Spread 2 teaspoons of the herb mixture over each fillet and season well. Marinate for 1 hour. Combine the remaining herb mixture with the remaining lime juice in a screwtop jar. Set aside until needed.

2 Bring a large saucepan of water to the boil. Add the rice and cook for 12 minutes, stirring occasionally. Drain well.

3 Meanwhile, heat a barbecue plate to medium and lightly brush with oil. Brush the zucchini and mushrooms with the remaining oil. Place the chicken on the chargrill plate and cook on each side for 4–5 minutes, or until cooked through. Add the vegetables during the last 5 minutes of cooking, and turn frequently until browned on the outside and just softened. Cover with foil until ready to serve.

3 Divide the rice among four serving bowls. Cut the chicken fillets into long thick strips, then arrange on top of the rice. Shake the dressing well and drizzle over the chicken and serve with the chargrilled vegetables.

MIRIN AND SAKE CHICKEN

Preparation time 10 minutes +
Total cooking time 15 minutes
Serves 4

4 large boneless, skinless chicken breast fillets
2 tablespoons mirin
2 tablespoons sake
1 tablespoon oil
5 cm (2 in) piece fresh ginger, finely sliced
3 teaspoons soy sauce
salad leaves, to serve

1 Put the chicken in a non-metallic dish. Combine the mirin, sake and oil and pour over the chicken. Marinate for 15 minutes, then drain. Reserve the marinade.
2 Cook the chicken on a hot, lightly oiled barbecue grill or flat plate for 4 minutes each side, or until tender.
3 Put the ginger in a pan and add the reserved marinade. Boil for about 7 minutes, or until thickened. Drizzle the soy sauce over the chicken and top with the ginger. Serve immediately with salad leaves.

THAI SPICED CHICKEN WITH POTATO ROSTI

Preparation time 15 minutes +
Total cooking time 15 minutes
Serves 6

600 g (1 lb 5 oz) boneless, skinless chicken breast
   fillet, cut into strips
1 tablespoon chopped lemongrass
2 tablespoons lime juice
1½ tablespoons oil
2 garlic cloves, crushed
1 tablespoon grated fresh ginger
2 teaspoons sweet chilli sauce
2 spring onions (scallions), chopped
1 lime, cut into 6 wedges

Potato rosti
600 g (1 lb 5 oz) potatoes
3 tablespoons plain (all-purpose) flour
1 egg, lightly beaten

1 Put the chicken in a shallow, non-metallic dish. Mix together the lemongrass, lime juice, oil, garlic, ginger, sweet chilli sauce and spring onion. Pour over the chicken pieces, cover and refrigerate for at least 2 hours.

2 To make the potato rosti, peel and grate the potatoes. Squeeze the excess moisture from the potato with your hands until it feels quite dry. Mix the potato with the flour and egg and season well. Divide into six equal portions. Cook on a hot barbecue flat plate for 10 minutes, or until golden brown on both sides, flattening them down with the back of a spatula during cooking.

3 Drain the chicken and reserve the marinade. Cook on a barbecue grill or flat plate for 3 minutes each side, or until tender and golden brown. Brush with the reserved marinade while cooking. Serve with the rosti and a squeeze of lime juice.

CHICKEN WITH CHILLI JAM

Preparation time 10 minutes
Total cooking time 10 minutes
Serves 4

2 teaspoons fish sauce
2 tablespoons oyster sauce
3 tablespoons coconut milk
½ teaspoon sugar
2½ tablespoons vegetable oil
6 garlic cloves, finely chopped
1–1½ tablespoons chilli jam, to taste
500 g (1 lb 2 oz) skinless chicken breast fillets,
  finely sliced
1 handful holy basil leaves
1 long red or green chilli, seeded and finely sliced,
  for garnish

1 Mix the fish sauce, oyster sauce, coconut milk and sugar in a small bowl.

2 Heat the oil in a wok or frying pan and stir-fry half the garlic over a medium heat until light brown. Add half the chilli jam and stir-fry for another 2 minutes or until fragrant. Add half of the chicken and stir-fry over a high heat for 2–3 minutes. Remove from the wok. Repeat with the remaining garlic, chilli jam and chicken. Return all the chicken to the wok.

3 Add the fish sauce mixture to the wok and stir-fry for a few more seconds or until the chicken is cooked. Taste, then adjust the seasoning if necessary. Stir in the basil leaves. Garnish with chilli slices.

Note Chilli jam, or roasted chilli paste, is used as a relish, condiment and ingredient in various Thai dishes. Here it adds a more complex sweet, chilli flavour than just using chillies. Add the smaller amount before tasting, then add a little more if you need to.

SAGE AND RICOTTA-STUFFED CHICKEN

Preparation time 10 minutes

Total cooking time 16 minutes

Serves 4

250 g (9 oz/1 cup) fresh ricotta cheese, well
  drained
1 tablespoon shredded sage leaves
2 garlic cloves, crushed
1½ teaspoons grated lemon zest
40 g (1½ oz) finely grated parmesan cheese
4 boneless, skinless chicken breast fillets
8 thin slices prosciutto
olive oil, for brushing

1 Mix together the ricotta, sage, garlic, zest and Parmesan until they are well combined. Use a sharp knife to cut a large pocket into the side of each chicken breast and fill each pocket with a quarter of the ricotta mixture. Pin the pockets closed with toothpicks and wrap each breast in two slices of prosciutto, securing it with a toothpick.

2 Heat a barbecue flat plate to medium direct heat, brush the chicken parcels with olive oil and season them with freshly ground black pepper. Cook them for 8 minutes on each side, or until they are cooked through. Serve on a bed of baby spinach leaves or a green salad.

MEDITERRANEAN CHICKEN SKEWERS

Preparation time 10 minutes +
Total cooking time 8 minutes
Makes 8 skewers

2 large boneless, skinless chicken breast fillets,
    cut into 32 cubes
24 cherry tomatoes
6 cap mushrooms, cut into quarters
2 garlic cloves, crushed
zest of 1 lemon, grated
2 tablespoons lemon juice
2 tablespoons olive oil
1 tablespoon oregano leaves, chopped

1 Soak eight wooden skewers in water to prevent scorching. Thread a piece of chicken onto each skewer, followed by a tomato, then a piece of mushroom. Repeat twice for each skewer and finish with a piece of chicken. Put the skewers in a shallow, non-metallic dish.
2 Combine the garlic, lemon zest, lemon juice, olive oil and chopped oregano, pour over the skewers and toss well. Marinate for at least 2 hours, or overnight if time permits.
3 Cook the skewers on a hot, lightly oiled barbecue grill or flat plate for 4 minutes on each side, basting occasionally, until the chicken is cooked.

MIDDLE EASTERN CHICKEN WITH BURGHUL

Preparation time 15 minutes +
Total cooking time 20 minutes
Serves 4

350 g (12 oz/2 cups) burghul (bulgur)
2 skinless chicken breast fillets
2 teaspoon olive oil
1 red onion, thinly sliced
300 g (10½ oz) can chickpeas, drained and rinsed
70 g (2½ oz/½ cup) unsalted pistachio kernels
1 tomato, chopped
juice of 1 orange
4 tablespoon finely chopped flat-leaf (Italian)
   parsley

1 Put the burghul in a bowl, cover with water and leave to soak for 15 minutes, or until the burghul has softened. Drain and use clean hands to squeeze dry.

2 Meanwhile, trim the chicken and thinly slice. Heat a large frying pan over high heat, add half the oil and swirl to coat. Add the chicken in batches and stir-fry for 3–5 minutes, or until cooked. Remove from the pan and keep warm.

3 Add the remaining oil to the pan and cook the onion, stirring, for 2 minutes, then add the chickpeas, pistachio kernels and tomato. Cook, stirring, for 3–5 minutes, or until the chickpeas are warmed through.

4 Pour in the orange juice, return the chicken and its juices to the pan and cook until half the juice has evaporated. Stir in the parsley. Season well with salt and freshly ground black pepper and serve with the burghul.

SPICY CHICKEN STIR-FRY

Preparation time 20 minutes +
Total cooking time 15 minutes
Serves 4

4 dried shiitake mushrooms
250 g (9 oz) flat rice stick noodles
oil spray
1 red onion, cut into thin wedges
2 garlic cloves, crushed
2 cm x 2 cm (¾ in x ¾ in) piece fresh ginger,
    julienned
1 tablespoon chilli jam
400 g (14 oz) skinless chicken breast fillet,
    cut into strips
½ red capsicum (pepper), cut into thin strips
800 g (1 lb 12 oz/1 bunch) gai larn (Chinese
    broccoli), cut into 5 cm (2 in) lengths
115 g (4 oz) fresh or tinned baby corn, halved on
    the diagonal
150 g (5½ oz/1½ cups) snowpeas (mangetout),
    halved on the diagonal
4 tablespoons soy sauce
2 tablespoons mirin
1 large handful coriander (cilantro) leaves

1 Place the mushrooms in a heatproof bowl and cover with 375 ml (13 fl oz/1½ cups) boiling water and stand for 15 minutes. Drain, reserving the liquid and squeezing out any excess liquid. Remove the stalks and thinly slice the caps. Place the noodles in a heatproof bowl, pour over boiling water to cover and stand for 5 minutes, or until tender. Drain.

2 Meanwhile, heat a non-stick wok over a high heat and spray with the oil. Add the onion and cook for 2–3 minutes. Add the garlic, ginger and chilli jam and cook for a further 1 minute, adding 1–2 tablespoons of the reserved mushroom liquid to mix in the chilli jam.

3 Add the chicken and cook for about 4–5 minutes, or until almost cooked through. Add the capsicum, gai larn, corn, snowpeas, mushrooms and 3 tablespoons reserved mushroom liquid and stir-fry for 2–3 minutes, or until the vegetables are tender. Add the soy sauce, mirin, coriander and noodles and season with ground white pepper. Toss until well combined and serve immediately.

CARDAMOM CHICKEN

Preparation time 20 minutes +
Total cooking time 30 minutes
Serves 4

1.5 kg (3 lb 5 oz) chicken or chicken pieces
25 cardamom pods
4 garlic cloves, crushed
3 cm (1¼ in) piece of ginger, grated
300 ml (10½ fl oz) thick natural yoghurt
1½ teaspoons ground black pepper
grated zest of 1 lemon
2 tablespoons ghee or oil
400 ml (14 fl oz) coconut milk
6 green chillies, pricked all over
2 tablespoons chopped coriander leaves
3 tablespoons lemon juice

1 If using a whole chicken, cut it into eight pieces by removing both legs and cutting between the joint of the drumstick and thigh. Cut down either side of the backbone and remove the backbone. Turn the chicken over and cut through the cartilage down the centre of the breastbone. Cut each breast in half, leaving the wing attached to the top half. Trim off the wing tips. Remove the skin if you prefer.

2 Remove the seeds from the cardamom pods and crush them in a spice grinder or pestle and mortar. In a blender, mix the garlic and ginger with enough of the yoghurt (about 2 tablespoons) to make a paste, or, if you prefer, mix them with a spoon. Add the cardamom, pepper and grated lemon rind. Spread this over the chicken pieces, cover, and leave in the fridge overnight.

3 Heat the ghee or oil in a karhai or heavy-based frying pan over low heat and brown the chicken pieces all over. Add the remaining yoghurt and coconut milk to the pan, bring to the boil, then add the whole chillies and the coriander leaves. Simmer for 20–30 minutes or until the chicken is cooked through. Season with salt, to taste, and stir in the lemon juice.

CHICKEN IN GARLIC SAUCE

Preparation time 20 minutes

Total cooking time 30 minutes

Serves 6

1 kg (2 lb 4 oz) boneless, skinless chicken thighs

1 tablespoon sweet paprika (pimentón)

2 tablespoons olive oil

8 garlic cloves, unpeeled

3 tablespoons fino sherry

125 ml (4 fl oz/½ cup) chicken stock

1 bay leaf

2 tablespoons chopped flat-leaf (Italian) parsley

1 Trim any excess fat from the chicken and cut the thighs into thirds. Combine the paprika with some salt and pepper in a bowl, add the chicken and toss to coat.

2 Heat half the oil in a large frying pan over high heat and cook the garlic cloves for 1–2 minutes, or until brown. Remove from the pan. Cook the chicken in batches for 5 minutes, or until brown all over. Return all the chicken to the pan, add the sherry, boil for 30 seconds, then add the stock and bay leaf. Reduce the heat and simmer, covered, over low heat for 10 minutes.

3 Meanwhile, squeeze the garlic pulp from their skins and pound with the parsley into a paste using a mortar and pestle or a small bowl and the back of a spoon. Stir into the chicken, then cover and cook for 10 minutes, or until tender. Serve hot.

3 Pound the garlic pulp and the parsley together to form a paste.

Note This dish is a great example of a modern Spanish recipe that takes typical and traditional ingredients — in this particular case, lots of garlic and sherry — and combines them in a way that is so impressive the dish will soon enter your repertoire of everyday meals.

CHICKEN WITH CRISPY HOLY BASIL LEAVES

Preparation time 15 minutes +
Total cooking time 10 minutes
Serves 4

500 g (1 lb 2 oz) skinless chicken breast fillets,
　thinly sliced
4–5 garlic cloves, finely chopped
4–5 small red or green bird's eye chillies, lightly
　crushed
1 tablespoon fish sauce
2 tablespoons oyster sauce
vegetable oil, for deep-frying
2 handfuls of holy basil leaves
2 tablespoons vegetable or chicken stock, or
　water
½ teaspoon sugar
1 red capsicum (pepper), cut into bite-sized
　pieces
1 medium onion, cut into thin wedges

1 Mix the chicken, garlic, chillies, fish sauce
and oyster sauce in a bowl. Cover with
plastic wrap and marinate in the refrigerator
for at least 30 minutes.
2 Heat 5 cm (2 in) oil in a wok or deep
frying pan over a medium heat. When the
oil seems hot, drop a few basil leaves into it.
If they sizzle immediately, the oil is ready.
Deep-fry three-quarters of the basil leaves
for 1 minute or until they are all crispy. Lift
out with a slotted spoon and drain on paper
towels. Discard the remaining oil.
3 Heat 2 tablespoons oil in the same wok or
frying pan and stir-fry half the chicken over a
high heat for 3–4 minutes. Remove from the
pan and repeat with the remaining chicken.
Return all the chicken to the wok.
4 Add the stock and sugar to the wok, then
the capsicum and onion, and stir-fry for
another 1–2 minutes. Stir in the fresh basil
leaves. Taste, then adjust the seasoning if
necessary. Garnish with the basil leaves.
Note This is one of the most common dishes
you will come across in Thailand. Holy basil
comes in two colours, red and green. It has a
hot, slightly sharp flavour and is often used
in conjunction with chillies in stir-fries. Serve
with plenty of rice.

CHICKEN WITH CASHEW NUTS

Preparation time 15 minutes
Total cooking time 15 minutes
Serves 4

1–2 dried long red chillies
1 tablespoon fish sauce
2 tablespoons oyster sauce
3 tablespoons chicken or vegetable stock
½–1 teaspoon sugar
4 tablespoons vegetable oil
80 g (2¾ oz/½ cup) cashew nuts
4–5 garlic cloves, finely chopped
500 g (1 lb 2 oz) skinless chicken breast fillets, finely sliced
½ red capsicum (pepper), cut into thin strips
½ carrot, sliced diagonally
1 small onion, cut into 6 wedges
2 spring onions (scallions), cut into 1 cm (½ in) lengths
ground white pepper, to sprinkle

1 Take the stems off the dried chillies, cut each chilli into 1 cm (½ inch) pieces with scissors or a knife and discard the seeds.
2 Mix the fish sauce, oyster sauce, stock and sugar in a small bowl.
3 Heat the oil in a wok over a medium heat and stir-fry the cashew nuts for 2–3 minutes or until light brown. Remove with a slotted spoon and drain on paper towels.
4 Stir-fry the chillies in the same oil over a medium heat for 1 minute. They should darken but not blacken and burn. Remove from the pan with a slotted spoon.
5 Heat the same oil again and stir-fry half the garlic over a medium heat until light brown. Add half the chicken and stir-fry over a high heat for 4–5 minutes or until the chicken is cooked. Remove from the wok and repeat with the remaining garlic and chicken. Return all the chicken to the wok.
6 Add the capsicum, carrot, onion and the sauce mixture to the wok and stir-fry for 1–2 minutes. Taste, then adjust the seasoning if necessary.
7 Add the cashew nuts, chillies and spring onions and toss well. Sprinkle with ground pepper.

CHICKEN WITH GOAT'S CHEESE AND COUSCOUS

Preparation time 15 minutes +

Total cooking time 20 minutes

Serves 4

4 chicken breast fillets

150 g (5½ oz) goat's cheese, roughly chopped

150 g (5½ oz) semi-dried tomatoes, finely chopped

3 tablespoons shredded basil

185 g (6½ oz/1 cup) couscous

1 tablespoon lemon juice

1 tablespoon olive oil

lemon wedges, to serve

1 Cut a pocket lengthways into the thickest part of each chicken breast, without cutting all the way through. Combine the goats cheese, tomato and 2 tablespoons basil. Divide the mixture into four and press into the chicken breast pockets. Secure with toothpicks.

2 Heat the oil in a large non-stick frying pan, add the chicken breasts and cook over medium heat for 8–10 minutes on each side, or until golden and cooked through. Cut the chicken into slices on the diagonal.

3 Meanwhile, place the couscous into a large heatproof bowl. Cover with the lemon juice and 250 ml (9 fl oz/1 cup) boiling water. Stand for about 5 minutes, then fluff with a fork and fold in the remaining basil.

4 To serve, place the slices of chicken on a bed of the couscous and garnish with the lemon wedges.

CHICKEN WITH CHARDONNAY MUSHROOM SAUCE

Preparation time 5 minutes
Total cooking time 20 minutes
Serves 4

60 g (2¼ oz) butter
4 chicken breast fillets
2 thin slices prosciutto
1 garlic clove, crushed
200 g (7 oz) button mushrooms, sliced
170 ml (5½ fl oz/⅔ cup) Chardonnay
1–2 tablespoons chopped fresh tarragon
110 g (3¾ oz/½ cup) mascarpone

1 Melt half the butter in a frying pan, add the chicken and cook over medium heat for 3–4 minutes each side, or until golden brown and cooked through. Transfer to a warm serving dish. Cut the prosciutto in half widthways and place half a slice over each chicken fillet, cover with foil and keep warm.
2 Melt the remaining butter in the pan, add the garlic and mushrooms, and cook, stirring, over medium heat for 2–3 minutes, or until the mushrooms are soft. Add the Chardonnay and tarragon, bring to the boil and cook over high heat for 5 minutes, or until the wine is reduced by half.
3 Stir in the mascarpone and heat gently until warmed through. Do not boil or it will split. Season and spoon over the chicken. Garnish with fresh tarragon leaves and serve immediatcly with steamed vegetables, if desired.

CHICKEN FALAFEL WITH TABOULEH CONES

Preparation time 30 minutes +
Total cooking time 20 minutes
Makes 24

45 g (1½ oz/¼ cup) burghul (bulgar)
4 pieces lavash or other unleavened bread
2 spring onions (scallions), thinly sliced
1 large tomato, seeded and finely chopped
1 small Lebanese (short) cucumber, chopped
1 large handful flat-leaf (Italian) parsley, chopped
1 tablespoon lemon juice
1 tablespoon virgin olive oil
1 tablespoon olive oil
1 onion, finely chopped
1 garlic clove, crushed
2 teaspoons ground coriander
1 teaspoon cumin seeds
½ teaspoon ground cinnamon
250 g (9 oz) minced (ground) chicken
300 g (10½ oz) tinned chickpeas, rinsed, drained and mashed
1 handful mint, chopped
1 handful flat-leaf (Italian) parsley, extra, chopped
2 tablespoons plain (all-purpose) flour
60 g (2¼ oz/¼ cup) Greek-style yoghurt

1 Soak the burghul in hot water for 20 minutes. Slice the bread into thirds widthways, then cut in half. Keep the bread covered with a damp cloth. Cut 24 pieces of baking paper the same size as the bread. Roll the paper up around the bottom half of the bread to form a cone and secure. Twist at the bottom. You will need 24 bread cones.

2 To make the tabouleh, drain the burghul in a fine mesh sieve, pressing out as much water as possible. Transfer to a bowl and mix with the spring onion, tomato, cucumber, parsley, lemon juice and virgin olive oil, and season.

3 Heat the olive oil in a frying pan, add the onion and garlic and cook, stirring over medium–low heat, for 5 minutes, or until the onion is soft. Add the spices and cook for another minute.

4 Put the onion mixture, minced chicken, chickpeas, mint and extra parsley in a bowl, season and mix. Shape into 24 firm falafel patties. Toss the falafel in the flour.

5 Fill a deep-fryer or heavy-based saucepan one-third full of oil and heat to 180°C (350°F), or until a cube of bread dropped into the oil turns golden in 15 seconds. Cook the falafels in batches for 3–4 minutes each side, or until golden and heated through. Drain on crumpled paper towels.

6 To assemble the cones, put 1 falafel in each bread cone, top with tabouleh and about ½ teaspoon yoghurt.

FRIED CRISPY CHICKEN

Preparation time 20 minutes +
Total cooking time 30 minutes
Serves 4

4 chicken leg quarters or 8 drumsticks
4 garlic cloves, chopped
3 coriander (cilantro) roots, finely chopped
2 teaspoons ground turmeric
1 teaspoon caster (superfine) sugar
2 tablespoons chilli sauce, plus extra to serve
oil, for deep-frying

1 Remove the skin from the chicken pieces. Put the chicken in a large saucepan with enough water to cover it. Cover and simmer for 15 minutes, or until cooked through. Drain and allow to cool.

2 Put the garlic, coriander root, turmeric, 1 teaspoon pepper, 1 teaspoon salt, sugar and chilli sauce in a mortar and pestle or food processor and pound or process into a smooth paste. Brush over the chicken, coating it thoroughly. Cover and refrigerate for 30 minutes.

3 Heat the oil in a heavy-based frying pan, add the chicken in batches and cook until dark brown, turning frequently. Drain on paper towels. Serve hot or cold with chilli sauce, if desired.

BUTTER CHICKEN

Preparation time 10 minutes
Total cooking time 35 minutes
Serves 4–6

2 tablespoons peanut oil
1 kg (2 lb 4 oz) chicken thighs, quartered
60 g (2¼ oz) butter or ghee
2 teaspoons garam masala
2 teaspoons sweet paprika
2 teaspoons ground coriander
1 tablespoon finely chopped fresh ginger
¼ teaspoon chilli powder
1 cinnamon stick
6 cardamom pods, bruised
350 g (12 oz) tomato passata (puréed tomatoes)
1 tablespoon sugar
60 g (2¼ oz/¼ cup) plain yoghurt
125 ml (4 fl oz/½ cup) pouring (whipping) cream
1 tablespoon lemon juice
poppadoms, to serve

1 Heat a wok to very hot, add 1 tablespoon oil and swirl to coat the base and side. Add half the chicken and stir-fry for about 4 minutes, or until nicely browned. Remove from the wok. Add a little extra oil, if needed, and brown the remaining chicken. Remove from the wok and set aside.

2 Reduce the heat to medium, add the butter and stir until melted. Add the garam masala, paprika, coriander, ginger, chilli powder, cinnamon stick and cardamom pods, and stir-fry for 1 minute, or until the spices are fragrant. Return the chicken to the wok and mix in until coated in the spices.

3 Add the puréed tomatoes and sugar and simmer, stirring, for 15 minutes, or until the chicken is tender and the sauce is thick. Stir in the yoghurt, cream and lemon juice and simmer for about 5 minutes, or until the sauce has thickened slightly. Serve with some poppadoms.

CANTONESE LEMON CHICKEN

Preparation time 15 minutes
Total cooking time 25 minutes
Serves 4

500 g (1 lb 2 oz) skinless chicken breast fillets
1 egg yolk, lightly beaten
2 teaspoons soy sauce
2 teaspoons dry sherry
3 teaspoons cornflour (cornstarch)
60 g (2¼ oz/½ cup) cornflour (cornstarch), extra
2½ tablespoons plain (all-purpose) flour
oil, for deep-frying
4 spring onions (scallions), thinly sliced

Lemon sauce
4 tablespoons lemon juice
2 tablespoons sugar
1 tablespoon dry sherry
2 teaspoons cornflour (cornstarch)

1 Cut the chicken into long strips, about 1 cm (½ in) wide, and then set aside. Combine the egg, 1 tablespoon water, soy sauce, sherry and cornflour in a bowl and mix. Pour the egg mixture over the chicken, mixing well, and set aside for 10 minutes.

2 Sift the extra cornflour and plain flour together onto a plate. Roll each piece of chicken in the flour, coating each piece evenly, and shake off the excess. Place the chicken in a single layer on a plate.
3 Fill a wok one-third full of oil and heat to 180°C (350°F), or until a cube of bread dropped into the oil browns in 15 seconds. Lower the chicken pieces into the oil, in batches, and cook for 2 minutes, or until golden brown. Remove the chicken and drain. Repeat with the remaining chicken. Set aside. Reserve the oil in the wok.
4 To make the lemon sauce, combine 2 tablespoons water, the lemon juice, sugar and sherry in a small saucepan. Bring to the boil over medium heat, stirring until the sugar dissolves. Stir the cornflour into 1 tablespoon water and mix to a paste, then add to the lemon juice mixture, stirring until the sauce boils and thickens. Set aside.
5 Just before serving, reheat the oil in the wok to very hot, add all the chicken pieces and deep-fry for 2 minutes, or until very crisp and a rich golden brown. Remove the chicken with a slotted spoon and drain. Pile the chicken onto a serving plate, drizzle over the sauce and sprinkle with spring onion.

CHICKEN WITH ALMONDS AND ASPARAGUS

Preparation time 15 minutes

Total cooking time 15 minutes

Serves 4–6

2 teaspoons cornflour (cornstarch)

4 tablespoons chicken stock

¼ teaspoon sesame oil

2 tablespoons oyster sauce

1 tablespoon soy sauce

3 garlic cloves, crushed

1 teaspoon finely chopped fresh ginger

pinch ground white pepper

2½ tablespoons peanut oil

50 g (1¾ oz/⅓ cup) blanched almonds

2 spring onions (scallions), cut into 3 cm (1¼ in) lengths

500 g (1 lb 2 oz) boneless, skinless chicken thighs, cut into thin strips

1 small carrot, thinly sliced

155 g (5½ oz) asparagus, trimmed and cut into 3 cm (1¼ in) lengths

60 g (2¼ oz/¼ cup) tinned bamboo shoots, sliced

steamed rice, to serve

1 To make the stir-fry sauce, put the cornflour and stock in a small bowl and mix to form a paste, then stir in the sesame oil, oyster sauce, soy sauce, garlic, ginger and white pepper. Set aside until needed.

2 Heat a wok over high heat, add 2 teaspoons of the peanut oil and swirl to coat the base and side. Add the almonds and stir-fry for 1–2 minutes, or until golden — be careful not to burn them. Remove from the wok and drain on crumpled paper towel.

3 Heat another teaspoon of the peanut oil in the wok and swirl to coat. Add the spring onion and stir-fry for 30 seconds, or until wilted. Remove from the wok and set aside. Heat 1 tablespoon of the peanut oil in the wok over high heat, add the chicken in two batches and stir-fry for 3 minutes, or until the chicken is just cooked through. Set aside with the spring onion.

4 Add the remaining peanut oil to the wok, then add the carrot and stir-fry for 1–2 minutes, or until just starting to brown. Toss in the asparagus and the bamboo shoots and stir-fry for a further 1 minute. Remove all the vegetables from the wok and set aside with the chicken and spring onion.

5 Stir the stir-fry sauce briefly, then pour into the wok, stirring until the mixture thickens. Return the chicken and vegetables to the wok and stir thoroughly for a couple of minutes until they are coated in the sauce and are heated through. Sprinkle with the almonds before serving. Serve with rice.

CHICKEN KAPITAN

Preparation time 35 minutes
Total cooking time 30 minutes
Serves 4–6

30 g (1 oz) small dried shrimp
4 tablespoons oil
4–8 red chillies, seeded and finely chopped
4 garlic cloves, finely chopped
3 lemongrass stems (white part only), finely
   chopped
2 teaspoons ground turmeric
10 candlenuts
2 large onions, chopped
500 g (1 lb 2 oz) boneless, skinless chicken
   thighs, chopped
250 ml (9 fl oz/1 cup) coconut milk
125 ml (4 fl oz/½ cup) coconut cream
2 tablespoons lime juice
steamed rice, to serve

1 Put the shrimp in a clean frying pan and dry-fry over low heat, shaking the pan regularly, for 3 minutes, or until the shrimp are dark orange. Transfer the shrimp to a mortar and pestle and pound until finely ground. Set aside.

2 Put half the oil with the chilli, garlic, lemongrass, turmeric and candlenuts in a food processor and process in short bursts until very finely chopped, scraping down the sides of the bowl with a rubber spatula.
3 Heat the remaining oil in a wok or frying pan, add the onion and ¼ teaspoon salt and cook over low heat for 8 minutes, or until golden, stirring regularly. Take care not to let the onion burn.
4 Add the spice mixture and nearly all the ground shrimp meat, setting a little aside to use as garnish. Stir for 5 minutes. If the mixture begins to stick to the bottom of the pan, add 2 tablespoons coconut milk to the mixture. It is important to cook the mixture thoroughly to develop the flavours.
5 Add the chicken to the wok and stir. Cook for 5 minutes, or until the chicken begins to brown. Stir in the remaining coconut milk and 250 ml (9 fl oz/1 cup) water, and bring to the boil. Reduce the heat and simmer for 7 minutes, or until the chicken is cooked. Add the coconut cream and bring the mixture back to the boil, stirring. Add the lime juice and serve sprinkled with the ground shrimp. Serve with steamed rice.

CHICKEN KARAAGE

Preparation time 20 minutes +
Total cooking time 30 minutes
Makes 20 pieces

1.5 kg (3 lb 5 oz) chicken
125 ml (4 fl oz/½ cup) Japanese soy sauce
3 tablespoons mirin
2 tablespoons sake
1 tablespoon finely chopped fresh ginger
4 garlic cloves, crushed
oil, for deep-frying
cornflour (cornstarch), to coat
lemon wedges, to serve

1 Using a cleaver or a large kitchen knife, remove the wings from the chicken and chop them in half across the joint. Cut the chicken into 16 even-sized pieces by cutting it in half down the centre, then across each half to form four even pieces. Cut each quarter into four pieces, trying to retain some skin on each piece. You should have 20 pieces in total, including the four wing pieces.

2 Combine the soy sauce, mirin, sake, ginger and garlic in a large non-metallic bowl. Add the chicken and toss to coat well. Cover and refrigerate overnight, turning occasionally to evenly coat the chicken in the marinade.

3 Preheat the oven to 150°C (300°F/Gas 2). Fill a wok or deep heavy-based saucepan one-third full with oil and heat to 180°C (350°F), or until a cube of bread dropped into the oil browns in 15 seconds. While the oil is heating, drain the chicken and coat thoroughly in well-seasoned cornflour, shaking lightly to remove any excess.

4 Deep-fry the chicken, in batches, for 4–5 minutes, or until crisp and golden and the chicken is just cooked through and tender. Drain well on crumpled paper towel. Keep the cooked chicken warm in the oven while you cook the remainder. Serve hot with lemon wedges.

GENERAL TSO'S CHICKEN

Preparation time 15 minutes +
Total cooking time 10 minutes
Serves 4–6

2 tablespoons Chinese rice wine
1 tablespoon cornflour (cornstarch)
4 tablespoons dark soy sauce
3 teaspoons sesame oil
900 g (2 lb) boneless, skinless chicken thighs,
    cut into 3 cm (1¼ in) cubes
2 pieces dried citrus peel
125 ml (4 fl oz/½ cup) peanut oil
1½–2 teaspoons chilli flakes
2 tablespoons finely chopped fresh ginger
60 g (2¼ oz/1 cup) thinly sliced spring onions
    (scallions), plus extra, to garnish
2 teaspoons sugar
steamed rice, to serve

1 Combine the rice wine, cornflour,
2 tablespoons of the dark soy sauce and
2 teaspoons of the sesame oil in a large non-metallic bowl. Add the chicken, toss to coat
in the marinade, then cover and marinate in
the refrigerator for 1 hour.

2 Meanwhile, soak the dried citrus peel in
warm water for 20 minutes. Remove from
the water and finely chop — you will need
1½ teaspoons chopped peel.

3 Heat the peanut oil in a wok over high
heat. Using a slotted spoon, drain the
chicken from the marinade, then add to the
wok in batches and stir-fry for 2 minutes at
a time, or until browned and just cooked
through. Remove from the oil with a slotted
spoon and leave to drain in a colander.

4 Drain all the oil except 1 tablespoon from
the wok. Reheat the wok over high heat,
then add the chilli flakes and ginger. Stir-fry
for 10 seconds, then return the chicken
to the wok. Add the spring onion, sugar,
chopped citrus peel, remaining soy sauce
and sesame oil and ½ teaspoon salt and stir-fry for a further 2–3 minutes, or until well
combined and warmed through. Garnish
with the extra spring onion and serve with
steamed rice.

Note This dish is named after a 19th-century
Chinese general.

CLAYPOT CHICKEN AND VEGETABLES

Preparation time 20 minutes +
Total cooking time 25 minutes
Serves 4

500 g (1 lb 2 oz) boneless, skinless chicken thighs
1 tablespoon soy sauce
1 tablespoon dry sherry
6 dried Chinese mushrooms
2 tablespoons peanut oil
2 small leeks, white part only, sliced
5 cm (2 in) piece ginger, grated
125 ml (4 fl oz/½ cup) chicken stock
1 teaspoon sesame oil
250 g (9 oz) orange sweet potato, sliced
3 teaspoons cornflour (cornstarch)
steamed rice, to serve

1 Wash the chicken under cold water and pat it dry with paper towel. Cut the chicken into small pieces. Put it in a dish with the soy sauce and sherry, cover and marinate for 30 minutes in the refrigerator.
2 Cover the mushrooms with hot water and soak for 20 minutes. Drain and squeeze to remove any excess liquid. Remove the stems and chop the caps into shreds.
3 Drain the chicken, reserving the marinade. Heat half the oil in a wok, swirling gently to coat the base and side. Add half the chicken pieces and stir-fry briefly until seared on all sides. Transfer the chicken to a flameproof clay pot or casserole dish. Stir-fry the remaining chicken and add it to the clay pot.
4 Heat the remaining oil in the wok. Add the leek and ginger and stir-fry for 1 minute. Add the mushrooms, remaining marinade, stock and sesame oil and cook for 2 minutes. Transfer to the clay pot with the sweet potato and cook, covered, on the top of the stove over low heat for about 20 minutes.
5 Dissolve the cornflour in a little water and add it to the pot. Cook, stirring over high heat, until the mixture boils and thickens. Serve the chicken and vegetables at once with steamed rice.
Note Like all stews, this is best cooked 1–2 days ahead and stored, covered, in the refrigerator to allow the flavours to mature.

GLAZED HOISIN CHICKEN STIR-FRY

Preparation time 15 minutes +
Total cooking time 15 minutes
Serves 4

½ teaspoon sesame oil

1 egg white

1 tablespoon cornflour (cornstarch)

700 g (1 lb 9 oz) boneless, skinless chicken
   thighs, cut into small cubes

2 tablespoons peanut oil

2 garlic cloves, chopped

1 tablespoon finely shredded fresh ginger

1 tablespoon brown bean sauce

1 tablespoon hoisin sauce

1 tablespoon Chinese rice wine

1 teaspoon light soy sauce

4 spring onions (scallions), finely sliced

steamed rice, to serve

1 Combine the sesame oil, egg white and cornflour in a large non-metallic bowl. Add the chicken, toss to coat in the marinade, then cover with plastic wrap and marinate in the refrigerator for at least 15 minutes.

2 Heat a wok over high heat, add the peanut oil and swirl to coat the base and side. Add the chicken in three batches and stir-fry for 4 minutes at a time, or until cooked through. Remove the chicken from the wok and set aside.

3 Reheat the wok over high heat, add a little extra oil if necessary, then add the garlic and ginger and stir-fry for 1 minute. Return the chicken to the wok and add the bean sauce and hoisin sauce and cook, stirring, for 1 minute. Add the rice wine, soy sauce and spring onion and cook for 1 minute, or until the sauce is thick and glossy and coats the chicken. Serve with steamed rice.

KUNG PAO CHICKEN

Preparation time 15 minutes +
Total cooking time 15 minutes
Serves 4

1 egg white
2 teaspoons cornflour (cornstarch)
½ teaspoon sesame oil
2 teaspoons Chinese rice wine
1½ tablespoons soy sauce
600 g (1 lb 5 oz) boneless, skinless chicken
    thighs, cut into small cubes
3 tablespoons chicken stock
2 teaspoons Chinese black vinegar
1 teaspoon soft brown sugar
2 tablespoons vegetable oil
3 long dried red chillies, cut in half lengthways
3 garlic cloves, finely chopped
2 teaspoons finely grated fresh ginger
2 spring onions (scallions), thinly sliced
50 g (1¾ oz/⅓ cup) unsalted raw peanuts,
    roughly crushed

1 Lightly whisk together the egg white,
cornflour, sesame oil, rice wine and
2 teaspoons of the soy sauce in a large non-
metallic bowl. Add the chicken and toss to
coat in the marinade. Cover and marinate in
the refrigerator for 30 minutes.
2 To make the stir-fry sauce, combine the
stock, vinegar, sugar and the remaining soy
sauce in a small bowl.
3 Heat a wok over high heat, add about
1 tablespoon of the vegetable oil and swirl to
coat the base and side. Stir-fry the chicken
in batches for about 3 minutes, or until
browned. Remove from the wok.
4 Heat the remaining oil in the wok, then
add the chilli and cook for 15 seconds, or
until it starts to change colour. Add the
garlic, ginger, spring onion and peanuts and
stir-fry for 1 minute. Return the chicken
to the wok along with the stir-fry sauce
and stir-fry for 3 minutes, or until heated
through and the sauce has thickened slightly.
Serve immediately.
Note This dish is said to have been created
for an important court official called Kung
Pao (or Gong Bao), who was stationed in the
Sichuan province of China.

NONYA LIME CHICKEN

Preparation time 20 minutes
Total cooking time 25 minutes
Serves 4–6

Curry paste
70 g (2½ oz/⅔ cup) red Asian shallots
4 garlic cloves
2 lemongrass stems, white part only,
    chopped
2 teaspoons finely chopped fresh galangal
1 teaspoon ground turmeric
2 tablespoons sambal oelek
1 tablespoon shrimp paste

3 tablespoons vegetable oil
1 kg (2 lb 4 oz) boneless, skinless chicken thighs,
    cut into 3 cm (1¼ in) cubes
400 ml (14 fl oz) coconut milk
1 teaspoon finely grated lime zest
125 ml (4 fl oz/½ cup) lime juice

6 kaffir lime leaves, finely shredded, plus extra,
    to garnish
2 tablespoons tamarind purée
steamed rice, to serve
lime wedges, to garnish

1 Combine the curry paste ingredients in a food processor or blender and blend until a smooth paste forms.
2 Heat a non-stick wok until very hot, add the oil and swirl to coat the base and side. Add the curry paste and stir-fry for 1–2 minutes, or until fragrant. Add the chicken and stir-fry for 5 minutes, or until browned. Add the coconut milk, lime zest and juice, makrut leaves and tamarind purée.
3 Reduce the heat and simmer for about 15 minutes, or until the chicken is cooked and the sauce has reduced and thickened slightly. Season with salt. Serve with steamed rice, lime wedges and extra kaffir lime leaves.

CHICKEN WITH PEACH, RED CAPSICUM AND BEAN SALSA

Preparation time 20 minutes +
Total cooking time 15 minutes
Serves 4

canola or olive oil spray
4 skinless chicken breast fillets
3 fresh peaches
150 g (5½ oz) baby green beans, trimmed
3 tablespoons white wine vinegar
1 tablespoon caster (superfine) sugar
2 teaspoon grated fresh ginger
1 garlic clove, crushed
½ teaspoon ground cumin
3 tablespoons chopped coriander (cilantro) leaves
3 tablespoons chopped mint
1 red capsicum (pepper), diced
1 small red onion, finely diced
1 small red chilli, finely chopped

1 Lightly spray a chargrill pan or barbecue hotplate with oil and cook the chicken breasts for 5 minutes on each side, or until tender and cooked through.
2 Meanwhile, to peel the peaches, plunge them into a bowl of boiling water. Refresh under cold water, then slip the skins from the peaches. Remove the stones, then dice.
3 Blanch the beans in a saucepan of boiling water for 2 minutes, then drain and refresh. Combine the vinegar, sugar, ginger, garlic, cumin, coriander and mint in a small bowl.
4 Put the capsicum, onion, chilli, peaches and beans in a large bowl. Gently stir through the vinegar herb mixture and serve at once with the chicken.

SPICY CHICKEN BURGERS

Preparation time 10 minutes +
Total cooking time 10 minutes
Serves 4

500 g (1 lb 2 oz) lean minced (ground) chicken
4 spring onions (scallions), finely chopped
4 tablespoons chopped coriander (cilantro) leaves
2 garlic cloves, crushed
¼ teaspoon cayenne pepper
1 egg white, lightly beaten
1 tablespoon olive or canola oil
1 lemon, halved
150 g (5½ oz) tabouleh
4 wholegrain bread rolls, halved

1 Mix together the chicken, spring onion, coriander, garlic, cayenne pepper and egg white and season with salt and freshly ground black pepper. Shape the mixture into four patties. Refrigerate for 20 minutes before cooking.

2 Heat the oil in a large non-stick frying pan over medium heat. Add the patties and cook for about 5 minutes on each side, or until browned and cooked through.

3 Squeeze the lemon on the cooked patties and drain well on crumpled paper towels. Add the patties to the halved wholegrain buns and fill with the tabouleh. Serve with a green salad and some chilli sauce, if you like.

TANDOORI CHICKEN SKEWERS AND RICE

Preparation time 20 minutes +
Total cooking time 15 minutes
Serves 4

1½ tablespoons tandoori spice powder
125 g (4½ oz/½ cup) low-fat plain yoghurt
1 tablespoons lemon juice
4 x 200 g (7 oz) skinless chicken fillets, cut into
    2 cm (¾ in) strips
300 g (10½ oz/1½ cups) basmati rice
2 teaspoons oil
1 small onion, finely diced
2 garlic cloves, crushed
1 teaspoon ginger, finely grated
½ teaspoons ground turmeric
1 teaspoon cumin seeds
4 bruised cardamom pods
1 stick cinnamon
500 ml (17 fl oz/2 cups) chicken stock
2 tablespoons currants
oil spray
mango chutney, lemon wedges and coriander
    (cilantro), to serve

1 Soak 8 bamboo skewers in cold water for 30 minutes. Place the spice powder, yoghurt, lemon juice and chicken in a non-metallic bowl. Mix well to combine, then cover and refrigerate for 2 hours.

2 For the pilaf, rinse the rice under cold water until it runs clear. Heat the oil over a medium heat in a saucepan, add the onion, garlic, ginger, turmeric and cumin seeds. Cook for 5 minutes, or until softened, and then add the rice, cardamom, cinnamon and chicken stock.

3 Bring to the boil, reduce the heat to low, cover and cook for 12 minutes. Remove from the heat, add the currants and stir through. Season well and set aside, covered.

4 Meanwhile, weave the chicken pieces onto the skewers so they are evenly distributed, but not too close together. Heat a chargrill pan or frying pan over a medium heat and spray with the oil. Add the skewers, and cook for 12–15 minutes, turning, so that they cook evenly. Serve the skewers on the rice pilaf with mango chutney, lemon wedges and coriander leaves.

CHICKEN AND NOODLES WITH HONEY AND LIME DRESSING

Preparation time 20 minutes

Total cooking time 5 minutes

Serves 4

Dressing

3 tablespoons honey

4 tablespoons light soy sauce

zest and juice from 2 limes

2 Asian shallots, finely chopped

1 teaspoon grated fresh ginger

1 small red chilli, seeded and finely chopped

500 g (1 lb 2 oz) Singapore noodles

1 barbecued chicken, skin and fat removed

150 g (5½ oz) snowpeas (mangetout), trimmed and cut in half on the diagonal

180 g (6½ oz/2 cups) bean sprouts

2 celery sticks, cut into thin, long shreds

2 large handfuls mint

1 Combine the dressing ingredients in a small bowl.

2 Place the noodles in a bowl, pour over boiling water and leave for 1 minute to soften. Drain. Refresh under cold water, then cut into short lengths using scissors. Place in a large mixing bowl.

3 Shred the flesh from the chicken. Blanch the snowpeas in a saucepan of boiling water. Boil for 1 minute, then drain and refresh. Add the snowpeas to the noodles. Add the chicken meat to the noodles.

4 Add the bean sprouts, celery, mint leaves and dressing and toss well to combine. Serve immediately.

FISH & SEAFOOD

With the wonderful array of fish and seafoods available, we have no excuse for not having an excellent diet. Most seafood has a low fat content as well as valuable vitamins, minerals, protein and fatty acids. All types of seafood should melt in your mouth so here are a few recipes to help you attain that goal.

FISH BASICS

Fish is often thought to be a perfect food: it is low in calories, high in protein and contains omega 3. It is also easy to cook and can be married with lots of different flavours.

BUYING FISH

Fresh fish should smell like the sea and they should not actually smell 'fishy'. They should be firm, have shiny scales and bright, clear eyes. Really fresh fish may have gaping mouths and open gill flaps. Some fish, such as salmon and trout, are covered in a clear slime. Oily fish deteriorate faster than white fish so be vigilant when buying them.

TYPES OF FISH

There are thousands of species of fish, mostly saltwater, but many freshwater. It is important to choose the right type of fish to suit the particular recipe or cooking method. The fish below are grouped into families — if a particular fish is unavailable, select another fish from within the same family.

Herring family These sleek, silver fish vary in size from small anchovies and whitebait (herring fry) to larger herrings. This family also includes sardines, pilchards and sprats.

Deep sea fish They include hoki, grenadier, orange roughy, redfish and scabbard fish. They tend to have white flesh and can be interchanged with many of the cod family.

Eels Conger and Moray eels have skin rather than scales and are sea fish. They are usually sold as steaks and have firm flesh. Buy skinned eels.

Reef fish They include barracuda, bourgeois, capitaine, emperor, grouper, parrotfish, pomfret and snapper. They are best eaten on the bone or in fillets.

Surface-feeding fish These large shoaling fish vary in size but tend to have a meaty flesh. They include tuna, bluefish, mackerel, horse mackerel, jack, kingfish, mahi mahi, marlin, swordfish and yellowtail.

Cod family They include cod, haddock, coley, pollack, whiting and ling. They have flaky white flesh with little fat.

Flat fish These fish have two eyes on top of their head and tend to have firm, white flesh. They include dab, Dover sole, brill, flounder, halibut, lemon sole and turbot. Best eaten off the bone but easy to fillet.

Salmon family Salmon and sea trout are migrating fish, but nowadays often farmed. All can be filleted; whole or larger fish are used as cutlets.

Inshore fish These John Dory, gurnard, monkfish (anglerfish), rascasse, red mullet, sea bass, sea bream and wrasse. They have a delicate flavour and are best cooked on the bone as the fillets are usually small. The tail of the monkfish is the only part eaten.

Freshwater fish Trout is the most common and is always available fresh, but others include catfish, freshwater bream, carp, char, perch, pike, sturgeon and tilapia.

Boneless fish These fish have cartilage rather than bones. They include shark, dogfish, skates and rays. Shark and dogfish are interchangeable in recipes. They are usually eaten as fish and chips.

SCALES AND SKIN

Fish with scales need to have them removed as they are hard and unpleasant to eat. Fish with skin are also best with the skin removed as it is very tough.

GUTTING AND TRIMMING

Fish need to be gutted fairly quickly as their digestive juices can break down and start to decompose their flesh. Once gutted, remove any visible blood lines that run along the length of the spine, then rinse well. For the same reason, snip out the gills.

FILLETING

Fish can be filleted either by the fishmonger or by yourself. Round fish give two fillets, one on each side of the fish. Flat fish give four fillets, two on each side or two large fillets.

SKINNING

Depending on the recipe, you may or may not need to skin your fish. Remove the skin before cooking, or if cooking a whole fish, carefully peel it off after cooking.

BONING

Fish can also be boned leaving a whole fish with no bones and a pocket in the flesh, which can be stuffed. Pocket boning is suitable for fish such as trout and mackerel. To pinbone a fish, remove any small bones by running your fingers over the fillet to locate them. Pull them out using your fingers or a pair of tweezers.

STORAGE

Prepare whole fish by scaling, gutting and cleaning, then rinsing under cold water. Pat dry to remove any traces of scales or intestinal lining. Place in a covered container (or in a freezer bag on a plate) in the coldest part of the fridge and use within 2–3 days. Whole fish can be frozen for up to 6 months (oily fish such as tuna, mullet, Atlantic salmon and sardines, can be frozen for up to 3 months). Fillets and cutlets should be frozen in bags in smaller portions for up to 3 months.

COOKING

Use a slice or tongs to turn fish during cooking and try not to pierce the flesh.

Don't salt skinned fish until just before you cook it as it tends to draw moisture out.

Fish cooks much faster than meat, and at a lower temperature.

Fish can be eaten raw, cooked in acid or salt, or cooked using heat. The important thing is to cook fish until it is just done. Large fish may benefit from being cooked in a moist heat, such as poaching or steaming. Make sure the fish is at room temperature when you cook it.

A fish is properly cooked when the flesh has turned opaque and may be more flaky in appearance. If the flesh is not visible, it will feel firm and flaky through the skin when you press it.

Some seafood, such as tuna and Atlantic salmon, is best served while it is still rare in the centre.

METHODS OF COOKING

Grilling and barbecuing Both these methods are suitable for cooking fish steaks, smaller whole fish and fillets. Make sure the grill is fully preheated to the highest setting. For barbecuing, baste fish well to keep it moist.

Baking and roasting Both these methods are suitable for cooking whole fish, steaks and fish fillets. Roasting cooks fish at a higher temperature and is particularly good for pieces of fillet such as salmon or whole fish.

Frying This method is suitable for small whole fish, fillets and steaks. When deep-frying, immerse whole or pieces of fish in the hot fat and cook them quickly.

Poaching This method is suitable for whole fish and fillets. Poaching is a gentle way of cooking fish by submerging them in a barely bubbling liquid such as court bouillon or milk. Poaching is especially suitable for large whole fish such as salmon as it stops the flesh drying out. Poaching is a good low-fat way of cooking fish.

Steaming This method is suitable for cooking fillets, parcels of fish and small whole fish. Steaming cooks the fish in a gentle heat and can also be used for adding aromatic flavours to the fish. Use a bamboo steamer and put the fish on a piece of baking paper or a plate. If you are using flavourings such as herbs, put the herbs in the bottom of the steamer, then put the fish on top of them. When steaming, choose pieces of fish that will hold their shape and will not become too fragile.

Searing and cooking on a griddle This method is suitable for cooking fillets with the skin on or whole fish and steaks cut from firm-fleshed fish such as tuna or swordfish. This method cooks the fish on a high heat and gives the fish a crisp skin.

SEAFOOD BASICS

Seafood has unfairly earned the tag 'difficult to cook', partly because in some cases it can require varying amounts of preparation for cooking.

BUYING SEAFOOD

Each type of seafood has particular characteristics that we can look at as a good indication of the freshness.

Prawns/shrimp, crabs, lobsters, bugs, freshwater crayfish No discolouration or 'blackness', particularly at the joints. Bodies, claws, nippers etc. should be fully intact. Bodies should be free of water or liquid and should be heavy in relation to size.

Prawns perish easily, so they are often frozen on board the ships from which they are fished. They can be bought shell on or shelled, head on or off, cooked or uncooked.

Choose fresh prawns with a pleasant smell, and firm shells. Avoid any that smell of ammonia or with dark discolouration around the head or legs.

Live crustaceans should be active and moving freely. Nippers and claws should be intact, not broken or loose. Never buy a dead uncooked crab. Look for lively crabs that feel heavy for their size. Crabs with worn barnacles and feet will not have just moulted — these crabs will have more meat.

Cooked crabs are also highly perishable, so buy with care. Make sure they smell fresh and are undamaged and their legs and feet are drawn into the body.

Molluscs (invertebrates with soft unsegmented bodies and often a shell) Always buy mussels from a reputable source.

Oysters, scallops Shells should be tightly closed, or close quickly after a tap on the bench, be intact and look lustrous. Flesh should be firm and 'plump'.

Octopus, cuttlefish, squid Flesh should be firm and resilient and spring back when touched. Head, tentacles and body should be intact and not loose.

TYPES OF SEAFOOD

Abalone Also known as ormer or ear shell. The foot or adductor muscle is eaten. Abalone is sold fresh, dried and frozen.

Clams Can be classed as either soft- or hard-shelled. Good raw or cooked. Clams must be bought live, then shucked and cleaned before use.

Cockles Cockles can be eaten raw or cooked and must be bought live.

Conchs and whelks Conchs are single-shelled molluscs. The flesh often needs to be tenderized by beating or marinating it. Whelks are smaller than conchs. Only the large adductor muscle ('foot') is eaten.

Crab Crab meat is sweet, delicate and versatile and food lovers compare it to lobster.

Crayfish Often used to refer to the rock or spiny lobster or crawfish.

Cuttlefish A relation of the squid and octopus. Like the squid, cuttlefish contain ink sacs that may be used in cooking. They have 10 large tentacles and an internal shell.

Lobster Generally, large crustaceans found in cold waters. Lobsters are often dark blue or almost black in colour when alive and turn red when cooked. Lobster flesh is firm, delicate and slightly sweet.

Mussels The flesh of female mussels is orange while that of the male is a pale whitish colour. Small mussels are more tender and have a better flavour.

Oysters A bivalve more cultivated than taken from the wild. Oysters are often eaten raw from their shells, but can be cooked.

Periwinkles (winkles) Small, blackish-brown single-shelled mollusc found on both sides of the Atlantic.

Prawns Crustaceans found all over the world living in fresh, briny and saltwater of varying temperatures called prawns in most countries, but shrimps in North and South America. Prawns vary in size, have two long antennae and five pairs of legs. Their flesh is translucent and can be coloured pink, yellow, grey, brown, red or dark red, depending on the species. They become opaque and turn pink once cooked. See also shrimp.

Scallops There are many varieties and their shells vary in size and roundness. Usually just the muscle and roe are eaten.

Sea Urchin Hidden inside the spiny sea urchin are five orange roe (corals). Cut the top off and scoop out the corals and eat raw or cook with pasta or eggs.

Shrimp These are small crustaceans similar to prawns but members of a different family. The colour of raw shrimps varies greatly but most will assume a pale to bright pink or brown colour on cooking.

Squid These range in length. The edible part of the squid is its tentacles and its long body. Squid have an ink sac. The black ink is used to give colour and flavour to pasta.

FREEZING

Ideally, all seafood is best eaten fresh. However, you can freeze it when it is very fresh.

Don't defrost frozen seafood at room temperature: thaw in the fridge. Some seafood, such as crumbed fish fillets, calamari or prawns (shrimp), can be cooked from frozen. Avoid refreezing seafood as this alters the flavour and texture.

Prawns (shrimp) Do not peel. Place in a plastic container and cover with water—this forms a large ice block which insulates the prawns and prevents freezer burn. Freeze for up to 3 months. When required, thaw in the refrigerator overnight.

Other seafood Freeze for up to 3 months. Wrap large crustaceans such as crayfish, lobsters and crabs in foil, then place in an airtight freezer bag for freezing. Octopus, squid and cuttlefish should be gutted and can be frozen for up to 3 months. Oysters shouldn't be frozen as the flavour will alter.

COOKING SEAFOOD

Seafood lends itself to steaming, poaching, baking, barbecuing and grilling (broiling), stewing and casseroling, stir-frying, deep or shallow frying, as well as marinating or coating. Seafood should never be overcooked or it will be dry, tough or rubbery.

Most seafood is cooked when it loses its translucent appearance and turns opaque.

Molluscs can be cooked briefly or eaten raw. The shells can be prised open—you may need to cut the muscle, or they can be steamed open.

Small octopus can be barbecued, grilled (broiled) or fried, but larger ones need to be tenderized by the fishmonger, then need long simmering in liquid. When tenderized, the tentacles curl up.

Small cuttlefish and squid can be fried and the bodies are ideal for stuffing. Large cuttlefish and squid require long simmering.

The most humane way of handling a live crab is to freeze it to make it lose consciousness — this will take about 45 minutes. Drop it into a large pot of boiling, salted water and simmer for 15 minutes per 500 g (1 lb 2 oz). Drain and leave to cool.

Though oysters are most often served raw, they can also be cooked. Shuck and add to stews or soups, leave in the shell and top with creamy sauces, or grill or steam dressed with Asian flavours. Shucked oysters can also be deep-fried, shallow-fried and poached and are traditionally used in steak pies or to stuff carpetbag steaks. Be careful when combining oysters with spirits as they may cause the oyster flesh to harden inside the gut, causing discomfort.

Whichever way prawns are cooked, they should not be overcooked or they will become tough and rubbery; 2–3 minutes is sufficient to cook average-sized prawns. If adding cooked prawns to a dish, add them at the last minute.

Tuna

Swordfish

Sole

Sardines

Whitebait

Sea bream

Red mullet

Prawns

Crab

Mussels

Rock lobster

Clams

Scallops

Squid

Octopus

TUNA SKEWERS WITH MOROCCAN SPICES AND CHERMOULA

Preparation time 10 minutes +
Total cooking time 5 minutes
Serves 4

800 g (1 lb 12 oz) tuna steaks, cut into cubes
2 tablespoons olive oil
½ teaspoon ground cumin
2 teaspoons grated lemon zest
couscous, to serve

Chermoula
3 teaspoons ground cumin
½ teaspoon ground coriander
2 teaspoons paprika
pinch of cayenne pepper
4 garlic cloves, crushed
15 g (½ oz) chopped flat-leaf (Italian) parsley
30 g (1 oz) chopped coriander (cilantro) leaves

4 tablespoons lemon juice
125 ml (4 oz/½ cup) olive oil

1 If using wooden skewers, soak for 30 minutes beforehand to prevent scorching. Place the tuna in a shallow non-metallic dish. Combine the olive oil, ground cumin and lemon zest and pour over the tuna. Toss to coat and leave to marinate for 10 minutes.
2 To make the chermoula, place the cumin, coriander, paprika and cayenne in a large frying pan and cook over medium heat for 30 seconds, or until fragrant. Combine with the remaining ingredients and leave for the flavours to develop.
3 Thread the tuna onto the skewers. Cook on a hot, lightly oiled barbecue grill or flat plate until cooked to your taste (about 1 minute on each side for rare and 2 minutes for medium). Serve on couscous with the chermoula drizzled over the skewers.

TUNA BURGERS WITH HERBED MAYONNAISE

Preparation time 15 minutes

Total cooking time 8 minutes

Serves 4

4 garlic cloves, crushed

2 egg yolks

250 ml (9 fl oz/1 cup) light olive oil

3 tablespoons chopped flat-leaf (Italian) parsley

1 tablespoon chopped dill

2 teaspoons Dijon mustard

1 tablespoon lemon juice

1 tablespoon red wine vinegar

1 tablespoon baby capers in brine, drained

4 anchovy fillets in oil, drained

4 x 150 g (5½ oz) tuna steaks

2 tablespoons olive oil

2 red onions, thinly sliced

4 large round bread rolls, halved and buttered

100 g (3½ oz) mixed lettuce leaves

1 Put the garlic and egg yolks in a food processor and process them together for 10 seconds. With the motor running, add the oil in a very thin, slow stream. When the mixture starts to thicken start pouring the oil a little faster until all of the oil has been added and the mixture is thick and creamy. Add the parsley, dill, mustard, lemon juice, vinegar, capers and anchovies, and process until the mixture is smooth. Refrigerate the mayonnaise until you need it.

2 Preheat the chargrill plate to high direct heat. Brush the tuna steaks with 1 tablespoon of olive oil and cook them for 2 minutes on each side, or until they are almost cooked through. Add the remaining olive oil to the onion, toss to separate and coat the rings, and cook on the flat plate for 2 minutes, or until the onion is soft and caramelized. Toast the rolls, buttered-side down, on the chargrill plate for 1 minute, or until they are marked and golden.

3 Put some lettuce, a tuna steak, some of the onion and a dollop of herbed mayonnaise on one half of each roll. Season and top with the other half of the roll.

SWEET CHILLI OCTOPUS

Preparation time 10 minutes
Total cooking time 5 minutes
Serves 4

1.5 kg (3 lb 5 oz) baby octopus
250 ml (9 fl oz/1 cup) sweet chilli sauce
4 tablespoons lime juice
4 tablespoons fish sauce
60 g (2¼ oz/⅓ cup) soft brown sugar
lime wedges, to serve

1 Cut off the octopus heads, below the eyes, with a sharp knife. Discard the heads and guts. Push the beaks out with your index finger, remove and discard. Wash the octopus thoroughly under running water and drain on crumpled paper towels. If the octopus tentacles are large, cut into quarters.
2 Mix together the sweet chilli sauce, lime juice, fish sauce and sugar.
3 Cook the octopus on a very hot, lightly oiled barbecue grill or flat plate, turning often, for 3–4 minutes, or until it just changes colour. Brush with a quarter of the sauce during cooking. Take care not to overcook the octopus or it will toughen. Serve with the sauce and lime wedges.

HONEY AND LIME PRAWN KEBABS WITH MANGO SALSA

Preparation time 10 minutes +
Total cooking time 5 minutes
Serves 4

3 tablespoons clear runny honey
1 small red chilli, seeded and finely chopped
2 tablespoons olive oil
grated zest and juice of 2 limes
1 large garlic clove, crushed
2 cm (¾ in) piece fresh ginger, peeled and finely grated
1 tablespoon chopped coriander (cilantro) leaves
32 tiger or king prawns (shrimp), peeled and deveined, tails intact

Mango salsa
2 tomatoes
1 small just-ripe mango, diced
½ small red onion, diced
1 small red chilli, seeded and finely chopped
grated zest and juice of 1 lime
2 tablespoons chopped coriander (cilantro) leaves

1 In a small bowl, whisk together the honey, chilli, oil, lime zest and lime juice, garlic, ginger and coriander.

2 Put the prawns in a non-metallic dish, add the marinade and toss well. Cover and refrigerate for several hours, turning the prawns occasionally.

3 Before you start cooking, soak eight bamboo skewers in cold water for about 30 minutes. While the skewers are soaking, make the salsa. Score a cross in the base of each tomato and put them in a heatproof bowl. Cover with boiling water, leave for 30 seconds, then plunge in cold water and peel the skin away from the cross. Remove the seeds, dice the flesh, saving any juices, and put the tomato with all its juices in a bowl. Mix in the mango, onion, chilli, lime zest, lime juice and coriander.

4 Heat the grill (broiler) to high. Thread 4 prawns onto each skewer and grill for 4 minutes, or until pink and cooked through, turning halfway through cooking and basting regularly with the leftover marinade. Serve at once with the salsa.

BARBECUED CHERMOULA PRAWNS

Preparation time 10 minutes +
Total cooking time 10 minutes
Serves 4

1 kg (2 lb 4 oz) raw prawns (shrimp)
3 teaspoons hot paprika
2 teaspoons ground cumin
30 g (1 oz) flat-leaf (Italian) parsley
15 g (½ oz) coriander (cilantro) leaves
100 ml (3½ fl oz) lemon juice
145 ml (5 fl oz) olive oil
280 g (10 oz/1½ cups) couscous
1 tablespoon grated lemon zest
lemon wedges, to serve

1 Peel the prawns, leaving the tails intact, and discard the heads. Gently pull out the dark vein from the backs, starting at the head end. Place the prawns in a large bowl. Dry-fry the paprika and cumin in a frying pan for about 1 minute, or until fragrant. Remove from the heat.

2 Blend or process the spices, parsley, coriander, lemon juice and 125 ml (4 fl oz/ ½ cup) of the oil until finely chopped. Add a little salt and pepper. Pour over the prawns and mix well, then cover with plastic wrap and refrigerate for 10 minutes. Heat a chargrill pan or barbecue plate to hot.

3 Meanwhile, to cook the couscous, bring 250 ml (9 fl oz/1 cup) water to the boil in a saucepan, and stir in the couscous, lemon zest, the remaining oil and ¼ teaspoon salt. Remove from the heat, cover and leave for 5 minutes. Fluff the couscous with a fork, adding a little extra olive oil if needed.

4 Cook the prawns on the chargrill plate for about 3–4 minutes, or until cooked through, turning and brushing with extra marinade while cooking (take care not to overcook). Serve the prawns on a bed of couscous, with a wedge of lemon.

MALAYSIAN BARBECUED SEAFOOD

Preparation time 15 minutes +
Total cooking time 8 minutes
Serves 4

1 onion, grated
4 garlic cloves, chopped
5 cm (2 in) piece of fresh ginger, grated
3 lemongrass stems, white part only, chopped
2 teaspoons ground or grated fresh turmeric
1 teaspoon shrimp paste
4 tablespoons vegetable oil
¼ teaspoon salt
4 medium calamari tubes
2 thick white boneless fish fillets
8 raw king prawns (shrimp)
banana leaves, to serve
2 limes, cut into wedges
strips of lime zest, to garnish
mint leaves, to garnish

1 Combine the onion, garlic, ginger, lemongrass, turmeric, shrimp paste, oil and salt in a small food processor. Process in short bursts until the mixture forms a paste.

2 Cut the calamari in half lengthways and lay it on the bench with the soft inside facing up. Score a very fine honeycomb pattern into the soft side, taking care not to cut all the way through, and then cut into large pieces. Wash all the seafood under cold running water and pat dry with paper towels.

3 Brush lightly with the spice paste, then place on a tray, cover and refrigerate for 15 minutes.

4 Lightly oil a chargrill plate and heat. When the plate is hot, arrange the fish fillets and prawns on the plate. Cook, turning once only, for about 3 minutes each side or until the fish flesh is just firm and the prawns turn bright pink to orange. Add the calamari pieces and cook for about 2 minutes or until the flesh turns white and rolls up. Take care not to overcook the seafood.

5 Arrange the seafood on a platter lined with the banana leaves, add the lime wedges and serve immediately, garnished with strips of lime zest and some fresh mint.

SWORDFISH WITH TOMATO BUTTER AND GRILLED ASPARAGUS

Preparation time 15 minutes +
Total cooking time 10 minutes
Serves 4

100 g (3½ oz) butter, softened
50 g (½ oz/⅓ cup) semi-dried (sun-blushed) tomatoes, finely chopped
2 tablespoons baby capers in brine, drained and crushed
1½ tablespoons shredded basil leaves
4 garlic cloves, crushed
3 tablespoons extra virgin olive oil
300 g (10½ oz) slender asparagus spears, trimmed
4 swordfish steaks

1 Put the butter in a bowl with the tomato, capers, basil and two cloves of crushed garlic, and mash it all together. Shape the flavoured butter into a log, then wrap it in baking paper and twist the ends to close them off. Refrigerate until the butter is firm, then cut it into 1 cm (½ in) slices and leave it, covered, at room temperature until needed.

2 Mix 2 tablespoons of the oil and the remaining garlic in a small bowl. Toss the asparagus spears with the oil until they are well coated, season them with salt and pepper, and leave for 30 minutes.

3 Preheat a ridged barbecue grill plate to high direct heat. Brush the swordfish steaks with the remaining oil and cook them for 2–3 minutes on each side or until they are just cooked through. Don't overcook the fish as residual heat will continue to cook the meat after it has been removed from the barbecue. Put a piece of the tomato butter on top of each steak as soon as it comes off the barbecue and season to taste. Cook the asparagus on the chargrill plate, turning it regularly, for 2–3 minutes, or until it is just tender. Serve the asparagus immediately with the fish.

BARBECUED SQUID WITH SALSA VERDE

Preparation time 10 minutes +
Total cooking time 4 minutes
Serves 4

4 cleaned squid tubes
3 tablespoons olive oil
3 garlic cloves, crushed
150 g (5½ oz) mixed lettuce leaves
250 g (9 oz/1 punnet) cherry tomatoes, halved

Salsa verde
2 large handfuls flat-leaf (Italian) parsley
2 tablespoons chopped dill
2 tablespoons extra virgin olive oil
2 tablespoons olive oil
1 tablespoon Dijon mustard
2 garlic cloves, crushed
1 tablespoon red wine vinegar
1 tablespoon baby capers, rinsed and
    drained
4 anchovy fillets, drained

1 Open out the squid tubes by cutting through one side so you have one large piece, the inside facing upwards. Pat dry with paper towels. Using a sharp knife, and being careful not to cut all the way through, score the flesh on the diagonal in a series of lines about 5 mm (¼ in) apart, then do the same in the opposite direction to form a crisscross pattern. Cut the squid into 4 cm (1½ in) pieces and put in a non-metallic bowl.
2 Combine the oil and garlic and pour over the squid, tossing to coat well. Cover and marinate in the refrigerator for 30 minutes.
3 Put all the salsa verde ingredients in a food processor and blend until just combined. Set aside until ready to use.
4 Preheat a barbecue flat plate to high. Drain the squid and cook for 1–2 minutes, or until curled up and just cooked through. Put the squid in a bowl with the salsa verde and toss until well coated. Arrange the lettuce and tomatoes on four serving plates, top with the squid, then season and serve at once.

MUSSELS WITH DILL AND CAPERS

Preparation time 5 minutes

Total cooking time 4 minutes

Serves 4

125 ml (4 fl oz/½ cup) cream

zest of 1 lemon

4 tablespoons dill sprigs

2 tablespoons baby capers, rinsed and drained

10 pitted black olives

1 kg (2 lb 4 oz) black mussels, scrubbed

3 tablespoons white wine

2 garlic cloves, crushed

70 g (2½ oz) butter, chopped

4 spring onions (scallions), finely sliced

1 Preheat a kettle or covered barbecue to medium direct heat. Mix together the cream, lemon zest, dill, capers and olives.

2 Put the mussels in a large frying pan on the barbecue, pour the wine over and lower the lid. Cook for 1–2 minutes, or until the mussels start to open.

3 Add the garlic and butter, and toss them through the mussels using tongs. Pour the cream and dill mixture over the mussels, then cover and cook for another minute, or until the mussels fully open.

4 Toss to coat the mussels thoroughly in the sauce, then discard any unopened mussels. Serve immediately, garnished with the spring onion.

PRAWNS WITH GARLIC AND CHILLI

Preparation time 5 minutes
Total cooking time 5 minutes
Serves 4

125 ml (4 fl oz/½ cup) olive oil
6 garlic cloves, crushed
1 red onion, finely chopped
3–4 dried chillies, cut in half, seeds removed
1.125 kg (2 lb 7 oz/about 32) large prawns
   (shrimp), peeled
4 tomatoes, finely chopped
a handful parsley or coriander (cilantro), chopped

1 Heat the oil in a large frying pan or shallow casserole. Add the garlic, onion and chilli, cook for a few minutes until softened, then add the prawns and cook them for about 4 minutes, by which time they should be pink all over.

2 When the prawns are cooked, add the tomato and cook for a minute or two just to heat through. Season with salt and stir the herbs through.

3 Take the pan to the table straight away (the prawns will continue cooking in the heat), remembering to put it on a heatproof mat. Eat with bread to mop up the juices.

TUNA MORNAY

Preparation time 10 minutes
Total cooking time 25 minutes
Serves 4

60 g (2¼ oz) butter
2 tablespoons plain (all-purpose) flour
500 ml (17 fl oz/2 cups) milk
½ teaspoon dry mustard
90 g (3¼ oz/¾ cup) grated Cheddar cheese
600 g (1 lb 5 oz) tinned tuna in brine, drained
2 tablespoons finely chopped parsley
2 eggs, hard-boiled and chopped
4 tablespoons fresh breadcrumbs
paprika, for dusting

1 Preheat the oven to 180°C (350°F/Gas 4). Melt the butter in a small saucepan, add the flour and stir over low heat for 1 minute. Take the pan off the heat and slowly pour in the milk, stirring with your other hand until you have a smooth sauce. Return the pan to the heat and stir constantly until the sauce boils and thickens. Reduce the heat and simmer for another 2 minutes. Remove the pan from the heat, whisk in the mustard and two-thirds of the cheese — don't stop whisking until you have a smooth, rich cheesy sauce.

2 Roughly flake the tuna with a fork, then tip it into the cheesy sauce, along with the parsley and egg. Season with a little salt and pepper, then spoon the mixture into four 250 ml (9 fl oz/1 cup) ovenproof ramekins.

3 Make the topping by mixing together the breadcrumbs and the rest of the cheese, then sprinkle it over the mornay. Add a hint of colour by dusting the top very lightly with paprika. Place in the oven until the topping is golden brown, about 20 minutes.

SHELLFISH STEW

Preparation time 15 minutes

Total cooking time 25 minutes

Serves 6

16 mussels

12 large prawns (shrimp)

435 ml (15¼ fl oz/1¾ cups) cider or dry white wine

50 g (1¾ oz) butter

1 garlic clove, crushed

2 shallots, finely chopped

2 celery stalks, finely chopped

1 large leek, white part only, thinly sliced

250 g (9 oz) small chestnut mushrooms, sliced

1 bay leaf

300 g (10½ oz) salmon fillet, skinned and cut into chunks

400 g (14 oz) sole fillet, skinned and cut into thick strips widthways

300 ml (10½ fl oz) thick (double/heavy) cream

3 tablespoons finely chopped parsley

1 Scrub the mussels and remove their beards. Throw away any that are open and don't close when tapped on the bench. Peel and devein the prawns.

2 Pour the cider into a large saucepan and bring to a simmer. Add the mussels, cover the pan and cook for 3–5 minutes, shaking the pan every now and then. Place a fine sieve over a bowl, tip in the mussels, then transfer them to a plate, throwing away any that haven't opened. Strain the cooking liquid again through the sieve.

3 Add the butter to the cleaned saucepan and melt over moderate heat. Add the garlic, shallot, celery and leek and cook for 7–10 minutes, or until the vegetables are just soft. Add the mushrooms and cook for a further 4–5 minutes until softened. While the vegetables are cooking, remove the mussels from their shells.

4 Add the strained liquid to the vegetables in the saucepan, add the bay leaf and bring to a simmer. Add the salmon, sole and prawns and cook for 3–4 minutes until the fish is opaque and the prawns are pink. Stir in the cream and cooked mussels and simmer for 2 minutes. Season and stir in the parsley.

STIR-FRIED SCALLOPS WITH SUGAR SNAP PEAS

Preparation time 5 minutes
Total cooking time 4 minutes
Serves 4

2 tablespoons oil
2 large garlic cloves, crushed
3 teaspoons finely chopped fresh ginger
300 g (10½ oz) sugar snap peas
500 g (1 lb 2 oz) scallops without roe
2 spring onions (scallions), cut into 2 cm (¾ in) lengths
2½ tablespoons oyster sauce
2 teaspoons soy sauce
½ teaspoon sesame oil
2 teaspoons sugar

1 Heat a wok over medium heat, add the oil and swirl to coat the surface of the wok. Add the garlic and ginger, and stir-fry for 30 seconds, or until fragrant.
2 Add the peas to the wok and cook for 1 minute, then add the scallops and spring onion and cook for 1 minute, or until the spring onion is wilted. Stir in the oyster and soy sauces, sesame oil and sugar and heat for 1 minute. Serve with rice.

SWEET CHILLI PRAWNS

Preparation time 5 minutes

Total cooking time 8 minutes

Serves 4

1 kg (2 lb 4 oz) raw prawns (shrimp), tails
   intact

2 tablespoons peanut oil

1 cm x 3 cm (½–1¼ in) piece fresh ginger, cut into
   julienne strips

2 garlic cloves, finely chopped

5 spring onions (scallions), cut into 3 cm (1¼ in)
   lengths

4 tablespoons chilli garlic sauce

2 tablespoons tomato sauce

2 tablespoons Chinese rice wine (see Notes)

1 tablespoon Chinese black vinegar or rice
   vinegar (see Notes)

1 tablespoon soy sauce

1 tablespoon soft brown sugar

1 teaspoon cornflour mixed with 125 ml (4 fl oz/
   ½ cup) water

finely chopped spring onion (scallion), to garnish

1 Peel and devein the prawns, leaving the tails intact. Heat a wok until very hot, then add the oil and swirl to coat the side. Heat over high heat until smoking, then quickly add the ginger, garlic and spring onion and stir-fry for 1 minute. Add the prawns and cook for 2 minutes, or until they are just pink and starting to curl. Remove the prawns from the wok with tongs or a slotted spoon.

2 Put the chilli garlic sauce, tomato sauce, rice wine, vinegar, soy sauce, sugar and cornflour paste in a small jug and whisk together. Pour the sauce into the wok and cook, stirring, for 1–2 minutes, or until it thickens slightly. Return the prawns to the wok for 1–2 minutes, or until heated and cooked through. Garnish with the finely chopped spring onion. Serve immediately with rice or thin egg noodles.

Notes Chinese rice wine has a rich sweetish taste. Chinese black vinegar is made from rice and has a sweet, mild taste. It is available in Asian food stores.

SOUTHERN INDIAN SEAFOOD CURRY

Preparation time 15 minutes
Total cooking time 20 minutes
Serves 4

2 tablespoons vegetable oil
½ teaspoon fenugreek seeds
10 fresh curry leaves
2 green chillies, split lengthways
1 red onion, sliced
1 tablespoon tamarind concentrate
½ teaspoon ground turmeric
½ teaspoon paprika
½ teaspoon salt
½ teaspoon ground black pepper
375 ml (13 fl oz/1½ cups) coconut milk
750 g (1 lb 10 oz) mixed seafood, such as snapper or firm white fish fillets, cut into pieces; prawns (shrimp), peeled and deveined, tails intact; scallops; squid, sliced into rings
400 g (14 oz) tinned chopped tomatoes

1 Heat the oil in a saucepan, add the fenugreek seeds and cook over medium heat until they pop. Add the curry leaves, chillies and onion and cook for 8 minutes, or until the onion is soft.

2 Add the tamarind, turmeric, paprika, salt, pepper, and half the coconut milk. Bring to the boil, reduce the heat to a simmer and add the seafood. Cook for 8 minutes, or until it changes colour, turning the seafood during cooking.

3 Add the tomatoes and the remaining coconut milk. Cover and cook for a further 4 minutes, or until the seafood is tender. Serve immediately.

BARBECUE FISH WITH GREEN BEAN SALAD

Preparation time 10 minutes +
Total cooking time 5 minutes
Serves 4

Marinade
3 tablespoons grapeseed oil
2 teaspoons grated lemon zest
2 tablespoons lemon juice
2 teaspoons baharat

Green bean salad
225 g (8 oz) green beans, trimmed
1 zucchini (courgette)
1 small carrot, peeled
½ red onion, finely sliced into wedges
salad dressing
2 tablespoons grapeseed oil
1 tablespoon lemon juice
1 teaspoon honey
½ teaspoon baharat

4 firm white fish fillets (800 g/1 lb 12 oz), such as
   snapper
olive oil

100 g (3½ oz) mixed salad leaves or baby rocket
   (arugula) leaves
lemon wedges, to serve

1 To make the marinade, combine the oil, lemon zest and juice and the baharat in a non-metallic dish. Coat the fish in the marinade and set aside for 30 minutes.
2 To make the salad, shred or finely slice the beans. Using a vegetable peeler, cut the zucchini and carrot into fine strips. Put all the ingredients into a large bowl. Combine the salad dressing ingredients and just prior to serving, pour over the salad and toss well.
3 Preheat a barbecue flat plate or grill plate. Lightly coat with the oil. Cook the fillets for 1 minute on each side to seal, then lower the heat and cook for 2–3 minutes on each side, or until just cooked through. The cooking time will depend on the thickness of the fillets. Brush with the marinade one or two times.
4 To serve, divide the salad leaves or rocket onto serving plates, pile the bean salad over and top each with a fish fillet. Serve with lemon wedges.

CATALAN FISH STEW

Preparation time 15 minutes
Total cooking time 30 minutes
Serves 6–8

Catalan fish stew
300 g (10½ oz) red mullet fillets
400 g (14 oz) firm white fish fillets
300 g (10½ oz) cleaned calamari
1.5 litres (52 fl oz/6 cups) fish stock
4 tablespoons olive oil
1 onion, chopped
6 garlic cloves, chopped
1 small fresh red chilli, chopped
1 teaspoon paprika
pinch saffron threads
150 ml (5 fl oz) white wine
425 g (15 oz) tinned crushed tomatoes
16 raw prawns (shrimp), peeled, tails intact
2 tablespoons brandy
24 black mussels, cleaned
1 tablespoon chopped fresh parsley

Picada
2 tablespoons olive oil
2 slices day-old bread, cubed
2 garlic cloves
5 blanched almonds, toasted
2 tablespoons fresh flat-leaf (Italian) parsley

1 Cut the fish and calamari into small pieces. Place the stock in a large saucepan and bring to the boil for 15 minutes, or until liquid has reduced a little.

2 To make the picada, heat the oil in a frying pan and cook the bread, stirring, for 2 minutes, or until golden, adding the garlic for the last minute. Place all of the ingredients in a food processor and process, gradually adding stock to make a smooth but not too runny paste.

3 Heat 2 tablespoons of the oil in a saucepan, add the onion, garlic, chilli and paprika, and cook, stirring, for 1 minute. Add the saffron, wine, tomatoes and stock. Bring to the boil, then reduce the heat and simmer. Heat the remaining oil in a frying pan and fry the fish and the calamari for 3–5 minutes. Remove from the pan. Add the prawns, cook for 1 minute, then pour in the brandy. Carefully ignite the brandy and let the flames burn down. Remove prawns from the pan.

4 Add the mussels to the pan and simmer, covered, for 2–3 minutes, or until opened. Discard any that do not open. Add all the seafood and the picada to the pan, stirring until the sauce has thickened. Season, sprinkle with the parsley and serve.

SWORDFISH WITH TOMATO SALSA AND GARLIC MASH

Preparation time 10 minutes

Total cooking time 20 minutes

Serves 4

500 g (1 lb 2 oz) potatoes, cubed
2 large vine-ripened tomatoes
2 tablespoons finely shredded fresh basil
1 tablespoon balsamic vinegar
3 garlic cloves, finely chopped
145 ml (4¾ fl oz) olive oil
4 swordfish steaks (about 200 g/7 oz each)

1 Cook the potato in a large saucepan of boiling water for 12–15 minutes, or until tender.

2 To make the salsa, score a cross in the base of each tomato. Place in a heatproof bowl and cover with boiling water. Leave for 30 seconds, then plunge into iced water and peel away from the cross. Cut the tomatoes in half, scoop out the seeds and discard. Finely dice the flesh, then combine with the basil, vinegar, 2 cloves garlic and 2 tablespoons oil. Season.

3 Heat 3 tablespoons of the olive oil in a large non-stick frying pan over medium–high heat. Season the swordfish well, then add to the frying pan and cook for 2–3 minutes on each side for medium–rare, or until cooked to your liking.

4 Just before the swordfish is ready, drain the potato. Add the remaining olive oil and garlic, and season to taste with salt and pepper. Mash until smooth with a potato masher.

5 To serve, put the swordfish steaks on four serving plates and top with the tomato salsa. Serve the garlic mash on the side

DEEP-FRIED CALAMARI IN CHICKPEA BATTER WITH PARSLEY SALAD

Preparation time 10 minutes +
Total cooking time 5 minutes
Serves 4

Deep-fried calamari
150 g (5½ oz) besan (chickpea flour)
1½ teaspoons smoked paprika
1½ teaspoons ground cumin
½ teaspoon baking powder
250 ml (9 fl oz/1 cup) soda water
oil, for deep-frying
6 cleaned squid hoods, cut into rings

Parsley salad
¼ preserved lemon, rinsed, pith
and flesh removed
3 tablespoons lemon juice
3 tablespoons extra virgin olive oil
1 garlic clove, finely chopped
1 handful fresh flat-leaf parsley
harissa, to serve (optional)

1 To make the batter, sift the besan, paprika, cumin and baking powder into a bowl, add ¼ teaspoon pepper, mix together and make a well in the centre. Gradually add the soda water, whisking the mixture until smooth. Season with salt. Cover, then leave for 30 minutes.

2 Cut the lemon rind into very thin slivers. To make the dressing, whisk the lemon juice, extra virgin olive oil and chopped garlic together.

3 Fill a large heavy-based saucepan or wok one-third full of oil and heat until a cube of bread dropped into the oil browns in 15 seconds.

4 Dip the calamari into the batter, allowing any excess to drip back into the bowl. Cook in batches for 30–60 seconds, or until pale gold and crisp all over. Drain on paper towels. Keep warm.

5 Add the parsley and lemon slivers to the dressing, tossing to coat the leaves. Divide the leaves among four bowls. Top with the calamari rings and serve with harissa.

SALT AND PEPPER SQUID

Preparation time 5 minutes

Total cooking time 4 minutes

Serves 4

500 g (1 lb 2 oz) cleaned squid tubes

2 tablespoons lemon juice

2 garlic cloves, finely chopped

95 g (3¼ oz/½ cup) potato flour

1 tablespoon sichuan peppercorns, toasted and ground

1 tablespoon ground black pepper

1½ teaspoons ground white pepper

1½ tablespoons sea salt flakes, crushed

1 teaspoon caster (superfine) sugar

peanut oil, for deep-frying

lemon wedges, to serve

1 Cut the squid tubes in half lengthways then lay flat on the bench with the inside facing up. Score a shallow criss-cross pattern over this side only. Cut into 5 x 3 cm (2 x 1¼ in) rectangles.

2 Combine the lemon juice and garlic, then add the squid and toss to coat. Refrigerate for 1 hour, then drain off the marinade and discard. Combine the potato flour, peppers, salt and sugar and set aside.

3 Fill a deep-fryer or large heavy-based saucepan one-third full with the oil and heat to 180°C (350°F), or until a cube of bread dropped in the oil browns in 15 seconds.

4 Coat the squid in the flour mixture, pressing lightly into it to help adhere. Deep-fry the squid pieces in batches for 1½–2 minutes, or until lightly golden and curled. Drain well on paper towel and serve with lemon wedges.

FISH FILLETS WITH FENNEL AND RED CAPSICUM SALSA

Preparation time 10 minutes

Total cooking time 30 minutes

Serves 4

750 g (1 lb 10 oz) small new potatoes

1 teaspoon fennel seeds

125 ml (4 fl oz/½ cup) olive oil

2 tablespoons drained baby capers

1 small red capsicum (pepper), seeded and finely diced

250 g (9 oz) mixed salad leaves, washed and picked over

2 tablespoons balsamic vinegar

4 white fish fillets (blue eye cod or John Dory), (about 200 g/7 oz each)

1 Cook the potatoes in a saucepan of boiling water for 15–20 minutes, or until tender. Drain and keep warm.

2 Meanwhile, to make the salsa, dry-fry the fennel seeds in a frying pan over medium heat for 1 minute, or until fragrant. Remove the seeds and heat 1 tablespoon oil in the same pan over medium heat. When the oil is hot but not smoking, flash-fry the capers for 1–2 minutes, or until crisp. Remove from the pan. Heat 1 tablespoon oil and cook the capsicum, stirring, for 4–5 minutes, or until cooked through. Remove and combine with the fennel seeds and fried capers.

3 Place the salad leaves in a serving bowl. To make the dressing, combine the balsamic vinegar and 3 tablespoons of the olive oil in a bowl. Add 1 tablespoon to the salsa, then toss the rest through the salad leaves.

4 Wipe the frying pan, then heat the remaining oil over medium–high heat. Season the fish well. When the oil is hot, but not smoking, cook the fish for 2–3 minutes each side, or until cooked through. Serve immediately with the salsa, potatoes and salad.

PRAWNS WITH SPICY TAMARIND SAUCE

Preparation time 10 minutes

Total cooking time 30 minutes

Serves 4

80 g (2¾ oz/½ cup) raw cashew nuts

250 g (9 oz/1¼ cups) jasmine rice

2 garlic cloves, finely chopped

1½ tablespoons fish sauce

1 tablespoon sambal oelek

1 tablespoon peanut oil

1 kg (2 lb 4 oz) raw prawns (shrimp), peeled and
   deveined with tails intact

2 teaspoons tamarind concentrate

1½ tablespoons grated palm sugar

350 g (12 oz) choy sum, cut into 10 cm (4 in)
   lengths

1 Preheat the oven to 180°C (350°F/Gas 4). Spread the cashews on a baking tray and bake for 5–8 minutes, or until light golden — watch carefully, as they burn easily.

2 Meanwhile, bring a large saucepan of water to the boil. Add the rice and cook for 12 minutes, stirring occasionally. Drain well.

3 Place the garlic, fish sauce, sambal oelek and toasted cashews in a blender or food processor, adding 2–3 tablespoons of water, if needed, and blend to a rough paste.

4 Heat a wok until very hot, add the oil and swirl to coat. Add the prawns, toss for 1–2 minutes, or until starting to turn pink. Remove from the wok. Add the cashew paste and stir-fry for 1 minute, or until it starts to brown slightly. Add the tamarind, sugar and about 4 tablespoons water, then bring to the boil, stirring well. Return the prawns to the wok and stir to coat. Cook for 2–3 minutes, or until the prawns are cooked through.

5 Place the choy sum in a paper-lined bamboo steamer and steam over a wok or saucepan of simmering water for 3 minutes, or until tender. Serve with the prawns and rice.

SALMON AND DILL POTATO PATTIES WITH LIME MAYONNAISE

Preparation time 15 minutes

Total cooking time 20 minutes

Serves 4

400 g (14 oz) new potatoes, cut in half

2 teaspoons grated lime zest

310 g (11 oz/1¼ cups) whole-egg mayonnaise

425 g (15 oz) tinned salmon, drained, boned

1 tablespoon chopped fresh dill

2 spring onions (scallions), thinly sliced

1 egg

80 g (2¾ oz/1 cup) fresh breadcrumbs

3 tablespoons oil

200 g (7 oz) rocket (arugula) leaves

lime wedges, to serve

1 Cook the potatoes in a large saucepan of boiling water for 12–15 minutes, or until tender. Drain well and cool.

2 Meanwhile, combine the lime zest and 250 g (9 oz/1 cup) of the mayonnaise.

3 Transfer the potato to a large bowl, then mash roughly with the back of a spoon, leaving some large chunks. Stir in the salmon, dill and spring onion and season. Mix in the egg and the remaining mayonnaise. Divide into eight portions, forming palm-size patties. Press lightly into the breadcrumbs to coat.

4 Heat the oil in a non-stick frying pan and cook the patties, turning, for 3–4 minutes, or until golden brown. Drain on paper towels. Serve with a dollop of lime mayonnaise, rocket leaves and lime wedges.

BLUE EYE CUTLETS IN A SPICY TOMATO SAUCE

Preparation time 10 minutes
Total cooking time 25 minutes
Serves 4

4 blue eye cutlets, 2.5 cm (1 in) thick (about
   250 g/9 oz each)
250 g (9 oz/1 cup) long-grain rice
2 tablespoons oil
1 teaspoon coriander seeds, lightly crushed
1 teaspoon black mustard seeds
1½ tablespoons sambal oelek
400 g (14 oz) tinned diced tomatoes
1 teaspoon garam masala
300 g (10½ oz) baby English spinach leaves

1 Preheat the oven to 180°C (350°F/Gas 4). Pat the cutlets dry with paper towels. Bring a large saucepan of water to the boil. Add the rice and cook for 12 minutes, stirring occasionally. Drain well.

2 Meanwhile, heat 1 tablespoon of the oil in a saucepan over medium heat. When hot, add the coriander and mustard seeds — the mustard seeds should start to pop after 30 seconds. Add the sambal oelek and cook for 30 seconds, then stir in the tomatoes and the garam masala. Bring to the boil, then reduce the heat to low and simmer, covered, for 6–8 minutes, or until the sauce thickens.

3 Heat the remaining oil in a large non-stick frying pan over medium heat. Add the cutlets and cook for 1 minute each side, or until evenly browned but not cooked through. Transfer to a large ceramic baking dish. Spoon the tomato sauce over the cutlets and bake for 10 minutes, or until the fish is cooked through.

4 Meanwhile, wash the spinach and put in a saucepan with just the water clinging to the leaves. Cook, covered, for 1 minute, or until wilted. Serve the fish cutlets topped with sauce, with the spinach and the rice.

THAI GINGER FISH WITH CORIANDER BUTTER

Preparation time 15 minutes

Total cooking time 10 minutes

Serves 4

60 g (2¼ oz) butter, at room temperature
1 tablespoon finely chopped coriander (cilantro)
    leaves
2 tablespoons lime juice
1 tablespoon oil
1 tablespoon grated palm sugar
4 fresh long red chillies, seeded and chopped
2 stems lemongrass, trimmed
4 firm white fish fillets (blue eye or John Dory),
    (about 200 g/7 oz each)
1 lime, thinly sliced
1 tablespoon finely shredded fresh ginger

1 Thoroughly mix the butter and coriander and roll it into a log. Wrap the log in plastic wrap and chill in the refrigerator until required.

2 Preheat the oven to 200°C (400°F/Gas 6). Combine the lime juice, oil, palm sugar and chilli in a small non-metallic bowl and stir until the sugar has dissolved. Cut the lemongrass into halves.

3 Place a piece of lemongrass in the centre of a sheet of foil large enough to fully enclose one fillet. Place a fish fillet on top and smear the surface with the lime juice mixture. Top with some lime slices and ginger shreds, then wrap into a secure parcel. Repeat with the remaining ingredients to make four parcels.

4 Place the parcels in an ovenproof dish and bake for 8–10 minutes, or until the fish flakes easily when tested with a fork.

5 To serve, place the parcels on plates and serve open with slices of coriander butter, steamed rice and steamed greens.

TUNA STEAKS WITH OLIVE MAYONNAISE

Preparation time 10 minutes

Total cooking time 6 minutes

Serves 4

345 ml (12 fl oz) olive oil

2 egg yolks, at room temperature

25 ml (1 fl oz) lemon juice

40 g (1½ oz/⅓ cup) pitted black olives, chopped

200 g (7 oz) baby rocket (arugula) leaves

1 tablespoon finely chopped fresh rosemary

4 tuna steaks (about 200 g/7 oz each)

ready-made potato wedges, to serve (optional)

1 Process the egg yolks in a food processor, adding 3 tablespoons of the oil drop by drop. With the motor running, pour in 185 ml (6 fl oz/¾ cup) of the oil in a thin stream until the mixture thickens and becomes creamy. With the motor still running, add 1 teaspoon of the lemon juice, season with salt and blend for 30 seconds. Stir in the olives, cover and refrigerate.

3 To make the salad, toss the rocket leaves, 2 tablespoons oil and 1 tablespoon lemon juice in a bowl.

4 Press the rosemary into the tuna steaks. Heat the remaining tablespoon of oil in a large frying pan and sear the tuna steaks over medium–high heat for 2–3 minutes on each side, or until cooked to your liking. Serve with a dollop of olive mayonnaise, some potato wedges and rocket salad.

Note To save time, use 250 g (9 oz/1 cup) of good-quality whole-egg mayonnaise.

SWORDFISH WITH ANCHOVY AND CAPER SAUCE

Preparation time 5 minutes

Total cooking time 4 minutes

Serves 4

Sauce

1 large garlic clove

1 tablespoon capers, rinsed and finely
  chopped

50 g (1¾ oz) anchovy fillets, finely chopped

1 tablespoon finely chopped rosemary or dried
  oregano

finely grated zest and juice of ½ lemon

4 tablespoons extra virgin olive oil

1 large tomato, finely chopped

4 swordfish steaks

1 tablespoon extra virgin olive oil

crusty Italian bread, to serve

1 Put the garlic in a mortar and pestle with
a little salt and crush it. To make the sauce,
mix together the garlic, capers, anchovies,
rosemary or oregano, lemon zest and juice,
oil and tomato. Leave for 10 minutes.

2 Preheat a griddle or grill (broiler) to very
hot. Using paper towels, pat the swordfish
dry and lightly brush with the olive oil.
Season with salt and pepper. Sear the
swordfish over high heat for about 2 minutes
on each side (depending on the thickness
of the steaks), or until just cooked. The best
way to check if the fish is cooked is to pull
apart the centre of one steak — the flesh
should be opaque. (Serve with the cut
side underneath.)

3 If the cooked swordfish is a little oily, drain
it on paper towels, then place on serving
plates and drizzle with the sauce. Serve with
Italian bread to mop up the sauce.

CAJUN PRAWNS WITH SALSA

Preparation time 10 minutes
Total cooking time 6 minutes
Serves 4

Cajun spice mix
1 tablespoon garlic powder
1 tablespoon onion powder
2 teaspoons dried thyme
2 teaspoons ground white pepper
1½ teaspoons cayenne pepper
½ teaspoon dried oregano

Tomato salsa
4 roma (plum) tomatoes, seeded and chopped
1 Lebanese (short) cucumber, peeled, chopped
2 tablespoons finely diced red onion
2 tablespoons chopped coriander (cilantro)
1 tablespoon chopped flat-leaf (Italian) parsley
1 garlic clove, crushed
2 tablespoons olive oil
1 tablespoon lime juice

1.25 kg (2 lb 12 oz) large raw prawns (shrimp)
100 g (3½ oz) butter, melted

60 g (2¼ oz) watercress, washed and
   picked over
4 spring onions (scallions), chopped
lemon wedges, to serve

1 Combine all the ingredients for the Cajun spice mix with 2 teaspoons cracked black pepper.
2 To make the tomato salsa, combine the tomato, cucumber, onion, coriander and parsley in a bowl. Mix the garlic, oil and lime juice together and season well. Add to the bowl and toss together.
3 Peel and devein the prawns, leaving the tails intact. Brush the prawns with the butter and sprinkle generously with the spice mix. Cook on a barbecue hotplate or under a hot grill (broiler), turning once, for 2–3 minutes each side, or until a crust forms and the prawns are pink and cooked.
4 Lay some watercress on serving plates, then spoon the salsa over the leaves. Arrange the prawns on top and sprinkle with some chopped spring onion. Serve with lemon wedges on the side.

BOMBAY-STYLE FISH

Preparation time 30 minutes +
Total cooking time 8 minutes
Serves 4

2 garlic cloves, crushed
3 small green chillies, seeded and finely chopped
½ teaspoon ground turmeric
½ teaspoon ground cloves
½ teaspoon ground cinnamon
½ teaspoon ground cayenne pepper
1 tablespoon tamarind purée
170 ml (5½ fl oz/⅔ cup) oil
800 g (1 lb 12 oz) pomfret, sole or leatherjacket fillets, skinned
310 ml (10¾ fl oz/1¼ cups) coconut cream
2 tablespoons chopped coriander (cilantro) leaves

1 Mix together the garlic, chilli, spices, tamarind and 125 ml (4 fl oz/½ cup) of the oil. Place the fish fillets in a shallow dish and spoon the marinade over them. Turn the fish over, cover and refrigerate for 30 minutes.

2 Heat the remaining oil in a large heavy-based frying pan and add the fish in batches. Cook for 1 minute on each side. Return all the fish to the pan, then reduce the heat to low and add any remaining marinade and the coconut cream. Season with salt and gently cook for 3–5 minutes, or until the fish is cooked through and flakes easily.

3 If the sauce is too runny, lift out the fish, simmer the sauce for a few minutes, then pour it over the fish. Garnish with the coriander leaves.

INDIAN-STYLE BUTTER PRAWNS

Preparation time 15 minutes
Total cooking time 20 minutes
Serves 4

1 kg (2 lb 4 oz) large raw prawns (shrimp)
100 g (3½ oz) butter
2 large garlic cloves, crushed
1 teaspoon ground cumin
1 teaspoon paprika
1½ teaspoons garam masala
2 tablespoons good-quality ready-made tandoori
    paste
2 tablespoons tomato paste
300 ml (10½ fl oz) thick cream
1 teaspoon sugar
90 g (3¼ oz/⅓ cup) plain yoghurt
2 tablespoons chopped coriander (cilantro) leaves
1 tablespoon flaked almonds, toasted
lemon wedges, to serve

1 Peel and devein the prawns, leaving the tails intact. Melt the butter in a large saucepan over medium heat, then add the garlic, cumin, paprika and 1 teaspoon of the garam masala and cook for 1 minute, or until fragrant. Add the tandoori paste and tomato paste, and cook for a further 2 minutes. Stir in the cream and sugar, then reduce the heat and simmer for 10 minutes, or until the sauce thickens slightly.

2 Add the prawns to the pan and cook for 8–10 minutes, or until they are pink and cooked through. Remove the pan from the heat and stir in the yoghurt, the remaining garam masala and half the coriander. Season.

3 Garnish with the flaked almonds and remaining coriander and serve with steamed rice and lemon wedges.

Note This dish is very rich so we recommend that you serve it with steamed vegetables or a fresh salad.

BARBECUED OCTOPUS

Preparation time 15 minutes +
Total cooking time 5 minutes
Serves 6

170 ml (5½ fl oz/⅔ cup) olive oil
10 g (¼ oz) chopped oregano
3 tablespoons chopped flat-leaf (Italian) parsley
1 tablespoon lemon juice
3 small red chillies, seeded and finely chopped
3 garlic cloves, crushed
1 kg (2 lb 4 oz) baby octopus
lime wedges, to serve

1 To make the marinade, combine the oil, herbs, lemon juice, chilli and garlic in a large bowl and mix well.

2 Use a small, sharp knife to remove the octopus heads. Grasp the bodies and push the beaks out from the centre with your index finger, then remove and discard. Slit the heads and remove the gut. If the octopus are too large, cut them into smaller portions.

3 Mix the octopus with the herb marinade. Cover and refrigerate for several hours, or overnight. Drain and reserve the marinade.

3 Cook on a very hot, lightly oiled barbecue or in a very hot frying pan for 3–5 minutes, or until the flesh turns white. Turn frequently and brush generously with the marinade during cooking. Serve immediately with lime wedges.

SINGAPORE PEPPER CRAB

Preparation time 10 minutes
Total cooking time 15 minutes
Serves 4

Stir-fry sauce
2 tablespoons dark soy sauce
2 tablespoons oyster sauce
1 tablespoon grated palm sugar or light brown
   sugar

2 kg (4 lb 8 oz) blue crabs
1–2 tablespoons peanut oil
170 g (6 oz) butter
2 tablespoons finely chopped garlic
1 tablespoon finely chopped ginger
1 small red chili, seeded and finely chopped
1½ tablespoons ground black pepper
1 scallion, green part only, thinly sliced
   diagonally

1 Mix the ingredients for the sauce in a small bowl and set aside.
2 Wash the crabs well with a stiff brush. Pull back the apron and remove the top shell from each crab (it should come off easily). Remove the intestine and the gray, feathery gills. Using a large, sharp knife, cut the crab lengthwise through the center of the body to form two halves with the legs attached. Cut each half in half again, crosswise. Crack the thicker part of the legs with the back of a heavy knife or crab crackers.
3 Heat a wok over high heat, add a little oil, and swirl to coat. Add the crab in a few batches, stir-frying over very high heat for 4 minutes per batch or until the shells turn bright orange, adding more oil if needed. Remove from the wok. Reduce the heat to medium-high, add the butter, garlic, ginger, chili, and pepper, and stir-fry for 30 seconds, then add the stir-fry sauce and simmer for 1 minute or until glossy.
4 Return the crab to the wok, cover, and stir every minute for 4 minutes or until cooked. Sprinkle with the scallions and serve with rice. Provide bowls of warm water with lemon slices for rinsing sticky fingers.

TERIYAKI SALMON FILLETS

Preparation time 15 minutes +
Total cooking time 20 minutes
Serves 4

4 tablespoons soy sauce
4 tablespoons sake
4 tablespoons mirin
1 teaspoon sesame oil
2 tablespoons caster (superfine) sugar
2 teaspoon finely grated ginger
1 small garlic clove, crushed
4 x 200 g (7 oz) salmon fillets
oil spray
2 spring onions (scallions), chopped

1 Mix the soy sauce, sake, mirin, sesame oil, sugar, ginger and garlic together in a jug. Put the fish in a shallow, non-metallic dish and pour the marinade over the top. Turn the fish in the marinade so it is well coated. Cover and marinate in the fridge for at least 3 hours.

2 Heat a large, heavy-based frying pan and spray with the oil. Lift the fish out of the marinade and drain. Cook the fish for 1–2 minutes, or until browned on each side, then cook at a lower heat for 3 minutes, or until the fish is just cooked through.

3 Add the marinade and bring to a simmer, then remove the fish and simmer the sauce for 5 minutes, or until thick and sticky. Return the fish to the sauce to coat. Place the fish on a serving plate and pour over the sauce. Garnish with the spring onions and serve with rice.

Hints Bottled teriyaki sauces are available from Asian food shops or supermarkets but you will get a much better flavour if you make your own.

Use Japanese soy sauce rather than Chinese soy sauce for a full-bodied flavour.

Sake, mirin and sesame oil are available in supermarkets and Asian shops.

STEAMED WHOLE FISH WITH CHILLI, GARLIC AND LIME

Preparation time 10 minutes

Total cooking time 20 minutes

Serves 4–6

1–1.5 kg (2 lb 4 oz–3 lb 5 oz) whole snapper

1 lime, sliced

red chillies, finely chopped, to garnish

coriander (cilantro) leaves, to garnish

lime wedges, to garnish

Sauce

2 teaspoons tamarind concentrate

5 long red chillies, seeded and chopped

6 large garlic cloves, roughly chopped

6 coriander (cilantro) roots and stalks

8 red Asian shallots, chopped

1½ tablespoons oil

2½ tablespoons lime juice

130 g (4½ oz/¾ cup) shaved palm sugar or soft brown sugar

3 tablespoons fish sauce

1 Rinse the fish and pat dry with paper towels. Cut two diagonal slashes through the thickest part of the fish on both sides, to ensure even cooking. Place the lime slices in the fish cavity, cover with plastic wrap and chill until ready to use.

2 To make the sauce, combine the tamarind with 3 tablespoons water. Blend the chilli, garlic, coriander and shallots in a food processor until finely puréed — add a little water, if needed.

3 Heat the oil in a saucepan. Add the paste and cook over medium heat for 5 minutes, or until fragrant. Stir in the tamarind, lime juice and palm sugar. Reduce the heat and simmer for 10 minutes, or until thick. Add the fish sauce.

4 Place the fish on a sheet of baking paper in a large bamboo steamer and cover. Place over a wok of simmering water — ensure the base doesn't touch the water. Cook for 6 minutes per 1 kg (2 lb 4 oz) fish, or until the flesh flakes easily with a fork when tested.

5 Pour the sauce over the fish and garnish with the chilli, coriander and lime wedges. Serve with rice.

BASIC PAN-FRIED FISH

Preparation time 5 minutes
Total cooking time 8 minutes
Serves 4

2–3 tablespoons plain (all-purpose) flour
4 blue-eye fish cutlets or jewfish, warehou,
   snapper or other firm white fish

olive oil, for shallow-frying

1 Sift the flour together with a little salt and freshly ground black pepper onto a plate. Pat the fish dry with paper towels, then coat both sides of the cutlets with seasoned flour, shaking off any excess.
2 Heat about 3 mm (⅛ in) oil in a large frying pan until very hot. Put the fish into the hot oil and cook for 3 minutes on one side, then turn and cook the other side for 2 minutes, or until the coating is crisp and well browned. Reduce the heat to low and cook for another 2–3 minutes, or until the flesh flakes easily when tested with a fork.
3 Remove the fish from the pan and drain briefly on crumpled paper towels. If you are cooking in batches, keep warm while cooking the remaining cutlets. Serve immediately with a green salad or some steamed vegetables.

BEER-BATTERED FISH FILLETS WITH CHIPS

Preparation time 5 minutes

Total cooking time 10 minutes

Serves 4

30 g (1 oz/¼ cup) self-raising flour

30 g (1 oz/¼ cup) cornflour (cornstarch)

125 g (4½ oz/1 cup) plain (all-purpose) flour

250 ml (9 fl oz/1 cup) beer (use any type to vary the flavour)

oil, for deep-frying

4 large pontiac potatoes, cut into finger-size chips

4 flathead fillets (about 200 g/7 oz each), or other white fish fillets (snapper, blue eye or John Dory), skinned and pin-boned

2 lemons, cut into wedges

1 Preheat the oven to 180°C (350°F/Gas 4). Sift the self-raising flour, cornflour and 60 g (2¼ oz/½ cup) of the plain flour into a large bowl and make a well. Gradually whisk in the beer to make a smooth batter. Cover.

2 Fill a large heavy-based saucepan one-third full of oil and heat to 180°C (350°F), or until a cube of bread dropped into the oil browns in 15 seconds. Deep-fry batches of potato chips for 2–4 minutes, or until pale golden. Drain on paper towels. Deep-fry again for 3 minutes, or until golden and cooked through. Keep hot in the oven while you cook the fish.

3 Reheat the oil to 180°C (350°F). Stir the batter, then coat the fish fillets in the remaining plain flour, shaking off the excess. Dip the fillets into the batter, allowing the excess to drip off a little. Slowly ease the fillets into the hot oil, holding the tail out for a few seconds — turn with tongs if necessary. Cook for 4–5 minutes, or until golden brown and the fish is cooked through. Remove with a slotted spoon and drain on crumpled paper towels. Serve with the chips, lemon wedges and a green salad.

BAKED TUNA SICILIANA

Preparation time 15 minutes +
Total cooking time 20 minutes
Serves 4

4 tablespoons olive oil
2 tablespoons lemon juice
2½ tablespoons finely chopped basil
4 x 175 g (6 oz) tuna steaks or swordfish
60 g (2¼ oz) black olives, pitted and chopped
1 tablespoon baby capers, rinsed and
    patted dry
2 anchovies, finely chopped
400 g (14 oz) tomatoes, peeled, deseeded and
    chopped, or a 400 g (14 oz) tinned chopped
    tomatoes
2 tablespoons dry breadcrumbs
crusty bread, to serve

1 Mix 2 tablespoons of the olive oil with the lemon juice and 1 tablespoon of the basil. Season and pour into a shallow, non-metallic ovenproof dish, large enough to hold the tuna steaks in a single layer. Arrange the tuna in the dish and leave to marinate for 15 minutes, turning once. Preheat the oven to 220°C (425°F/Gas 7) and preheat the griller (broiler).

2 Combine the olives, capers, anchovies and tomatoes with the remaining oil and the remaining basil and season well. Spread over the tuna and sprinkle the breadcrumbs over the top. Bake for about 20 minutes, or until the fish is just opaque. Finish off by placing briefly under the hot griller until the breadcrumbs are crisp. Serve with bread to soak up the juices.

FISH PROVENÇALE

Preparation time 5 minutes

Total cooking time 12 minutes

Serves 4

1 small red capsicum (pepper), thinly sliced
250 g (9 fl oz/1 cup) bottled pasta sauce
1 tablespoon chopped thyme
40 g (1½ oz) butter
4 large skinless perch fillets or snapper
thyme sprigs, to garnish

1 Put the capsicum, pasta sauce and chopped thyme in a bowl and mix well.

2 Melt half the butter in a large non-stick frying pan over high heat and cook the fish for 1 minute, adding the remaining butter as you go. Turn the fish over and pour on the capsicum mixture. Simmer for 10 minutes, or until the fish is cooked. Season to taste and garnish with thyme sprigs. Serve with roasted potato slices and crusty bread to soak up the juices.

STEAMED WHOLE SNAPPER WITH ASIAN FLAVOURS

Preparation time 10 minutes

Total cooking time 25 minutes

Serves 2

800 g (1 lb 12 oz) whole snapper, scaled and
    gutted

3 lemongrass stems

handful of coriander (cilantro) leaves

small knob of fresh ginger, peeled and cut into
    thin matchsticks

1 large garlic clove, peeled and cut into thin slivers

2 tablespoons soy sauce

3 tablespoons oil

1 tablespoon fish sauce

1 small red chilli, deseeded and finely chopped

1 Score the fish with diagonal cuts on both sides. Cut each stem of lemongrass into three and lightly squash each piece with the end of the handle of a large knife. Put half of the lemongrass in the middle of a large piece of foil and lay the fish on top. Put the remaining lemongrass and half of the coriander leaves inside the cavity of the fish.

2 Mix the ginger, garlic, soy sauce, oil, fish sauce and chilli together. Drizzle the mixture over the fish and scatter with the remaining coriander leaves.

3 Enclose the fish in the foil and sit in a large bamboo or metal steamer over a pan of simmering water. Steam for 25 minutes, or until the flesh of the fish is opaque and white. Serve with stir-fried Asian greens and rice.

FRESH TUNA AND GREEN BEAN STIR-FRY

Preparation time 10 minutes

Total cooking time 12 minutes

Serves 4

300 g (10½ oz) small green beans, trimmed

2 tablespoons oil

600 g (1 lb 5 oz) piece of tuna, cut into small cubes

250 g (9 oz) punnet small cherry tomatoes

16 small black olives

2–3 tablespoons lemon juice

2 garlic cloves, finely chopped

8 anchovy fillets, rinsed, dried and finely chopped

3 tablespoons small basil leaves

1 Blanch the beans in a small saucepan of boiling water for 2 minutes. Drain and refresh under cold water to arrest the cooking, then set aside.

2 Heat a wok until very hot, add the oil and swirl it around to coat the side. Stir-fry the tuna in batches for about 5 minutes each batch, or until cooked on the outside but still a little pink on the inside. If necessary, heat a little more oil for each batch.

3 Add the cherry tomatoes, olives and beans to the wok, then gently toss for a minute or so until heated through. Add the lemon juice, garlic and anchovies and stir well. Season to taste with salt and freshly ground black pepper. Serve scattered with the basil leaves.

CRUNCHY FISH FILLETS WITH CHIVE MAYO

Preparation time 5 minutes

Total cooking time 6 minutes

Serves 4

160 g (5¾ oz/⅔ cup) good-quality ready-made
   mayonnaise
2 tablespoons chopped chives
1 tablespoon sweet chilli sauce
75 g (2½ oz/½ cup) cornmeal
4 x 200 g (7 oz) skinless perch fillets
3 tablespoons oil

1 For the chive mayo, combine the mayonnaise, chives and chilli sauce in a small bowl. Keep refrigerated until needed.

2 Put the cornmeal on a plate. Score four diagonal slashes in the skin side of each fish fillet, to prevent the fish curling during cooking. Press both sides of the fillets into the cornmeal to coat thoroughly.

3 Heat the oil in a frying pan over medium heat. Add the fish and cook for 3 minutes. Turn and cook for another 3 minutes, or until tender and the fish flakes easily. Remove and drain. Serve with the chive mayo.

THAI PRAWN CURRY

Preparation time 10 minutes
Total cooking time 12 minutes
Serves 4

Curry paste
1 small onion, roughly chopped
3 garlic cloves
4 dried red chillies
4 whole black peppercorns
2 tablespoons chopped lemongrass,
    white part only
1 tablespoon chopped coriander (cilantro) root
2 teaspoons grated lime zest
2 teaspoons cumin seeds
1 teaspoon sweet paprika
1 teaspoon ground coriander
2 tablespoons oil

1 tablespoon oil
2 tablespoons fish sauce

2 cm (¾ in) piece of fresh galangal, thinly sliced
4 kaffir lime leaves
400 ml (14 fl oz) tinned coconut cream
1 kg (2 lb 4 oz) prawns (shrimp), peeled and
    deveined, tails intact
sliced fresh red chillies, to garnish (optional)
coriander (cilantro) leaves, to garnish

1 To make the curry paste, put all the ingredients and 1 teaspoon salt in a small food processor. Whiz until the mixture forms a smooth paste.

2 Heat the oil in a pan. Add half the curry paste and stir over low heat for 30 seconds. Add the fish sauce, galangal, lime leaves and coconut cream, and stir until combined.

3 Add the prawns to the pan and simmer, uncovered, for 10 minutes, or until the prawns are cooked and the sauce has thickened slightly. Sprinkle with chilli and coriander leaves and serve with steamed rice.

GARLIC AND GINGER PRAWNS

Preparation time 25 minutes
Total cooking time 20 minutes
Serves 4

1 kg (2 lb 4 oz) large raw prawns (shrimp)
400 g (14 oz) fresh rice noodles
2 teaspoons canola oil
3–4 garlic cloves, finely chopped
5 cm (2 in) piece fresh ginger, cut into
   matchsticks
2–3 small red chillies, seeded and finely chopped
6 coriander (cilantro) roots, finely chopped, plus a
   few leaves to garnish
8 spring onions (scallions), cut into short lengths
½ red capsicum (pepper), thinly sliced
2 tablespoons lemon juice

125 ml (4 fl oz/½ cup) white wine
1 teaspoon crushed palm sugar or soft brown
   sugar
2 teaspoons fish sauce

1 To make the curry paste, put all the ingredients and 1 teaspoon salt in a small food processor. Whiz until the mixture forms a smooth paste.
2 Heat the oil in a pan. Add half the curry paste and stir over low heat for 30 seconds. Add the fish sauce, galangal, lime leaves and coconut cream, and stir until combined.
3 Add the prawns to the pan and simmer, uncovered, for 10 minutes, or until the prawns are cooked and the sauce has thickened slightly. Sprinkle with chilli and coriander leaves and serve with steamed rice.

FISH AND BLACK BEANS

Preparation time 20 minutes

Total cooking time 20 minutes

Serves 4

400 g (14 oz) fresh rice noodles

200 g (7 oz) Chinese broccoli (gai larn), cut into
5 cm (2 in) lengths

2 tablespoons light soy sauce

1½ tablespoons Chinese rice wine

½ teaspoon sesame oil

1 teaspoon cornflour (cornstarch)

550 g (1 lb 4 oz) skinless snapper or blue eye
fillets

2 teaspoon canola oil

5 garlic cloves, crushed

2 teaspoon finely chopped ginger

2 spring onions (scallions), finely chopped, plus
extra, thinly sliced on the diagonal, to garnish

2 small red chillies, finely chopped

2 tablespoons canned salted black beans, rinsed,
roughly chopped

170 ml (5½ fl oz) fish stock

1 Put the noodles in a large heatproof bowl, cover with boiling water and soak for 8 minutes, or until softened. Separate gently and drain.

2 Put the Chinese broccoli in a steamer, cover and steam over a wok or large saucepan of simmering water for 2 minutes, or until slightly wilted. Remove from the heat and keep warm.

3 To make the marinade, combine the soy sauce, rice wine, sesame oil and cornflour in a large non metallic bowl. Cut the fish into 4 cm (1½ in) pieces, checking for bones. Add to the marinade and toss to coat well.

4 Heat a wok over high heat, add the canola oil and swirl to coat. Add the garlic, ginger, spring onion, chilli and black beans and stir-fry for 1 minute. Add the fish and marinade and cook for 2 minutes, or until the fish is almost cooked through.

5 Remove the fish with a slotted spoon and keep warm. Add the stock to the wok and bring to the boil. Reduce the heat to low and bring to a simmer. Cook for 5 minutes, or until the sauce has slightly thickened. Return the fish to the wok, cover with a lid and simmer gently for 2–3 minutes, or until just cooked.

6 Divide the noodles among four plates, top with the Chinese broccoli and spoon the fish and black bean sauce on top. Garnish with the extra spring onion.

TUNA WITH LIME AND CHILLI SAUCE

Preparation time 20 minutes

Total cooking time 10 minutes

Serves 4

Sauce

2 large handfuls mint, chopped

2 large handfuls coriander (cilantro) leaves, chopped

1 teaspoon grated lime zest

1 tablespoon lime juice

1 teaspoon grated fresh ginger

1 jalapeno chilli, seeded and finely chopped

250 g (9 oz/1 cup) low-fat plain yoghurt

canola oil spray

4 tuna steaks

175 g (6 oz) asparagus, trimmed and cut into 5 cm (2 in) pieces

125 g (4½ oz) snowpeas (mangetout), trimmed

125 g (4½ oz) green beans, trimmed

4 wholegrain bread rolls, to serve

1 To make the sauce, mix together the mint, coriander, lime zest, lime juice, ginger and chilli. Fold in the yoghurt and season with salt and freshly ground black pepper.

2 Heat a chargrill pan over high heat and lightly spray with the oil. Cook the tuna steaks for 2 minutes on each side, or until cooked, but still pink in the centre.

3 Meanwhile, steam the vegetables for 2–3 minutes, or until just tender.

4 Top the tuna with the sauce. Serve with the vegetables and bread.

Hint Jalapeno chillies are smooth and thick-fleshed and are available both red and green. They are quite fiery, so you can use a less powerful variety of chilli if you prefer.

CHILLI SQUID WITH ASIAN SALAD

Preparation time 20 minutes +
Total cooking time 15 minutes
Serves 4

8 squid
270 g (9¾ oz) packet dried udon noodles
1 small red capsicum (pepper)
3 Asian shallots
200 g (7 oz) baby Asian salad leaves
180 g (6 oz/2 cups) bean sprouts
oil spray

Marinade
zest and juice from 1 lemon
2 tablespoons sweet chilli sauce
1 tablespoon grated palm sugar or soft brown
    sugar
1 teaspoon canola oil

Lemon dressing
3 tablespoons lemon juice
3 tablespoons rice wine vinegar
2 tablespoons grated palm sugar or brown sugar
1½ tablespoons fish sauce
1 small red chilli, seeded and chopped

1 To clean the squid, remove the head, insides and the beak. Wash the squid well under cold water and pull away the outer skin. Cut off the tentacles from the heads. Score the skin in a zigzag pattern and cut into 5 cm (2 in) pieces. Combine the marinade in a large, non-metallic bowl, and add the squid pieces and tentacles. Refrigerate for 30 minutes.

2 Meanwhile, cook the noodles in a large saucepan of boiling water for 10 minutes, or follow the manufacturer's directions. Drain, then rinse well in cold water and drain again. Cut the noodles into shorter lengths with scissors.

3 Seed and thinly slice the capsicum. Thinly slice the shallots on the diagonal. Place the salad leaves, capsicum, shallots, bean sprouts and noodles in a serving bowl.

4 Combine the lemon dressing ingredients in a bowl.

5 Drain the squid. Heat a barbecue flat plate or frying pan and lightly spray with the oil. Cook and toss the squid over a high heat for 2 minutes, or until cooked.

6 Add the squid to the salad and toss together with the lemon dressing.

PORK

Pork, sometimes referred to as 'the other white meat', is a very versatile meat. Not only is it quick and easy to cook with, it works well with a large range of cooking styles and different flavours from around the world. Pork is readily available and is best cooked until slightly pink in the middle, with the juices sealed in.

PORK BASICS

Pork is one of the oldest and most important meats worldwide, except in areas where Jewish or Muslim communities predominate. Pigs were domesticated in China about 5,000 years ago, and in Europe every family that could afford to had at least one pig.

They were (and still are in southern Europe) traditionally killed in November, when their offal was eaten fresh and most of the rest of the animal was cured, turned into sausages or preserved to be eaten throughout the rest of the year — nothing was wasted.

Pigs that are to be eaten as fresh pork, called porkers, are less than 6 months old and their meat varies in colour from pale pink to white, depending on their breed. Pork is eaten as joints, smaller cuts or as a whole sucking pig. It appears in most world cuisines, is very adaptable and carries flavours well.

BUYING

Pork should have firm white fat and pale pink flesh. Avoid any pork that looks wet or has waxy-looking fat.

The quality of pork varies greatly — animals that are reared organically or in a non-intensive manner tend to have better quality meat. Traditional breeds often have better flavoured meat than modern breeds, which are bred more for their leanness than flavour. Look for meat from such breeds as Tamworth, Welsh Saddleback and Gloucester Old Spot.

Pork is usually bought fresh after it has been hung for 2 to 3 days, but it is better hung for about 7 to 10 days so flavour can develop. Generally only the best cuts are aged.

COOKING

Nearly all cuts of pork are tender and can be grilled or roasted.

Pork from Western countries no longer needs to be well cooked as the threat of tapeworm has been eradicated. Pork from other countries may contain trichonella but this is killed off at the relatively low temperature of 58°C (136°F). If in doubt, cook your pork thoroughly.

Cooking pork at lower temperatures will keep the meat moist and prevent it from becoming tough.

Add a pig's trotter or piece of pork rind to stews and casseroles to give them a rich flavour and a gelatinous sauce. Remove the pork before serving the dish.

Dry out pork rind thoroughly if you want really crunchy crackling.

CUTS OF PORK

Front cuts Cuts from the front of the pig tend to be inexpensive and are good for using in braises and casseroles as they have a high gelatinous content. They include the hand and spring, spare rib, which can be cut into shoulder chops or spare rib chops.

Centre cuts The cuts from the underside or belly of the pig have an equal proportion of fat and meat and can be braised, roasted and casseroled. The pork from the belly makes good fatty mince for pâtés and terrines.

The top cuts include the loin and fillet. These can be cooked as whole pieces, on or off the bone, or cut into loin and chump chops or noisettes.

Back cuts The leg is sold either as a whole joint or cut into the knuckle and leg fillet. Both cuts are good for roasting.

OTHER PARTS

It is said that any part of a pig except the squeak can be eaten.

Pork fat is very useful, rendered down as lard or as sheets of fat for barding around lean cuts of meat.

Pig cheeks are good slow cooked as are trotters, which can be boned and stuffed.

Pig's head is made into brawn and the **ears** may be eaten whole or shredded.

The heart, kidneys and liver can be used as for other animals though their strong flavour is best in pâtés and terrines.

Pig's caul (fat) is used to wrap meat while it cooks.

ROASTING

The loin and leg of pork are the best for roasting. A whole loin should feed four people and a leg will feed a large gathering. If cooking a joint on the bone, ask your butcher to chine it (detach the backbone) for you, as this will make it easier to carve. Part of the attraction of roast pork is the crackling and this can be roasted either on the pork or separately, which will make sure it is crisp.

Roast pork at 180°C (350°F) for about 25–30 minutes per 500 g (1 lb 2 oz). Take the skin off, leaving about 1 cm fat on it, score the skin with a knife, rub it with salt and roast next to the pork. If your joint is particularly lean, rest the fat on top and remove it for the last 20 minutes to crisp — this will help baste the meat as it cooks.

Pork fat can be used to roast potatoes and the meat juices make good gravy. As well as this version of roast pork there is porchetta, a whole roast pig from Italy, and char siu, the Chinese version of roast pork.

SLOW COOKING

Though pork is a tender meat, it cooks particularly well slowly, especially when cuts with plenty of connective tissue, such as neck, are used, giving the dish a smooth, velvety texture from the gelatinous parts.

All cuts of pork can be braised, casseroled or pot-roasted. Most cuisines of the world have some slow-cooked pork recipes — the Chinese have especially good methods of cooking belly pork with soy and star anise until it is very tender, the French use it in cassoulet, the Americans use it in Boston baked beans, and in the Philippines, pork is cooked in vinegar to make adobo.

Slow cook pork for several hours in plenty of liquid to keep it tender and moist.

CHINING AND TRIMMING PORK

Step 1 Put the rack of pork ribs on a chopping board, ribs facing downwards. Using a sharp boning knife, cut down the side of the chine bone in one hand and the joint in the other and snap off the chine bone.

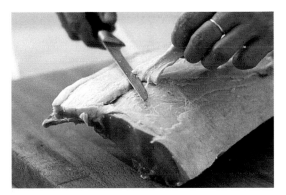

Step 2 Trim the layer of fat off the back of the joint leaving just enough to act as a protective layer and baste the joint.

Step 3 Trim the meat away from the very end of each rib bone, exposing the bone. This looks attractive and makes it easier to cut the meat after cooking. Cook the pork bone side down so the ribs act as a rack.

CHILLI PORK KEBABS

Preparation time 20 minutes +
Total cooking time 8 minutes
Makes 8

500 g (1 lb 2 oz) pork fillet
2 tablespoons sweet chilli sauce
2 tablespoons tomato sauce (ketchup)
2 tablespoons hoisin sauce
2 garlic cloves, crushed
3 tablespoons lemon juice
2 tablespoons honey
2 teaspoons grated fresh ginger
ready-made satay sauce, to serve (optional)

1 Trim the fat and sinew from the pork, cut into small cubes and put into a large non-metallic bowl.

2 Combine the sweet chilli sauce, tomato sauce, hoisin sauce, garlic, lemon juice, honey and ginger in a large ceramic or glass bowl. Pour over the pork and stir well. Cover with plastic wrap and refrigerate for several hours, or overnight if time permits.
3 Soak 8 wooden skewers in water for about 30 minutes to ensure they don't burn during cooking. Thread the pork cubes onto the skewers.
4 Heat a little oil on a heated barbecue hotplate and cook the skewers for 3–4 minutes each side over medium heat, or until just cooked through. Do not overcook. Brush with the remaining marinade while cooking.
5 Serve immediately with some ready-made satay sauce.

PORK AND POLENTA STACK

Preparation time 20 minutes +
Total cooking time 25 minutes
Serves 4

1.125 litres (39 fl oz/4½ cups) chicken stock
2 teaspoons balsamic vinegar
1 teaspoon Worcestershire sauce
1 teaspoon cornflour (cornstarch)
150 g (5½ oz/1 cup) instant polenta
2 tablespoons grated parmesan cheese
oil, for brushing
2 x 200 g (7 oz) pork fillets
chopped flat-leaf (Italian) parsley, to serve

1 In a small saucepan, combine 185 ml
(6 fl oz/¾ cup) of the stock with the vinegar,
Worcestershire sauce and cornflour. Stir over
medium heat until the mixture boils and
thickens, then set aside.
2 In another saucepan, bring the remaining
stock to the boil. Add the polenta and stir
constantly over medium heat for 7 minutes,
or until the mixture has thickened and the
polenta is soft. Stir in the parmesan, and
some salt and cracked black pepper to taste.
Pour into a lightly oiled 23 cm (9 in) square
cake tin and allow to cool. Refrigerate for
about 1 hour, or until firm.
3 Preheat a barbecue grill plate or flat plate
to medium. Turn the polenta out of the tin
and cut it into four squares. Lightly brush
both sides with oil and cook for about
3–4 minutes on each side, or until golden
all over. Set aside and keep warm.
4 Cut each pork fillet in half crossways.
Place between two sheets of plastic wrap
and rest cut-side-down on a chopping board,
then gently flatten them slightly with a
rolling pin or mallet.
5 Brush the hotplate with a little more
oil and cook the pork for 4 minutes on
each side, or until just cooked through.
Meanwhile, reheat the sauce.
6 Divide the polenta among four serving
plates and top with a slice of pork. Drizzle
with the warm sauce, sprinkle with parsley
and serve with mixed vegetables.

PORK, BOK CHOY AND BLACK BEAN STIR-FRY

Preparation time 20 minutes

Total cooking time 35 minutes

Serves 4

400 g (14 oz/2 cups) basmati rice, rinsed and
drained

400 g (14 oz) lean pork leg steaks

2 teaspoons sesame oil

2 onions, thinly sliced

2 garlic cloves, finely chopped

2–3 teaspoons chopped fresh ginger

1 red capsicum (pepper), cut into strips

1 tablespoon canned salted black beans, rinsed,
roughly chopped

500 g (1 lb 2 oz) baby bok choy (pak choy),
shredded

90 g (3¼ oz/½ cup) canned water chestnuts,
rinsed, drained and thinly sliced

2 tablespoons oyster sauce

1 tablespoon soy sauce

2 teaspoons fish sauce

1 Put the rice and 1 litre (35 fl oz/4 cups) water in a saucepan and bring to the boil over medium heat. Reduce the heat to low, cover with a lid and cook for 20 minutes, or until the rice is tender. Remove from the heat and leave to stand, covered, for 5 minutes.

2 Meanwhile, slice the pork steaks into strips across the grain. Heat a wok over medium–high heat until hot, add half the sesame oil and swirl to coat. Cook the onion, garlic and ginger over high heat for 3–4 minutes, being careful that the garlic doesn't burn. Add the capsicum and cook
for 2–3 minutes. Remove from the wok.

3 Heat the remaining sesame oil in the wok, add the pork in batches and stir-fry until browned. Reheat the wok between batches.

4 Return all the pork to the pan with the onion mixture, black beans, bok choy, water chestnuts and oyster, soy and fish sauces. Toss quickly, reduce the heat, cover and steam for 3–4 minutes, or until the bok choy has just wilted. Serve with the rice.

PORK LOIN WITH PICKLED EGGPLANT

Preparation time 20 minutes

Total cooking time 15 minutes

Serves 4

2 x 500 g (1 lb 2 oz) piece (about 10 cm/4 in long) pork loin fillet

2 tablespoons hoisin sauce

a large pinch five-spice powder

4 tablespoons oil

1 eggplant (aubergine), cut into wedges

2 tablespoons soy sauce

2 teaspoons sesame oil

2 tablespoons balsamic vinegar

¼ teaspoon caster (superfine) sugar

2 bok choy (pak choy), cut into quarters

1 Put the pork in a dish and add the hoisin sauce, five-spice powder and a tablespoon of oil. Rub the mixture over the pork and set it to one side.

2 Heat another 2 tablespoons of oil in a non-stick frying pan and add the eggplant. Fry it until it softens and starts to brown, then add the soy sauce, sesame oil, vinegar and sugar and toss everything together for a minute. Tip the eggplant out onto a plate and wipe out the frying pan.

3 Put the last tablespoon of oil in the frying pan and put it over a medium heat. Add the pork and fry it on all sides until it is browned and cooked through. The time this takes will depend on how thick your piece of pork is — when it is cooked, it will feel firm when pressed. Put the eggplant back in the pan to heat through.

4 Take out the pork and leave it to sit for a minute or two.

5 Cook the bok choy in a saucepan with a little bit of boiling water for 1 minute, then drain well.

6 Slice the pork into medallions and serve it with the pickled eggplant and bok choy.

CHINESE BARBECUED PORK WITH CHINESE BROCCOLI

Preparation time 10 minutes

Total cooking time 8 minutes

Serves 4

3 tablespoons chicken or vegetable stock

3 tablespoons oyster sauce

1 tablespoon kecap manis

1 kg (2 lb 4 oz) Chinese broccoli (gai larn), cut into 5 cm (2 in) lengths

1 tablespoon peanut oil

2 cm (¾ in) piece fresh ginger, cut into thin matchsticks

2 garlic cloves, crushed

500 g (1 lb 2 oz) Chinese barbecued pork (char siu), sliced

1 To make the stir-fry sauce, combine the stock, oyster sauce and kecap manis.
2 Put the Chinese broccoli in a steamer over a saucepan or wok of simmering water and cook for 5 minutes, or until just tender.
3 Heat a wok over high heat, add the oil and swirl to coat the base and side. Add the ginger and garlic and stir-fry for 30 seconds, or until fragrant. Add the Chinese broccoli and pork and toss to coat. Pour in the stir-fry sauce and toss together until heated through. Serve with steamed rice or noodles.

FIVE-SPICE PORK STIR-FRY

Preparation time 20 minutes
Total cooking time 20 minutes
Serves 4

375 g (13 oz) fresh thin egg noodles

1 tablespoon sesame oil

3 teaspoons grated fresh ginger

1½ teaspoons Chinese five-spice

2 teaspoons rice flour

500 g (1 lb 2 oz) pork loin fillet, thinly sliced across
   the grain

2 tablespoons vegetable oil

2 garlic cloves, crushed

1 red capsicum (pepper), thinly sliced

300 g (10½ oz) bok choy (pak choy), chopped

6 spring onions (scallions), sliced

2 tablespoons Chinese rice wine

2 tablespoons hoisin sauce

1 tablespoon soy sauce

1 Cook the noodles in a saucepan of boiling water for 1 minute. Drain, rinse and return to the saucepan. Stir in half of the sesame oil. Set aside.

2 Place the ginger, five-spice and rice flour in a bowl, season, then mix well. Add the pork and toss to coat.

3 Heat a wok over high heat, add half of the vegetable oil and swirl to coat the base and side. Add the pork in batches and stir-fry for 5 minutes at a time, or until tender. Remove from the wok and set aside. Add the remaining vegetable oil, garlic, capsicum, bok choy and spring onion and stir-fry for 3 minutes, or until softened.

4 Return the pork to the wok and stir in the rice wine, hoisin sauce, soy sauce and the remaining sesame oil and simmer for 2 minutes. Add the noodles and reheat gently before serving.

PORK CHOPS WITH APPLES AND CIDER

Preparation time 10 minutes

Total cooking time 15 minutes

Serves 4

1 tablespoon oil

2 onions, sliced

2 Golden Delicious apples, cored and cut into
  wedges

2 teaspoons caster (superfine) sugar

2 teaspoons butter

4 thick pork chops, snipped around the edges

3 tablespoons cider

3 tablespoons cream

1 Heat the oil in a large non-stick frying pan, add the onion and fry for about 5 minutes, or until soft and just beginning to brown. Tip the onion out onto a plate.

2 Add the apple wedges to the pan and fry them for a minute or two — they should not break up, but should gradually start to soften and brown. Add the sugar and butter and shake everything around in the pan over the heat until the apples start to caramelise. Transfer the apples to the plate with the onion.

3 Put the pork chops in the frying pan, add a little seasoning and fry them for about 4 minutes on each side, or until they are cooked through. Put the onion and apple back in the pan and heat them up, then add the cider and bring to a simmer. Once the liquid is bubbling, add the cream and shake the pan so everything is well combined. Let it bubble for a minute, then season well.

4 Serve with potatoes and a green salad — watercress goes particularly well.

PORK CHOPS PIZZAIOLA

Preparation time 15 minutes

Total cooking time 15 minutes

Serves 4

4 pork chops

4 tablespoons olive oil

600 g (1 lb 5 oz) ripe tomatoes

3 garlic cloves, crushed

3 basil leaves, torn into pieces

1 teaspoon finely chopped parsley, to serve

1 Using scissors or a knife, cut the pork fat at 5 mm (¼ in) intervals around the rind. Brush the chops with 1 tablespoon of the olive oil and season well.

2 Remove the stems from the tomatoes and score a cross in the bottom of each one.

Blanch in boiling water for 30 seconds. Transfer to cold water, peel the skin away from the cross and chop the tomatoes.

3 Heat 2 tablespoons of the oil in a saucepan over low heat and add the garlic. Soften without browning for 1–2 minutes, then add the tomato and season. Increase the heat, bring to the boil and cook for 5 minutes until thick. Stir in the basil.

4 Heat the remaining oil in a large frying pan with a tight-fitting lid. Brown the chops in batches over medium-high heat for 2 minutes on each side. Place in a slightly overlapping row down the centre of the pan and spoon the sauce over the top, covering the chops completely. Cover the pan and cook over low heat for about 5 minutes. Sprinkle with parsley to serve.

STICKY PORK FILLET

Preparation time 20 minutes +
Total cooking time 30 minutes
Serves 4

3 tablespoons Chinese rice wine
3 tablespoons char siu sauce
2 tablespoons hoisin sauce
1 tablespoon honey
3 garlic cloves, finely chopped
1 tablespoon finely grated fresh ginger
1 teaspoon Chinese five spice
1 teaspoon sesame oil
2 x 300 g (10½ oz) pork fillets, cut in half
400 g (14 oz) baby bok choy (pak choy), halved
    and rinsed

1 Combine the rice wine, sauces, honey, garlic, ginger, five spice and sesame oil in a shallow dish. Add the pork and toss until well coated. Cover and leave to marinate in the refrigerator.

2 Line the bottom basket of a double steamer with several pieces of baking paper and the top basket with a single layer. Punch the paper with holes. Lay the pork in a single layer in the bottom basket and cover with a lid. Sit the steamer over a wok or saucepan of boiling water and steam for 20 minutes, basting the pork regularly.

3 Lay the bok choy in the top steamer basket, cover and steam both baskets for a further 5 minutes. Remove the pork and cover. Pour the remaining marinade into a small saucepan, stir in 1–2 tablespoons of water and simmer over high heat for 5 minutes to reduce slightly.

4 Slice the pork fillets and arrange on plates or in bowls with the bok choy. Drizzle with the sauce and serve with steamed rice.

PORK, SNOWPEA AND SICHUAN PEPPER STIR-FRY

Preparation time 10 minutes
Total cooking time 15 minutes
Serves 4

2 teaspoons sichuan pepper
1 tablespoon sesame oil
1 tablespoon vegetable oil
2 garlic cloves, crushed
3 cm (1¼ in) piece fresh ginger, grated
300 g (10½ oz) pork fillet, cut into thin strips
200 g (7 oz) button mushrooms, sliced
3 tablespoons oyster sauce
2 teaspoons chilli bean paste (see Note)
1 teaspoon Chinese black vinegar (chinkiang) (see Note)
150 g (5½ oz) snowpeas (mangetout), trimmed
steamed jasmine rice, to serve

1 Heat the oven to 200°C (400°F/Gas 6). Put the sichuan pepper into a small ovenproof dish and roast for 5 minutes, or until fragrant. Cool and crush to a fine powder with a mortar and pestle.

2 Put the sesame and vegetable oils into a wok and heat until almost smoking. Add the garlic, ginger and sichuan pepper and stir-fry for 30 seconds.

3 Add the pork and stir-fry for 3 minutes, or until no longer pink. Add the sliced mushrooms, oyster sauce, chilli bean paste, black vinegar, and 3 tablespoons of water and simmer for 2 minutes.

4 Toss through the snowpeas and simmer for 2 more minutes. Serve immediately with steamed jasmine rice.

Note Chilli bean paste and Chinese black vinegar (chinkiang) are available from Asian supermarkets.

CHILLI PORK WITH CASHEWS

Preparation time 10 minutes

Total cooking time 8 minutes

Serves 4

2–3 tablespoons peanut oil

600 g (1 lb 5 oz) pork fillet, thinly sliced

4 spring onions (scallions), cut into 3 cm (1¼ in)
   lengths

50 g (1¾ oz/⅓ cup) toasted unsalted cashews

1 tablespoon fish sauce

1 tablespoon mushroom oyster sauce

1–2 tablespoons Thai chilli paste in soy bean oil
   or chilli jam

1 large handful Thai basil leaves, plus extra
   to garnish

1 Heat a wok over high heat, add about
1 tablespoon of peanut oil and swirl to coat.
Stir-fry the pork in batches for 2–3 minutes,
or until it starts to brown. Remove from the
wok and keep warm.

2 Heat the remaining oil, then stir-fry the
spring onion for 1 minute. Return the pork to
the wok, along with any juices, and stir-fry
for 2 minutes.

3 Stir in the cashews, fish sauce, oyster sauce
and chilli paste or jam. Toss for a further
2 minutes, or until the pork is tender and
coated with the sauce.

4 Remove from the heat and gently stir in
the Thai basil. Serve garnished with some
extra basil.

FIVE-SPICE PORK RIBS

Preparation time 10 minutes +
Total cooking time 30 minutes
Serves 4

1 kg (2 lb 4 oz) American-style pork ribs
shredded spring onions (scallions), to serve

Marinade
125 ml (4 fl oz/½ cup) tomato sauce (ketchup)
2 tablespoons Chinese rice wine or dry sherry
2 tablespoons light soy sauce
2 tablespoons honey
1 tablespoon sweet chilli sauce
2 teaspoons five-spice powder
2 garlic cloves, crushed

1 Slice the pork ribs into individual ribs. Combine the marinade ingredients in a non-metallic bowl. Add the ribs and toss well to coat. Cover and marinate in the refrigerator for several hours.

2 Preheat the oven to 180°C (350°F/Gas 4). Line a large baking tray with foil. Remove excess marinade from the ribs, reserving it for basting.

3 Put the ribs on a rack on the baking tray. Bake for about 30 minutes, or until cooked and golden brown.

4 Brush with the reserved marinade once or twice during cooking. Serve the ribs hot and generously garnish with spring onions if desired.

PORK NOISETTES
WITH PRUNES

Preparation time 15 minutes
Total cooking time 30 minutes
Serves 4

8 pork noisettes or 2 x 400 g (14 oz)
   pork fillets
16 prunes, pitted
1 tablespoon oil
45 g (1½ oz) butter
1 onion, finely chopped
155 ml (5 fl oz) white wine
280 ml (10 fl oz) chicken or brown stock
1 bay leaf
2 thyme sprigs
250 ml (9 fl oz/1 cup) double cream

1 Trim any excess fat from the pork, making sure you get rid of any membrane that will cause the pork to shrink. If you are using pork fillet, cut each fillet into four diagonal slices. Put the prunes in a small saucepan, cover with cold water and bring to the boil. Reduce the heat and simmer the prunes for 5 minutes. Drain well.

2 Heat the oil in a large heavy-based frying pan and add half the butter. When the butter starts foaming, add the pork and sauté on both sides until cooked. Transfer the pork to a warm plate, cover and keep warm. Pour off the excess fat from the pan.

3 Meanwhile, melt the remaining butter, add the onion and cook over low heat until softened but not browned.

4 Add the wine, bring to the boil and simmer for 2 minutes. Add the stock, bay leaf and thyme and bring to the boil. Reduce the heat and simmer for 10 minutes or until reduced by half.

5 Strain the stock into a bowl and rinse the frying pan. Return the stock to the pan, add the cream and prunes and simmer for 8 minutes, or until the sauce thickens slightly. Tip the pork back into the pan and simmer until heated through.

PORK WITH APPLE AND ONION WEDGES

Preparation time 15 minutes
Total cooking time 20 minutes
Serves 4

2 pork fillets, about 400 g (14 oz) each
12 pitted prunes
2 green apples, cored, unpeeled, cut into wedges
2 red onions, cut into wedges
50 g (1¾ oz) butter, melted
2 teaspoons caster (superfine) sugar
125 ml (4 fl oz/½ cup) cream
2 tablespoons brandy
1 tablespoon chopped chives

1 Trim the pork of any excess fat and sinew and cut each fillet in half. Make a slit with a knife through the centre of each fillet and push 3 prunes into each one. Brush the pork, the apple and onion wedges with the melted butter and sprinkle the apple and onion with the caster sugar.

2 Brown the pork on a hot, lightly oiled barbecue flat plate. Add the apple and onion wedges (you may need to cook in batches if your flat plate isn't large enough). Cook, turning frequently, for 5–7 minutes, or until the pork is cooked through and the apple and onion pieces are softened. Remove the pork, apple and onion from the barbecue and keep warm.

3 Mix together the cream, brandy and chives in a pan. Transfer to the stove top and simmer for 3 minutes, or until slightly thickened. Season with salt and black pepper.

4 Slice the meat and serve with the apple, onion wedges and brandy cream sauce.

STIR-FRIED HOISIN PORK AND GREENS WITH GINGERED RICE

Preparation time 20 minutes

Total cooking time 25 minutes

Serves 4

250 g (9 oz/1¼ cups) jasmine rice

500 g (1lb 2 oz) pork fillets, thinly sliced

1 tablespoon caster (superfine) sugar

2 tablespoons oil

125 ml (4 fl oz/½ cup) white wine vinegar

250 ml (9 fl oz/1 cup) hoisin sauce

2 tablespoons stem ginger in syrup, chopped

1.25 kg (2 lb 12 oz) mixed Asian greens (bok choy, choy sum or spinach)

1 Rinse the rice and place in a large saucepan. Add 435 ml (15¼ fl oz/1¾ cups) water and bring to the boil. Cover, reduce the heat to very low and cook for about 10 minutes. Remove from the heat and leave to stand, covered, for 10 minutes.

2 Meanwhile, place the pork in a bowl and sprinkle with the sugar. Toss to coat.

3 Heat a wok over high heat, add about 1 tablespoon oil and swirl to coat. Add the pork in batches and stir-fry for 3 minutes, or until brown. Remove from the wok

4 Add the vinegar to the wok and boil for 3–5 minutes, or until reduced by two-thirds. Reduce the heat, add the hoisin sauce and 1 tablespoon ginger, and simmer for 5 minutes. Season to taste. Remove from the wok.

5 Reheat the cleaned wok over high heat, add the remaining oil and swirl to coat. Add the greens and stir-fry for 3 minutes, or until crisp and cooked.

6 Stir the remaining ginger through the rice, then press into four round teacups or small bowls, smoothing the surface. Unmould the rice onto four plates, arrange the pork and greens on the side and drizzle the sauce over the top.

Note You can find stem ginger in Asian food stores. Substitute glacé ginger if unavailable.

CARAMEL PORK

Preparation time 10 minutes
Total cooking time 20 minutes
Serves 4

110 g (3¾ oz/½ cup) sugar
oil, for deep-frying
4 large red Asian shallots, very finely sliced
750 g (1 lb 10 oz) pork fillets, trimmed and cut
    into 2 cm (¾ in) cubes
1 egg white, beaten until frothy
125 g (4½ oz/1 cup) potato flour or cornflour
    (cornstarch)
5 spring onions (scallions), thinly sliced on the
    diagonal
3 garlic cloves, crushed
3 cm (1¼ in) piece fresh ginger, julienned
1 tablespoon soy sauce
1 tablespoon lime juice
3 teaspoons grated palm sugar

1 Put the sugar and 125 ml (4 fl oz/½ cup)
of water in a saucepan and stir over low
heat until the sugar has dissolved. Bring to
the boil and cook for 5 minutes, or until
thickened and syrupy. Stir in 150 ml (5 fl oz)
of water until combined. Return to the heat
and simmer for 10 minutes, or until the sauce
is thick and golden.

2 Meanwhile, fill a wok one-third full of
oil and heat to 180°C (350°F), or until a
cube of bread dropped in the oil browns in
15 seconds. Deep-fry the shallots for about
1 minute, or until golden. Drain on crumpled
paper towels.

3 Toss the pork in the egg white and then in
the flour, shaking off any excess. Add to the
wok in batches and deep-fry for 2 minutes,
or until golden and cooked through. Drain
on paper towels. Remove all but 1 tablespoon
of oil from the wok and cook the spring
onion, garlic and ginger for 1 minute. Add
the caramel sauce, soy sauce, lime juice and
palm sugar and stir until combined. Add the
pork and toss until coated. Serve sprinkled
with the fried shallots.

SWEET AND SOUR PORK

Preparation time 10 minutes
Total cooking time 20 minutes
Serves 6

Sauce
1 tablespoon oil
1 green capsicum (pepper), finely sliced
75 g (2½ oz/⅓ cup) sugar
3 tablespoons rice vinegar
1½ tablespoons light soy sauce
1½ tablespoons tomato paste (purée)
¼ teaspoon sesame oil
4 tablespoons chicken stock
3 teaspoons cornflour (cornstarch)

900 g (2 lb) piece centre-cut pork loin, cut into
    2 cm (¾ in) cubes
2 eggs, lightly beaten
100 g (3½ oz) cornflour (cornstarch), extra
oil, for deep-frying

1 To make the sauce, heat a wok over high heat, add the oil and swirl to coat. Add the capsicum and stir-fry for 1 minute. Add the sugar, rice vinegar, soy sauce, tomato paste, sesame oil and stock and bring to the boil, stirring.
2 Combine the cornflour with 1 tablespoon of water and stir to form a smooth paste. Add the mixture to the sauce and bring to the boil, stirring, until the sauce thickens. Remove from the heat and keep warm.
3 Put the pork in a large bowl with the beaten egg, extra cornflour and 3 teaspoons of cold water. Toss the pork until well coated in the mixture.
4 Fill a wok two thirds full of oil and heat to 180°C (350°F), or until a cube of bread browns in 15 seconds. Add the pork in batches and cook for 3–4 minutes, or until golden brown and crispy. Drain on crumpled paper towels.
4 Remove the oil from the wok and wipe clean. Return the sauce to the wok and heat through for about 1 minute. Add the pork, toss well to coat. Serve with steamed white rice, if desired.

JUNGLE PORK CURRY

Preparation time 20 minutes
Total cooking time 25 minutes
Serves 4

Curry paste
8–10 large dried red chillies
1 tablespoon shrimp paste
1 teaspoon white pepper
1 lemongrass stem, white part only, sliced
5 red Asian shallots, sliced
5 garlic cloves, crushed
1 tablespoon finely chopped galangal
2 teaspoons finely grated fresh ginger
2 small coriander (cilantro) roots, chopped

1 tablespoon peanut oil
1 garlic clove, finely chopped
500 g (1 lb 2 oz) pork fillet, thinly sliced
500 ml (17 fl oz/2 cups) chicken stock
1 tablespoon fish sauce
85 g (3 oz) Thai apple eggplants (aubergines),
    quartered, or Thai pea eggplants (aubergines)
100 g (3½ oz) snake beans, cut into 3 cm (1¼ in)
    lengths
60 g (2¼ oz/¼ cup) sliced bamboo
    shoots
4 kaffir lime leaves, torn

1 small handful Thai basil leaves, plus extra
    to serve
1 long red chilli, seeded and julienned

1 To make the curry paste, soak the dried
chillies in boiling water for 10 minutes. Drain
and chop. Wrap the shrimp paste in foil and
toast in a hot wok for 1 minute on each side.
Remove from the foil and put the shrimp
paste in a food processor with the chopped
chilli and remaining paste ingredients. Add
1 teaspoon of salt and blend until smooth.
Add a little water if necessary to form a
smooth paste.

2 Heat a wok over medium heat, add the
peanut oil and swirl to coat. Add the garlic
and 4 tablespoons of the curry paste and
cook, stirring, for 1–2 minutes, or until
fragrant.

3 Add the pork and stir-fry for 2–3 minutes,
or until browned. Pour in the stock and
fish sauce, stir to combine, then bring to
the boil. Add the eggplant, snake beans,
bamboo shoots and lime leaves, reduce the
heat and simmer for 5–8 minutes, or until the
vegetables are tender. Remove from the heat
and stir in the basil leaves. Garnish with the
chilli strips and extra basil leaves.

STEAMED PORK RIBS IN BLACK BEAN SAUCE

Preparation time 10 minutes
Total cooking time 20 minutes
Serves 4

400 g (14 oz) American-style pork ribs, chopped
    into individual ribs about 8 cm (3¼ in) long (ask
    your butcher to do this if you do not have a
    cleaver)
1½ tablespoons black beans, washed and slightly
    mashed with a fork
2 garlic cloves, chopped
1 cm (½ in) piece fresh ginger, finely chopped
1 tablespoon oyster sauce
2 teaspoons soy sauce
2 teaspoons sugar
1 tablespoon cornflour (cornstarch)
1 spring onion (scallion), cut into 2 cm (¾ in)
    lengths

1 Put the chopped ribs in a shallow heatproof dish that will fit into a bamboo steamer. Combine the black beans, garlic, ginger, oyster sauce, soy sauce and sugar in a small bowl and mix well. Stir in the cornflour. Add the mixture to the ribs and mix well with clean hands. Scatter the spring onion over the top.
2 Put the dish in the steamer and sit the steamer over a wok of boiling water. Steam, covered, for 20 minutes (replenish the water if necessary during steaming). During cooking, the steam will create a sauce for the ribs. Serve hot with steamed rice and some Asian greens, if desired.
Tip Make sure the lid on your steamer is tight fitting as you need a lot of steam to help create the sauce. If necessary, add about 1–2 tablespoons of boiling water to the dish.

PORK AND LIME SKEWERS

Preparation time 20 minutes +
Total cooking time 20 minutes
Serves 4

50 g (1¾ oz) shaved palm sugar or soft brown
    sugar
250 ml (9 fl oz/1 cup) light coconut cream
1 bird's eye chilli, seeded and finely chopped
grated zest of 1 large lime
3 tablespoons lime juice
1 kaffir lime leaf, finely shredded (see tip)
750 g (1 lb 10 oz) pork fillets, cut into 2 cm (¾ in)
    cubes
4 lime wedges

1 Soak eight bamboo skewers in cold water for about 30 minutes. Meanwhile, put the sugar, coconut cream and chilli in a large saucepan and stir over low heat until the sugar has dissolved. Pour into a large non-metallic bowl, allow to cool a little, then add the lime zest, lime juice and kaffir lime leaf. Add the pork, toss gently, then cover and marinate in the refrigerator for 20 minutes, turning occasionally.

2 Heat the grill (broiler) to medium. Thread the pork onto the skewers, reserving the marinade. Spread the skewers slightly apart on an oiled grill tray, then grill for 8–10 minutes or until cooked through, turning once.

3 While the pork is sizzling, put the reserved marinade in a small saucepan. Bring to the boil, then reduce the heat and simmer for 5 minutes. When the pork is done, spoon the sauce over the skewers and serve with the lime wedges. Delicious with rice.

Tip When shredding a kaffir lime leaf, first remove the large fibrous vein running down the middle of the leaf. A simple way to do this is to fold the leaf in half lengthways, then chop away the centre vein with a sharp knife.

GARLIC PORK CHOPS

Preparation time 10 minutes +
Total cooking time 15 minutes
Serves 4

1 kg (2 lb 4 oz) pork chops
8 garlic cloves, crushed
2 tablespoons fish sauce
1 tablespoon soy sauce
2 tablespoons oyster sauce
2 tablespoons chopped spring onion (scallion)

1 Put the pork chops in a large glass bowl and add the garlic, fish sauce, soy sauce, oyster sauce and ½ teaspoon freshly ground black pepper. Stir well so that all the meat is covered with the marinade. Cover and marinate in the refrigerator for 4 hours.

2 Heat a barbecue grill or hotplate to hot and cook the pork on all sides until browned and cooked through. Alternatively you can cook the pork under a hot grill (broiler). If the pork starts to burn, move it further away from the grill element.

3 Arrange the pork on a serving platter and scatter over the spring onion.

PORK WITH SWEET AND SOUR SAUCE

Preparation time 15 minutes
Total cooking time 15 minutes
Serves 4

225 g (8 oz) tinned pineapple slices in light syrup, each slice cut into 4 pieces (reserve the syrup)
1½ tablespoons plum sauce or tomato ketchup
2½ teaspoons fish sauce
1 tablespoon sugar
2 tablespoons vegetable oil
250 g (9 oz) pork, sliced
4 garlic cloves, finely chopped
¼ carrot, sliced
1 onion, cut into 8 slices
½ red capsicum (pepper), cut into bite-sized pieces
1 small cucumber, unpeeled, halved lengthways and cut into thick slices
1 tomato, cut into 4 slices, or 4–5 baby tomatoes
a few coriander (cilantro) leaves, to garnish

1 Mix all the pineapple syrup (6 tablespoons) with the plum sauce, fish sauce and sugar in a small bowl until smooth.
2 Heat the oil in a wok or deep frying pan over a medium heat and fry the pork until nicely browned and cooked. Lift out with a slotted spoon and drain on paper towels.
3 Add the garlic to the wok or pan and fry over a medium heat for 1 minute or until lightly browned. Add the carrot, onion and capsicum and stir-fry for 1–2 minutes. Add the cucumber, tomato, pineapple and pineapple syrup and stir together for another minute. Taste, then adjust the seasoning.
4 Return the pork to the pan and gently stir. Spoon onto a serving plate and garnish with coriander leaves.

PORK WITH GINGER

Preparation time 15 minutes
Total cooking time 10 minutes
Serves 4

15 g (½ oz) dried black fungus
1 tablespoon fish sauce
1½ tablespoons oyster sauce
4 tablespoons vegetable or chicken stock
½ teaspoon sugar
2 tablespoons vegetable oil
3–4 garlic cloves, finely chopped
500 g (1 lb 2 oz) lean pork, finely sliced
25 g (1 oz) ginger, julienned
1 small onion, cut into 8 wedges
2 spring onions (scallions), diagonally sliced
ground white pepper, for sprinkling
1 long red chilli, seeded and finely sliced
a few coriander (cilantro) leaves, to garnish

1 Soak the black fungus in hot water for 2–3 minutes or until soft, then drain.
2 Mix the fish sauce, oyster sauce, stock and sugar in a small bowl.
3 Heat the oil in a wok or frying pan and stir-fry half the garlic over a medium heat until light brown.
4 Add half the pork and stir-fry over a high heat for 2–3 minutes or until the pork is cooked. Remove from the wok. Repeat with the remaining garlic and pork. Return all the pork to the wok.
5 Add the ginger, onion, black fungus and the sauce mixture to the wok. Stir-fry for 1–2 minutes. Taste, then adjust the seasoning if necessary. Stir in the spring onions.
6 Spoon onto a serving plate and sprinkle with ground pepper, chilli slices and coriander leaves.

RED PORK CURRY WITH GREEN PEPPERCORNS

Preparation time 15 minutes

Total cooking time 25 minutes

Serves 4

3 tablespoons coconut cream

2 tablespoons red curry paste or bought paste

3 tablespoons fish sauce

1½ tablespoons palm sugar

500 g (1 lb 2 oz) lean pork, finely sliced

440 ml (15¼ fl oz/1¾ cups) coconut milk

280 g (10 oz) Thai eggplants (aubergines), cut in half or quarters, or 1 eggplant (aubergine), cubed

75 g (2½ oz) fresh green peppercorns, cleaned

7 kaffir lime leaves, torn in half

2 long red chillies, seeded and finely sliced, to garnish

1 Put the coconut cream in a wok or saucepan and simmer over a medium heat for about 5 minutes, or until the cream separates and a layer of oil forms on the surface. Stir the cream if it starts to brown around the edges.

2 Add the curry paste, stir well to combine and cook until fragrant. Add the fish sauce and palm sugar and cook for another 2 minutes or until the mixture begins to darken. Add the pork and stir for about 5–7 minutes.

3 Add the coconut milk to the saucepan or wok and simmer over a medium heat for another 5 minutes.

4 Add the eggplants and green peppercorns and cook for 5 minutes. Add the kaffir lime leaves. Taste, then adjust the seasoning if necessary. Transfer to a serving bowl and sprinkle with the chillies.

ROAST PORK FILLET WITH APPLE AND MUSTARD SAUCE AND GLAZED APPLES

Preparation time 30 minutes

Total cooking time 25 minutes

Serves 4

750 g (1 lb 10 oz) pork fillet
30 g (1 oz) butter
1 tablespoon oil
1 garlic clove, crushed
½ teaspoon freshly grated ginger
1 tablespoon seeded mustard
3 tablespoons apple sauce
2 tablespoons chicken stock
125 ml (4 fl oz/½ cup) pouring (whipping) cream
1 teaspoon cornflour (cornstarch)

Glazed apples
2 green apples
50 g (1¾ oz) butter
2 tablespoons soft brown sugar

1 Preheat the oven to 180°C (350°F/Gas 4). Trim the pork fillet, removing any fat or sinew from the outside. Tie the fillet with kitchen string at 3 cm (1¼ in) intervals to keep in shape.

2 Heat the butter and oil in a frying pan, add the pork fillet and cook until lightly browned all over. Remove and place on a rack in a baking dish. (Retain the cooking oils in the frying pan.) Add 125 ml (4 fl oz/ ½ cup) water to the baking dish and bake for 15–20 minutes. Leave in a warm place for 10 minutes before removing the string and slicing.

3 For the sauce, reheat the oils in the frying pan, add the garlic and ginger and stir for 1 minute. Stir in the mustard, apple sauce and stock. Slowly stir in the combined cream and cornflour and stir until the mixture boils and thickens.

4 For the glazed apples, cut the apples into 1 cm (½ in) slices. Melt the butter in the pan and add the sugar. Stir until the sugar dissolves. Add the apple slices and pan-fry, turning occasionally, until the apples are glazed and lightly browned.

5 Slice the pork and serve the apple and mustard sauce over it. Serve with the glazed apples.

PORK CHOPS IN MARSALA

Preparation time 10 minutes
Total cooking time 15 minutes
Serves 4

4 pork loin chops
2 tablespoons olive oil
125 ml (4 fl oz/½ cup) Marsala
2 teaspoons grated orange zest
3 tablespoons orange juice
3 tablespoons chopped flat-leaf (Italian) parsley

1 Pat dry the chops and season well. Heat the olive oil in a heavy-based frying pan over medium heat and cook the chops on both sides for 5 minutes each side, or until brown and cooked.

2 Add the Marsala, orange zest and juice and cook for 4–5 minutes, or until the sauce has reduced and thickened. Add the parsley and serve immediately.

Note Marsala is a fortified wine from Sicily, made by mixing grape juice with white wine, which is then left to mature in casks. Marsala has a sweet, smoky flavour that ranges from dry to sweet. Some may be flavoured with almond, cream or egg. Dry Marsala is best for use in cooking and appears in many sauces for various Italian dishes such as saltimbocca and chicken cacciatora. You can find it in most large supermarkets or delicatessens.

PORK WITH GARLIC AND PEPPER

Preparation time 10 minutes

Total cooking time 15 minutes

Serves 4

1½ teaspoons black peppercorns

1 whole bulb of garlic, cloves roughly chopped

8–10 coriander (cilantro) roots, roughly chopped

3 tablespoons vegetable oil

500 g (1 lb 2 oz) pork fillet, cut into 5 cm (2 in) squares

1 tablespoon fish sauce

1 tablespoon light soy sauce

½ teaspoon sugar

garlic and chilli sauce, to serve

1 Using a pestle and mortar or a small blender, pound or blend the black peppercorns (just roughly) and spoon them into a small bowl.

2 Pound or blend the garlic and coriander roots into a paste and mix with peppercorns.

3 Heat the oil in a wok or frying pan and stir-fry half the garlic and peppercorn paste over a medium heat for 1–2 minutes or until the garlic turns light brown and is fragrant.

Add half the pork and stir-fry over a high heat for a minute, then reduce the heat and cook for 2–3 minutes, or until the meat is cooked. Remove from the heat. Repeat with the remaining paste and pork. Return all the pork to the wok.

4 Add the fish sauce, light soy sauce and sugar to the wok. Stir-fry for 5 minutes or until the pork starts to turn brown. Serve immediately with garlic and chilli sauce.

PORK AND TOMATO BURGERS

Preparation time 10 minutes +
Total cooking time 15 minutes
Serves 4

350 g (12 oz) minced (ground) pork and veal
100 g (3½ oz) sun-dried tomatoes, chopped
3 spring onions (scallions), finely chopped
2 tablespoons chopped basil
1 red capsicum (pepper), seeded and
    sliced
olive oil, for cooking
1 tablespoon balsamic vinegar

1 Mix together the pork and veal, sun-dried tomato, spring onion and basil. Season well and knead for 2 minutes, or until a little sticky. Form into four burgers and refrigerate for at least 15 minutes.

2 Mix the capsicum with a little olive oil. Cook on a hot, lightly oiled barbecue grill or flat plate, tossing well and drizzling with the balsamic vinegar, until just softened. Set aside.

3 Wipe the barbecue clean and reheat. Brush the burgers with olive oil and cook for about 4–5 minutes each side, or until cooked. Serve with the chargrilled capsicum.

CARAMEL PORK AND PUMPKIN STIR-FRY

Preparation time 20 minutes
Total cooking time 30 minutes
Serves 4

250 g (9 oz/1¼ cups) jasmine rice
500 g (1 lb 2 oz) pork fillet, thinly sliced
2 garlic cloves, crushed
2–3 tablespoons peanut oil
300 g (10½ oz) butternut pumpkin, cut into
    2 cm x 4 cm (¾ x 1½ in) pieces about 5 mm
    (¼ in) thick
60 g (2¼ oz/⅓ cup) soft brown sugar
3 tablespoons fish sauce
3 tablespoons rice vinegar
2 tablespoons chopped coriander (cilantro) leaves
1.25 kg (2 lb 12 oz) mixed Asian greens (bok
    choy, choy sum, gai larn)

1 Bring a large saucepan of water to the boil. Add the rice and cook for 12 minutes, stirring occasionally. Drain.

2 Combine the pork with the garlic and 2 teaspoons of the peanut oil. Season with salt and plenty of pepper.

3 Heat a wok until very hot, add about 1 tablespoon oil and swirl to coat. When just starting to smoke, stir-fry the pork in two batches for about 1 minute per batch, or until the meat changes colour. Transfer to a plate.

4 Add the remaining oil to the wok and stir-fry the pumpkin for 4 minutes, or until tender but not falling apart. Remove and add to the pork.

5 Combine the sugar, fish sauce, rice vinegar and 125 ml (4 fl oz/½ cup) water in the wok and boil for about 10 minutes, or until syrupy. Return the pork and pumpkin to the wok and stir for 1 minute, or until well coated and heated through. Stir in the coriander.

5 Put the mixed Asian greens in a paper-lined bamboo steamer over a wok of simmering water for 3 minutes, or until wilted. Serve immediately with the stir-fry and rice.

BARBECUED ASIAN PORK RIBS WITH SPRING ONION RICE

Preparation time 15 minutes +
Total cooking time 30 minutes
Serves 4

1 kg (2 lb 4 oz) American-style pork ribs, cut into sections of 4–5 ribs
3 tablespoons hoisin sauce
1 tablespoon Chinese rice wine or dry sherry
3 tablespoons soy sauce
2 garlic cloves, chopped
2 tablespoons oil
3 spring onions (scallions), finely chopped
1 tablespoon grated fresh ginger
250 g (9 oz/1¼ cups) jasmine rice
600 g (1 lb 5 oz) baby bok choy (pak choy), leaves separated

1 Place the ribs in a non-metallic bowl. Combine the hoisin sauce, rice wine, soy sauce, garlic, 1 tablespoon oil, 2 tablespoons spring onion and half the ginger. Pour over the ribs and marinate for at least 10 minutes, or overnight in the refrigerator.

2 Bring a large saucepan of water to the boil. Add the rice and cook for 12 minutes, stirring occasionally. Drain.

3 Heat the remaining oil in a small pan over medium–low heat. When the oil is warm but not smoking, remove the pan from the heat and add the rest of the spring onion and ginger. Stir in ¼ teaspoon salt. Stir through the rice.

4 Heat a chargrill pan or barbecue plate and brush with oil. Remove the ribs from the marinade, reserving the marinade.

5 Cook the ribs in batches, if necessary, for about 8–10 minutes on each side, or until cooked through, basting with the marinade during cooking.

6 Before the ribs are cooked, bring the reserved marinade to the boil in a pan (add 4 tablespoons of water if necessary). Boil for 2 minutes, then add the bok choy. Cover and cook for 1–2 minutes, or until just wilted. Serve the ribs with the rice and bok choy, and drizzle with the marinade.

JAPANESE PORK AND CABBAGE STIR-FRY

Preparation time 15 minutes

Total cooking time 10 minutes

Serves 4

¼ teaspoon dashi granules

1½ tablespoons vegetable oil

500 g (1 lb 2 oz) pork loin fillet, very thinly sliced across the grain

4 spring onions (scallions), cut into 3 cm (1¼ in) lengths

135 g (4¾ oz/3 cups) shredded Chinese cabbage (wong bok)

3 tablespoons soy sauce

2 teaspoons mirin

3 teaspoons finely grated fresh ginger

2 garlic cloves, crushed

1–2 teaspoons sugar

black sesame seeds or thinly sliced spring onion (scallion), to garnish (optional)

1 Dissolve the dashi in 125 ml (4 fl oz/ ½ cup) hot water.

2 Heat a wok over high heat, add about 1 tablespoon of the oil and swirl to coat the base and side. Stir-fry the pork in three batches for 1 minute at a time, or until it just changes colour, then remove from the wok and set aside.

3 Add the remaining oil to the wok and swirl to coat, then add the spring onion and Chinese cabbage and stir-fry for 1 minute, or until softened, then set aside with the pork.

4 Combine the dashi broth, soy sauce, mirin, ginger, garlic and sugar in a bowl. Add to the wok, bring to the boil and cook for 1 minute. Return the pork and vegetables to the wok and stir-fry for 2–3 minutes, or until combined and the pork is just cooked through but still tender.

5 Garnish with black sesame seeds or thinly sliced spring onion.

PORK WITH SNAKE BEANS

Preparation time 10 minutes

Total cooking time 10 minutes

Serves 4

1 tablespoon oyster sauce

1 tablespoon light soy sauce

¼ teaspoon sugar

2 tablespoons vegetable oil

4 garlic cloves, finely chopped

350 g (12 oz) pork fillet, finely sliced

250 g (9 oz) snake beans, cut into 5 cm (2 in) pieces

½ long red chilli, seeded, shredded, to garnish

1 Combine the oyster sauce, light soy sauce, sugar and about 2 tablespoons water in a small bowl.

2 Heat the oil in a wok or frying pan and stir-fry the garlic over a medium heat until light brown.

3 Add the pork and stir-fry over a high heat for 3–5 minutes or until the pork is just cooked. Do not over cook. Add the beans and the sauce mixture and stir-fry for 4 minutes. Taste, then adjust the seasoning if necessary.

4 Transfer the pork and beans to a serving plate and scatter chilli slices over the top.

LAMB

Lamb has long been considered a festival food all around the world. It has strong associations with springtime, as well as many religious feast days. But lamb doesn't need to be reserved for special occasions. It's the perfect mid-week meat. Although it's quite tasty on its own, lamb works very well with all sorts of different flavours.

LAMB BASICS

Lamb is defined as meat from a young sheep, usually up to 1 year old, depending on local definitions. The meat from older sheep, either hogget (up to 20 months) or mutton (30–40 months) is darker in colour and stronger in flavour.

Lambs are raised in most parts of the world where there are grasslands, from Mongolia to Patagonia, and their meat (and milk) is widely utilized. Very young milk-fed (sucking) lambs are a speciality in Italy, France, Spain, Portugal and the Middle East and pré-salé lambs (those that feed on the salt marshes) are also reared in parts of France and Wales.

Many cuisines use whole lamb as a centrepiece for feast days and special occasions, such as the Muslim festival of Eid-el-Kurban, where a whole lamb is roasted. Usually the whole lamb is spit-roasted.

Lamb is also used to welcome spring in Europe — spring lamb tends to have a better flavour than those born in the autumn as their diet is richer in young grass and flowers.

New season lamb is generally considered to be better quality than older lamb, and frozen cuts from the other side of the world may be preferable to older lamb in its own country. Lamb mince is also used extensively in some cuisines in dishes such as shepherd's pie and moussaka as it is fattier and stays more moist than beef mince when cooked.

BUYING

Lamb is often hung and aged for a week to give it a better flavour and more tender texture; however, milk-fed lamb isn't hung.

Young lamb has a pinker flesh than older lamb or mutton, though what the lamb has been fed on can also affect the colour of the meat. Milk-fed lamb is very pale.

Lamb should have a healthy pink colour with waxy, dry, firm white fat.

Make sure that you buy the correct cut of lamb for your recipe, as cheaper cuts tend to be for longer, slower cooking and will not benefit from being grilled or pan-fried.

STORAGE

Cover pieces of lamb and store them in the fridge until ready to use. This will stop the surface of the meat from oxidizing and turning brown.

COOKING

Because lamb is a fatty meat, it is traditionally served with acidic accompaniments, such as mint sauce and redcurrant jelly, to cut through the fat, or strong herbs such as rosemary. In some cuisines, fruit and sweet root vegetables are used to complement the lamb's fattiness. Lamb is particularly good in tagines, navarins and hotpots.

CUTS OF LAMB

Cutlets from the best end of neck are grilled, while breasts, shoulder and legs are roasted, on the bone or stuffed. Cubed lamb is used in stews and ragùs.

Fronts cuts These range from the fatty neck or scrag end to the tender meat of the racks. Cuts include the breast, scrag end and middle neck, the shoulder (bone in or bone out), and the rack (sometimes called the 'best end of neck'), which can be bought in one piece, cut into chops and cutlets, or two racks can be joined to make a crown roast, or if inward facing, a guard of honour. The fattier cuts are good for slow cooking and casseroles and the racks and shoulder are good for roasting, grilling and pan-frying.

Centre cuts Cuts include the saddle (both loins and often the tail and kidneys), the loins (on the bone), chump chops and noisettes. These cuts are good for roasting or, when off the bone, for frying and grilling.

Back cuts The leg (gigot) as a whole is good for roasting, and the shank or knuckle end is good for slow cooking. Leg chops are cut from the top of the leg.

ROASTING

For roasting, choose joints such as saddle, rack (joined cutlets), crown roast (what the French call carre d'agneau), guard of honour, loin, shoulder or leg. A loin (six to seven chops) will feed three people and a chop loin (four to five chops) will feed two people.

Roast lamb is best cooked on the bone at 200°C (400°F/Gas 6)and will need to cook for about 20 minutes per 500 g (1 lb 2 oz), with 15 minutes standing time, for pink lamb. For well-cooked lamb, it will need 25 minutes per 500 g (1 lb 2 oz) with an extra 25 minutes cooking. If the skin and fat are not browned or crisp enough, grill them for a few seconds. A light covering of fat will baste the meat as it cooks, but remember to serve on hot plates as lamb fat congeals fast.

SLOW COOKING

Cuts such as scrag end, middle neck, shoulder, leg and shanks can all be slow cooked, though generally lamb is very tender. Shanks benefit from braising as they are leaner and tougher, but when casseroling fattier cuts, trim them as much as possible or let the finished dish go cold so you can lift off any fat before reheating it.

Many traditional British dishes such as Lancashire hotpot and Irish stew use cutlets and chops while French recipes use both these and cubed shoulder and leg to make navarins, daubes and casseroles. Indian and Arabic dishes also use cubed shoulder and leg in curries and spiced stews such as korma, and Moroccan and Middle Eastern cuisines use it in tagines. As for roasting, always serve lamb on a hot plate to stop the fat congealing.

TRIMMING A LEG OF LAMB

Step 1 Using a small knife, cut away any excess fat covering the leg of lamb. Cut through the tendon joining the meat to the knuckle and trim off any meat from the bone. Using a saw, cut off the knuckle end of the shank bone to neaten it.

Step 2 Next, turn the leg over and, using a boning knife, cut around the edges of the pelvic bone. Following its contour down to the ball and socket joint, cut through the tendons that join the two bones and then pull out the pelvic bone.

Step 3 Fold the flap of flesh back over the lamb and use a piece of string to tie it in place. Wind the string round the shank end and up both sides of the leg. Tie another piece of string across the joint.

STIR-FRIED LAMB WITH MINT AND CHILLI

Preparation time 5 minutes

Total cooking time 4 minutes

Serves 4

1 tablespoon oil

750 g (1 lb 10 oz) lamb fillet, thinly sliced (see Note)

4 garlic cloves, finely chopped

2 small fresh red chillies, thinly sliced

4 tablespoons oyster sauce

2½ tablespoons fish sauce

1½ teaspoons sugar

25 g (1 oz) chopped mint

1 small handful whole fresh mint leaves

1 Heat a wok over high heat, add the oil and swirl to coat. Add the lamb and garlic in batches and stir-fry for 1–2 minutes, or until the lamb is almost cooked. Return all the lamb to the wok. Stir in the chilli, oyster sauce, fish sauce, sugar and the chopped mint leaves, and cook for another 1–2 minutes. **2** Remove from the heat, fold in the whole mint leaves and serve immediately with rice. **Note** Make sure you slice the lamb across the grain.

LAMB WITH HOKKIEN NOODLES AND SOUR SAUCE

Preparation time 10 minutes

Total cooking time 15 minutes

Serves 4–6

450 g (1 lb) hokkien (egg) noodles

2 tablespoons vegetable oil

375 g (13 oz) lamb backstrap, thinly sliced

75 g (2½ oz) red Asian shallots, peeled and thinly sliced

3 garlic cloves, crushed

2 teaspoons finely chopped fresh ginger

1 small fresh red chilli, seeded and finely chopped

1½ tablespoons red curry paste

125 g (4½ oz) snowpeas (mangetout), trimmed and cut in half on the diagonal

1 small carrot, julienned

125 ml (4 fl oz/½ cup) chicken stock

15 g (½ oz) grated palm sugar or soft brown sugar

1 tablespoon lime juice

small whole basil leaves, to garnish

1 Cover the noodles with boiling water and soak for 1 minute. Drain and set aside.

2 Heat 1 tablespoon of the oil in a wok and swirl to coat. Stir-fry the lamb in batches over high heat for 2–3 minutes, or until it just changes colour. Remove to a side plate.

3 Add the remaining oil, then the shallots, garlic, ginger and chilli and stir-fry for 1–2 minutes. Stir in the curry paste and cook for 1 minute. Add the snowpeas, carrot and the lamb and combine. Cook over high heat, tossing often, for 1–2 minutes.

4 Add the stock, palm sugar and lime juice, toss to combine and cook for 2–3 minutes. Add the noodles and cook for 1 minute, or until heated through.

5 Divide among serving bowls and garnish with the basil.

LAMB BACKSTRAPS WITH SPICED LENTILS AND MINT RAITA

Preparation time 10 minutes +
Total cooking time 10 minutes
Serves 4

125 g (4½ oz/½ cup) plain yoghurt
2 tablespoons finely chopped mint
1 tablespoon garam masala
3 teaspoons ground cumin
½ teaspoon chilli powder
4 tablespoons oil
4 lamb backstraps or eye of loin fillets (about
    150 g/5½ oz each)
2 teaspoons grated fresh ginger
1 teaspoon ground turmeric
850 g (1 lb 14 oz) tinned lentils, drained and
    rinsed

1 Combine the yoghurt and half the mint in a small non-metallic bowl. Cover and set aside.

2 Dry-fry the garam masala in a frying pan over medium heat for 1 minute, or until fragrant. Remove, then dry-fry the cumin. Combine 2 teaspoons each of garam masala and cumin, the chilli and 2 tablespoons oil. Put the lamb in a non-metallic dish. Brush with the spiced oil, cover and marinate for 10 minutes.

3 Meanwhile, heat 1 tablespoon of the remaining oil in a saucepan. Add the ginger, turmeric and remaining cumin and cook for 30 seconds. Add the lentils and stir until heated through. Reduce the heat to low, add the remaining garam masala and season with salt. Cover and cook for 5 minutes, adding 3 tablespoons water if the lentils start to stick. Stir in the remaining mint.

4 Heat a large frying pan over medium-high heat and add the remaining oil. Cook the backstraps for 3–4 minutes each side for medium–rare, or until cooked to your liking. Leave for several minutes, then cut into 1 cm (¾ in) slices. Place some lentils on a plate, arrange the lamb slices on top and serve with mint raita.

MADRAS LAMB PILAU

Preparation time 15 minutes
Total cooking time 30 minutes
Serves 4

3 tablespoons oil
2 onions, thinly sliced
250 g (9 oz/1 cup) plain yoghurt
60 g (2¼ oz/¼ cup) Madras curry paste
400 g (14 oz/2 cups) basmati rice, well rinsed
8 large French-trimmed lamb cutlets
4 tablespoons chopped fresh mint
60 g (2¼ oz/¼ cup) slivered almonds, lightly
    toasted

1 Heat 2 tablespoons of the oil in a large saucepan, add the onions and cook over medium heat for 4–5 minutes, or until soft. Remove half with a slotted spoon, set aside and keep warm. Add 200 g (7 oz) of the yoghurt and 2 tablespoons of the curry paste to the pan. Cook, stirring, for 2 minutes. Stir in the rice until well coated. Pour in 500 ml (17 fl oz/2 cups) water, bring to the boil, then reduce the heat to medium–low and cook for 15–20 minutes, or until all the water has been absorbed and the rice is tender.
2 Meanwhile, smear the cutlets with the remaining curry paste and marinate for 5 minutes. Heat the remaining oil in a frying pan over high heat, then cook the cutlets for 3–4 minutes on each side, or until cooked to your liking. Remove from the heat, cover with foil and allow to rest. Combine the remaining yoghurt with 1 tablespoon of the mint.
3 To serve, stir the remaining mint through the rice, season, then divide among four serving plates. Top with the remaining onions, the lamb and the almonds. Serve with a dollop of the minted yoghurt on the side.

PAN-FRIED LAMB FILLETS WITH RED WINE

Preparation time 10 minutes
Total cooking time 30 minutes
Serves 4

600 g (1 lb 5 oz) small new potatoes
160 g (5¾ oz) snowpeas (mangetout), trimmed
2 tablespoons olive oil
4 lamb backstraps or eye of loin fillets (about
    200 g/7 oz each), trimmed
170 ml (5½ fl oz/⅔ cup) red wine
1 tablespoon redcurrant jelly
2 teaspoons chopped thyme
30 g (1 oz) butter, chilled and cut into cubes

1 Cook the potatoes in a large saucepan of lightly salted boiling water for about 15–20 minutes, or until tender. Add the snowpeas and cook for another minute. Drain the vegetables, return to the pan and toss gently with 1 tablespoon of the oil.
2 Meanwhile, heat the remaining oil in a large frying pan and cook the lamb fillets over medium–high heat for about 4–5 minutes each side, or until cooked, but still pink inside. Remove from the pan, cover and keep warm.
3 Add the wine, redcurrant jelly and thyme to the pan and bring to the boil. Boil rapidly for 5 minutes, or until reduced and syrupy. Stir in the butter.
4 To serve, slice the lamb on the diagonal, divide among four plates and spoon some sauce on top. Serve immediately with the vegetables.

LAMB CUTLETS WITH MINT GREMOLATA

Preparation time 10 minutes

Total cooking time 10 minutes

Serves 4

4 tablespoons mint leaves

1 tablespoon flat-leaf (Italian) parsley

2 garlic cloves

1½ tablespoons lemon zest (white pith removed),
    cut into thin strips

2 tablespoons extra virgin olive oil

8 French-trimmed lamb cutlets

2 carrots

2 zucchini (courgettes)

1 tablespoon lemon juice

1 To make the gremolata, finely chop the mint, parsley, garlic and lemon strips, then combine well.

2 Heat a chargrill pan or barbecue plate to very hot. Lightly brush barbecue plate with 1 tablespoon of the oil.

3 Cook the cutlets over medium heat for about 2 minutes on each side, or until cooked to your liking. Remove the cutlets and cover to keep warm. Allow to rest while cooking the vegetables.

3 Trim the ends from the carrots and zucchini and, using a sharp vegetable peeler, peel the vegetables lengthways into ribbons. Heat the remaining oil in a large saucepan, add the vegetables and toss over medium heat for 3–5 minutes, or until sautéed but still tender.

4 Divide the lamb cutlets among four serving plates, lightly sprinkle the cutlets with the gremolata and drizzle with the lemon juice. Serve immediately with the vegetable ribbons.

SUMAC-CRUSTED LAMB FILLETS WITH BABA GANOUJ

Preparation time 20 minutes
Total cooking time 30 minutes
Serves 4

2 tablespoons olive oil
750 g (1 lb 10 oz) small new potatoes
2–3 garlic cloves, crushed
3 tablespoons lemon juice
1 red capsicum (pepper), seeded and quartered lengthways
4 lamb backstraps or eye of loin fillets (about 200 g/7 oz each)
1 tablespoon sumac (see Note)
3 tablespoons finely chopped fresh flat-leaf parsley
250 g (9 oz) baba ganouj (eggplant/aubergine dip)

1 Heat the oil in a saucepan big enough to hold the potatoes in one layer. Cook the potatoes and garlic, turning frequently, for 3–5 minutes, or until golden. Add the lemon juice and reduce the heat to medium–low. Simmer, covered, for 15–20 minutes, or until tender, stirring occasionally. Season well.

2 Meanwhile, lightly oil a chargrill pan or barbecue plate and heat to very hot. Cook the capsicum skin-side-down for 1–2 minutes, or until the skin starts to blister and turn black. Cook the other side for 1–2 minutes. Place the capsicum in a plastic bag or bowl covered with plastic wrap.

3 Coat the lamb with sumac. Cook on the chargrill pan for 4–5 minutes each side, or until cooked to your liking. Remove and cover with foil. Peel the capsicum and slice into thin strips.

4 Stir the parsley through the potatoes. Divide the baba ganouj among four plates. Cut the lamb into 1 cm (¾ in) slices on the diagonal and arrange on the baba ganouj with the capsicum. Serve with the potatoes and a salad.

Note Sumac is available from Middle Eastern food stores. If unavailable, use the same amount of ground cumin.

LAMB KOFTAS IN PITTA BREAD

Preparation time 20 minutes +
Total cooking time 20 minutes
Serves 4

500 g (1 lb 2 oz) lean lamb
1 onion, roughly chopped
1 handful flat-leaf (Italian) parsley, roughly
    chopped
1 large handful mint, chopped
2 teaspoons lemon zest
1 teaspoon ground cumin
¼ teaspoon chilli powder
250 g (9 oz/1 cup) low-fat yoghurt
2 teaspoons lemon juice
oil spray
4 wholemeal (wholewheat) pitta breads

Tabbouleh
80 g (3 oz/½ cup) burghul
2 vine-ripened tomatoes
1 Lebanese (short) cucumber
60 g (2¼ oz) flat-leaf (Italian) parsley, chopped
1 large handful mint, chopped
2 French shallots, chopped
125 ml (4 fl oz/½ cup) Greek salad dressing

1 Roughly chop the lamb. Put the lamb and onion in a food processor and process until smooth. Add the parsley, mint, lemon zest and spices and process until well combined. Divide the mixture into 24 balls and place on a tray. Cover and refrigerate for 30 minutes.
2 Meanwhile, to make the tabbouleh, place the burghul in a bowl. Cover with boiling water, set aside for 10 minutes, or until softened. Drain, then squeeze dry. Seed and chop the tomatoes. Cut the cucumber into halves, seed and chop. Place in a bowl with the parsley, mint, tomatoes, cucumber and shallots. Stir through the fat-free dressing.
3 To make the yoghurt dressing, combine the yoghurt and lemon juice in a bowl. Cover and refrigerate.
4 Heat a large, non-stick frying pan and spray with the oil. Cook the lamb balls in 2 batches, spraying with the oil before each batch, until browned all over.
5 Preheat the oven to 180°C (350°F/Gas 4). Cut the pitta pocket breads in half, wrap in foil and place in the oven for 10 minutes.
6 To serve, divide the tabbouleh between the pitta bread halves, add 3 kofta balls to each and top with the yoghurt dressing.

LAMB, MINT AND CHILLI STIR-FRY

Preparation time 10 minutes

Total cooking time 20 minutes

Serves 4

250 g (9 oz/1¼ cups) jasmine rice
2 tablespoons oil
750 g (1 lb 10 oz) lamb backstrap or eye of loin
    fillets, sliced thinly
2 garlic cloves, finely chopped
1 small red onion, cut into wedges
1 fresh bird's eye chilli, finely chopped
3 tablespoons lime juice
2 tablespoons sweet chilli sauce
2 tablespoons fish sauce
1 handful fresh mint leaves

1 Bring a large saucepan of water to the boil. Add the rice and cook for 12 minutes, stirring occasionally. Drain well.

2 Meanwhile, heat a wok until very hot, add 1 tablespoon oil and swirl to coat. Add the lamb in batches and cook for 2 minutes, or until browned. Remove from the wok.

3 Heat the remaining oil in the wok, add the garlic and onion and stir-fry for 1 minute, then add the chilli and cook for 30 seconds. Return the lamb to the wok, then add the lime juice, sweet chilli sauce and fish sauce and stir-fry for 2 minutes over high heat. Stir in the mint and serve with the rice.

Note: You can use chicken breasts or pork loin, adding 80 g (2¾ oz/½ cup) cashews and using basil instead of mint.

SPRING ONION LAMB

Preparation time 10 minutes +
Total cooking time 20 minutes
Serves 4

600 g (1 lb 5 oz) lean lamb backstrap, sliced
   across the grain into thin slices
1 tablespoon Chinese rice wine or dry sherry
3 tablespoons soy sauce
½ teaspoon white pepper
6 spring onions (scallions)
300 g (10½ oz/1½ cups) long-grain rice
2 tablespoons oil
750 g (1 lb 10 oz) choy sum, cut into 10 cm (4 in)
   lengths
3 garlic cloves, crushed
1 tablespoon Chinese black vinegar
1 teaspoon sesame oil

1 Put the lamb in a non-metallic bowl
with the rice wine, 1 tablespoon soy sauce,
½ teaspoon salt and the white pepper and
mix. Cover and chill for 10 minutes. Slice the
spring onions diagonally.

2 Meanwhile, bring a large pan of water to
the boil. Add the rice and cook for
12 minutes, stirring occasionally. Drain.

3 Heat a wok over high heat, add
½ tablespoon oil and swirl to coat. Add the
choy sum, stir-fry, then add 1 clove garlic
and 1 tablespoon soy sauce. Cook for
3 minutes, or until crisp. Take the wok off
the heat, remove the greens and keep warm.

4 Wipe out the wok and heat over high heat,
then add 1 tablespoon oil and swirl. Add the
lamb in batches and stir-fry over high heat
for 1–2 minutes, or until brown. Remove
from the wok.

5 Add more oil to the wok. Add the spring
onion and remaining garlic and stir-fry for
1–2 minutes. Combine the vinegar, sesame
oil and the remaining soy sauce. Pour into
the wok, stirring for 1 minute. Return the
lamb to the wok and stir-fry for another
minute, or until heated through. Serve with
the stir-fried greens and rice.

LAMB WITH JUNIPER AND PORT SAUCE

Preparation time 10 minutes
Total cooking time 20 minutes
Serves 4

500 ml (17 fl oz/2 cups) chicken stock
150 g (5½ oz/1 cup) polenta
12 French trimmed lamb cutlets
1 tablespoon oil
185 ml (6 fl oz/¾ cup) port
5 juniper berries
50 g (1¾ oz) butter, cut into cubes

1 Bring the stock and 375 ml (13 fl oz/
1½ cups) of water to the boil in a large
saucepan. Add the polenta and stir. Cook

over a low heat, stirring, for 10 minutes, or
until smooth and creamy.
2 Meanwhile, rub each cutlet with oil and
salt and pepper. Cook in a heavy-based
frying pan over high heat for 2 minutes on
each side, or until cooked to your liking.
Remove the lamb from the pan and
keep warm.
3 Pour the port and 3 tablespoons of water
into the frying pan, stirring with a wooden
spoon. Add the juniper berries, reduce the
heat and simmer for 5 minutes, or until the
liquid has reduced by half. Add the butter,
one cube at a time, stirring constantly until
all the butter is incorporated.
4 Serve the lamb with the polenta, drizzled
with the sauce.

HERBED LAMB CUTLETS WITH PRESERVED LEMON COUSCOUS

Preparation time 10 minutes

Total cooking time 20 minutes

Serves 4

2 tablespoons finely chopped thyme leaves

2 teaspoons freshly ground black pepper

12 French-trimmed lamb cutlets

3 tablespoons virgin olive oil

2 tablespoons soy sauce

2 garlic cloves, crushed

oil, for brushing

preserved lemon couscous

1 tablespoon olive oil

185 g (6½ oz/1 cup) couscous

2 tablespoons thinly sliced preserved lemon zest

1 Sprinkle the thyme and pepper onto a plate. Use the mixture to coat both sides of each lamb cutlet, pressing it in well.

2 In a shallow non-metallic dish, whisk the oil, soy sauce and garlic until combined. Add the lamb cutlets, then cover and refrigerate for 20 minutes, turning once.

3 Preheat a barbecue grill plate or chargrill pan until very hot. Meanwhile, make the preserved lemon couscous. Bring 375 ml (13 fl oz/1½ cups) of water to the boil in a saucepan. Add the oil, then stir in the couscous and preserved lemon. Remove from the heat, cover and leave for 5 minutes. Before serving, fluff up the couscous with a fork.

4 Shake the excess marinade off the cutlets and set them slightly apart on the barbecue hotplate. Grill for 1–2 minutes on each side, or until cooked to your liking. Serve the cutlets with the preserved lemon couscous.

CHILLI MINT LAMB

Preparation time 10 minutes

Total cooking time 10 minutes

Serves 4

2 tablespoons peanut oil

500 g (1lb 2 oz) lamb sirloin or backstrap fillets, thinly sliced

150 g (5½ oz) snake beans, cut into 3 cm (1¼ in) lengths

2 garlic cloves, crushed

1 small red chilli, finely sliced (seeded optional)

1½ tablespoons fish sauce

1½ tablespoons lime juice

1 teaspoon chilli garlic sauce

2 teaspoons grated palm sugar

1 handful mint leaves, plus extra to garnish

1 Heat a wok over high heat, add about 1 tablespoon of oil and swirl to coat. Stir-fry the lamb in batches for 2–3 minutes, or until browned. Make sure the wok is hot before adding each batch. Remove and set aside.

2 Heat the remaining oil in the wok, add the snake beans and stir-fry for 1 minute, then add the garlic and chilli and toss for 30 seconds. Return the lamb to the wok with the fish sauce, lime juice, chilli sauce and sugar and stir-fry for 1–2 minutes, or until the lamb is heated through and coated with the sauce.

3 Remove the pan from the heat, gently stir in the mint leaves and serve, generously garnished with extra mint leaves.

LAMB STIR-FRY WITH ORANGE AND SICHUAN PEPPER

Preparation time 20 minutes +
Total cooking time 15 minutes
Serves 3–4

2 tablespoons soy sauce
125 ml (4 fl oz/½ cup) orange juice
¼ teaspoon bicarbarbonate of soda (baking soda)
2 teaspoons cornflour (cornstarch)
2 teaspoons crushed sichuan peppercorns
3 tablespoons peanut oil
350 g (12 oz) lamb fillet, thinly sliced
5 cm (2 in) piece fresh ginger, julienned
4 star anise
2 garlic cloves, crushed
10 thin spring onions (scallions), cut into 2.5 cm
    (1 in) lengths
200 g (7 oz) snowpeas (mangetout), trimmed and
    cut on the diagonal
2 small red chillies, finely sliced
2 tablespoons oyster sauce
2 tablespoons Chinese rice wine
½ teaspoon sugar

Coconut rice
200 ml (7 fl oz) coconut cream
200 g (7 oz/1 cup) basmati rice

1 Put the soy sauce, orange juice, bicarbonate of soda, cornflour, peppercorns and 1 tablespoon of oil in a bowl, add the lamb and marinate in the refrigerator for 30 minutes. Drain, reserving the marinade.

2 While the lamb is marinating, prepare the coconut rice. Mix the coconut cream with 200 ml (7 fl oz) of water and 1 teaspoon of salt in a large saucepan. Stir the rice, bring to the boil over high heat, then reduce the heat and simmer for 10 minutes.

3 Heat a wok over high heat, add about 1 tablespoon of oil and stir-fry the lamb in batches for 1–2 minutes, or until just seared.

4 Heat the remaining oil, add the ginger, star anise, garlic, spring onion, snowpeas and chilli and stir-fry for 30 seconds. Return the lamb to the wok with the marinade and the combined oyster sauce, rice wine and sugar. Stir-fry for 1 minute, then serve with the coconut rice.

SATAY LAMB

Preparation time 10 minutes

Total cooking time 15 minutes

Serves 4

3 tablespoons peanut oil

750 g (1 lb 10 oz) lamb loin fillets, thinly sliced across the grain

2 teaspoons ground cumin

1 teaspoon ground turmeric

1 red pepper (capsicum), sliced

3 tablespoons sweet chilli sauce

60 g (2¼ oz/¼ cup) crunchy peanut butter

250 ml (9 fl oz/1 cup) coconut milk

2 teaspoons soft brown sugar

1–2 tablespoons lemon juice, to taste

4 tablespoons chopped coriander (cilantro) leaves

40 g (1½ oz/¼ cup) unsalted peanuts, roasted, chopped, to serve

1 Heat a wok over high heat, add about 1 tablespoon oil and swirl. Add half the lamb and stir-fry for 3 minutes, or until browned. Remove. Repeat with 1 tablespoon oil and the remaining lamb.

2 Reheat the wok, add the remaining oil and cumin, turmeric and pepper, and stir-fry for 2 minutes, or until the pepper is tender.

3 Return the lamb to the wok. Stir in the chilli sauce, peanut butter, coconut milk and sugar. Bring to the boil, then reduce the heat and simmer for 5 minutes, or until the meat is tender. Remove from the heat and add the lemon juice. Stir in the coriander and sprinkle with the peanuts. Serve.

STICKY TAMARIND LAMB

Preparation time 10 minutes
Total cooking time 12 minutes
Serves 2

2 tablespoons lime juice
1 tablespoon tamarind concentrate
1 tablespoon fish sauce
2 tablespoons peanut oil
500 g (1 lb 2 oz) lean lamb sirloin or backstrap
    fillets, thinly sliced
150 g (5½ oz) sugar snap peas, trimmed
3 red Asian shallots, finely chopped
2 garlic cloves, crushed
2 tablespoons toasted unsalted peanuts, crushed

1 Combine the lime juice, tamarind concentrate and fish sauce in a small non-metallic bowl or jug.

2 Heat a non-stick wok over high heat, add 1 tablespoon of oil and swirl to coat. Stir-fry the lamb in batches for 2–3 minutes, or until well browned. Make sure the wok is hot before adding each batch. Remove and keep warm.

3 Heat the remaining oil in the wok, then quickly stir-fry the sugar snap peas over a high heat for about 1 minute, or until just tender. Remove from the wok.

4 Add the shallots and garlic to the wok and stir-fry for 30 seconds, or until fragrant. Add tamarind mixture, bring it to the boil and simmer for 2–3 minutes, or until reduced to a thick, sticky syrup.

5 Return the lamb and sugar snap peas to the wok and toss to coat well with the sauce. Serve immediately garnished with the crushed peanuts.

LAMB FILLET WITH PEA SAUCE

Preparation time 10 minutes

Total cooking time 10 minutes

Serves 4

2 tablespoons canola oil

800 g (1 lb 12 oz) lamb fillets

1 garlic clove, peeled and slivered

Pea sauce

155 g (5½ oz/1 cup) frozen peas

1 large handful parsley, chopped

3 spring onions (scallions), chopped

3 tablespoons pear juice

¼ teaspoon citric acid

3 tablespoons chicken stock

1 Preheat the oven to 350°F (180°C/Gas 4). Heat the oil in a roasting pan. Add the lamb fillets and garlic to the roasting pan. Bake for 8–10 minutes for medium or about 12–15 minutes for well done, or until cooked to your liking.

2 Meanwhile, make the pea sauce. Bring a small saucepan of water to a boil. Add the peas, parsley and scallions and cook for about 2 minutes, or until the peas have turned a bright green and are tender. Drain well, reserving about 4 tablespoons of the cooking liquid.

3 Purée the peas, reserved liquid, pear juice, citric acid and stock in a food processor or blender. Return the purée to the saucepan and heat over low heat until the sauce is heated through.

3 Remove the lamb from the oven. Slice the lamb and arrange on four serving plates. Spoon the pea sauce to the side. If desired, serve with roasted potatoes on the side.

GREEK-STYLE LAMB

Preparation time 10 minutes

Total cooking time 10 minutes

Serves 4

400 g (14 oz) lean lamb fillets

olive oil spray

1 teaspoon olive oil

1 large red onion, sliced

3 zucchini (courgettes), thinly sliced

200 g (7 oz) cherry tomatoes, halved

3 garlic cloves, crushed

60 g (2¼ oz/½ cup) pitted black olives in brine,
    drained and cut in half

2 tablespoons lemon juice

2 tablespoons finely chopped oregano

100 g (3½ oz) low-fat feta cheese, crumbled

50 g (1¾ oz/⅓ cup) pine nuts, lightly toasted

4 wholegrain bread rolls or stone-ground
    wholemeal pitta bread pockets, warmed

1 Trim the lamb, then cut across the grain into thin strips. Heat a large frying pan until hot and spray with the oil. Add the lamb in small batches and cook each batch over high heat for 1–2 minutes, or until browned. Remove all the lamb from the pan.

2 Heat the oil in the pan, then add the onion and zucchini. Cook, stirring, over high heat for 2 minutes, or until just tender. Add the cherry tomatoes and garlic. Cook for 1–2 minutes, or until the tomatoes have just softened. Return the meat to the pan and stir over high heat until heated through.

3 Remove the pan from the heat. Add the olives, lemon juice and oregano and toss until well combined.

4 Sprinkle with crumbled feta cheese and pine nuts before serving. Serve with the bread rolls or pitta bread pockets and a mixed green salad, if desired.

MONGOLIAN LAMB

Preparation time 10 minutes

Total cooking time 15 minutes

Serves 4–6

2 garlic cloves, crushed

2 teaspoons finely grated fresh ginger

3 tablespoons Chinese rice wine

3 tablespoons soy sauce

2 tablespoons hoisin sauce

1 teaspoon sesame oil

1 kg (2 lb 4 oz) lamb loin fillets, thinly sliced across the grain

4 tablespoons peanut oil

6 spring onions (scallions), cut into 3 cm (1¼ in) lengths

2 teaspoons chilli sauce

1½ tablespoons hoisin sauce, extra

1 Combine the garlic, ginger, Chinese rice wine, soy sauce, hoisin sauce and sesame oil in a large non-metallic bowl. Add the lamb and toss until well coated. Cover with plastic wrap and marinate in the refrigerator overnight, tossing occasionally.

2 Heat a wok over high heat, add about 1 tablespoon of the peanut oil and swirl to coat the wok. Add the spring onion and stir-fry for 1 minute, or until lightly golden. Remove, reserving the oil in the wok.

3 Lift the lamb out of the marinade with tongs, reserving the marinade. Add the meat in four batches and stir-fry for about 1–2 minutes per batch, or until browned but not completely cooked through, adding more oil and making sure the wok is very hot before cooking each batch. Return all the meat and any juices to the wok with the spring onion and stir-fry for 1 minute, or until meat is cooked through.

4 Remove the meat and spring onion from the wok with a slotted spoon and place in a serving bowl, retaining the liquid in the wok. Add any reserved marinade to the wok along with the chilli sauce and extra hoisin sauce, then boil for 3–4 minutes, or until the sauce thickens and becomes slightly syrupy. Spoon the sauce over the lamb, toss together well, then serve with steamed rice.

MALAYSIAN LAMB SKEWERS

Preparation time 30 minutes +
Total cooking time 10 minutes
Makes 8

500 g (1 lb 2 oz) lamb fillets
1 onion, roughly chopped
2 garlic cloves, crushed
2 cm (¾ in) piece lemongrass, white part only,
    roughly chopped
2 slices fresh galangal
1 teaspoon chopped fresh ginger
1 teaspoon ground cumin
½ teaspoon ground fennel
1 tablespoon ground coriander
1 teaspoon ground turmeric
1 tablespoon soft brown sugar
1 tablespoon lemon juice

1 If using wooden skewers, you will need to soak them in water for about 30 minutes to make sure they don't burn during the cooking process.

2 Trim any fat or sinew from the lamb fillets. Slice the meat across the grain into very thin strips. (If you have time, leave the meat in the freezer for 30 minutes, as this will make it easier to thinly slice.)

3 In a food processor, combine the onion, garlic, lemongrass, galangal, ginger, cumin, fennel, coriander, turmeric, brown sugar and lemon juice and process until a smooth paste is formed.

4 Transfer the paste to a shallow non-metallic dish and add the lamb, stirring to coat thoroughly. Cover and refrigerate for at least 30 minutes.

5 Thread the meat onto the skewers. Heat a little oil on a barbecue hotplate and cook the skewers for 3–4 minutes each side, or until cooked. Brush regularly with the remaining marinade while cooking.

SHISH KEBABS WITH CAPSICUM AND HERBS

Preparation time 20 minutes +
Total cooking time 5 minutes
Serves 4

1 kg (2 lb 4 oz) boneless leg of lamb
1 red capsicum (pepper)
1 green capsicum (pepper)
3 red onions
olive oil, for brushing

Marinade
1 onion, thinly sliced
2 garlic cloves, crushed
3 tablespoons lemon juice
4 tablespoons olive oil
1 tablespoon chopped thyme
1 tablespoon paprika
½ teaspoon chilli flakes
2 teaspoons ground cumin
20 g (¾ oz) chopped mint
15 g (½ oz) chopped flat-leaf (Italian) parsley

1 If using wooden skewers, soak them for about 30 minutes to prevent them from burning during cooking.

2 Trim the sinew and most of the fat from the lamb and cut the meat into 3 cm (1¼ in) cubes. Mix all the ingredients for the marinade in a large bowl. Season well, add the meat and mix well. Cover and refrigerate for 4–6 hours, or overnight.

3 Remove the seeds and membrane from the capsicums and cut the flesh into 3 cm (1¼ in) squares. Cut each red onion into six wedges. Preheat a barbecue flatplate to medium.

4 Remove the lamb from the marinade and reserve the liquid. Thread the meat onto the skewers, alternating with onion and capsicum pieces. Cook the skewers on a barbecue flatplate for 5–6 minutes, brushing with the marinade. Serve immediately with rice.

SOUVLAKI

Preparation time 20 minutes +
Total cooking time 10 minutes
Serves 4

1 kg (2 lb 4 oz) boned leg of lamb, trimmed and
    cut into 2 cm (¾ in) cubes
3 tablespoons olive oil
2 teaspoons finely grated lemon zest
4 tablespoons lemon juice
125 ml (4 fl oz/½ cup) dry white wine
2 teaspoons dried oregano
2 large garlic cloves, finely chopped
2 bay leaves
250 g (9 oz/1 cup) Greek-style yoghurt
2 garlic cloves, extra, crushed

1 If using wooden skewers, soak them for about 30 minutes to prevent them from burning during cooking.
2 Put the lamb in a non-metallic bowl with 2 tablespoons of the oil, the lemon zest and juice, wine, oregano, garlic, bay leaves and some black pepper. Toss, then cover and refrigerate overnight.
2 Put the yoghurt and extra garlic in a bowl, mix well and leave for 30 minutes.
3 Drain the lamb. Thread onto eight skewers and cook on a barbecue or chargrill plate, brushing with the remaining oil, for about 7–8 minutes, or until cooked to your liking. Serve with the yoghurt, some bread and a salad.

WARM LAMB AND SNOWPEA SALAD

Preparation time 30 minutes +
Total cooking time 15 minutes
Serves 4–6

2 tablespoons red curry paste
3 tablespoons chopped coriander (cilantro) leaves
1 tablespoon finely grated fresh ginger
1 tablespoon peanut oil
750 g (1 lb 10 oz) lamb loin fillets, thinly sliced
200 g (7 oz) snowpeas (mangetout), trimmed
600 g (1 lb 5 oz) thick fresh rice noodles
canola or olive oil spray
1 red capsicum (pepper), thinly sliced
1 Lebanese (short) cucumber, thinly sliced
6 spring onions (scallions), thinly sliced

Dressing
1 tablespoon peanut oil
3 tablespoons lime juice
2 teaspoons soft brown sugar
3 teaspoons fish sauce
3 teaspoons soy sauce
4 tablespoons chopped mint leaves
1 garlic clove, crushed

1 Combine the curry paste, coriander, ginger and oil in a bowl. Add the lamb and coat well. Cover and refrigerate for 2–3 hours.
2 Steam or boil the snowpeas until just tender, then refresh under cold water and drain.
3 Put the noodles in a large heatproof bowl, cover with boiling water and soak for 8 minutes, or until softened. Separate gently and drain.
4 To make the dressing, combine all the ingredients in a small bowl and whisk until well blended.
5 Heat a wok until very hot. Spray with the oil. Add half the lamb and stir-fry for 5 minutes, or until tender. Repeat with the remaining lamb.
6 Put the lamb, snowpeas, noodles, capsicum, cucumber and spring onion in a large bowl, drizzle with the dressing and toss together before serving.

LAMB KEBABS

Preparation time 15 minutes +
Total cooking time 20 minutes
Serves 4

750 g (1 lb 10 oz) boneless lamb from leg
1 onion, grated
1 teaspoon paprika
1 teaspoon ground cumin
2 tablespoons finely chopped flat-leaf (Italian)
   parsley
3 tablespoons olive oil
1 round of Moroccan bread or pitta breads, to
   serve

Harissa and tomato sauce
2 tomatoes
½ onion, grated
1 tablespoon olive oil
1 teaspoon harissa, or to taste, or ¼ teaspoon
   cayenne pepper
½ teaspoon sugar

1 Soak eight bamboo skewers in water for
2 hours, or use metal skewers.
2 Do not trim the fat from the lamb. Cut
the meat into 3 cm (1¼ in) cubes and put
in a bowl. Add the onion, paprika, cumin,
parsley, olive oil and a generous grind of

black pepper. Toss well to coat the lamb with
the marinade, then cover and leave in the
refrigerator to marinate for at least 2 hours.
3 To make the harissa and tomato sauce,
halve the tomatoes crossways and squeeze
out the seeds. Coarsely grate the tomatoes
into a bowl down to the skin, discarding
the skin. In a saucepan, cook the onion in
the olive oil for 2 minutes, stir in the harissa
or cayenne pepper, and add the grated
tomatoes, sugar and ½ teaspoon salt. Cover
and simmer for 10 minutes, then remove
the lid and simmer for a further 4 minutes,
or until the sauce reaches a thick, pouring
consistency. Transfer to a bowl.
4 Thread the lamb cubes onto the skewers,
leaving a little space between the meat cubes.
Heat the barbecue grill to high and cook for
5–6 minutes, turning and brushing with the
marinade. Alternatively, cook in a chargrill
pan or under the grill (broiler).
5 If serving the kebabs with Moroccan bread,
cut the bread into quarters and slit each piece
in half almost to the crust. Slide the meat
from the skewers into the bread pocket and
drizzle with a little of the tomato and harissa
sauce. If using pitta bread, do not split it;
just slide the lamb from the skewers onto the
centre, add the sauce and fold up the sides.

RACK OF LAMB WITH HERB CRUST

Preparation time 25 minutes
Total cooking time 25 minutes
Serves 4

2 x 6–rib racks of lamb, French-trimmed
1 tablespoon oil
80 g (2¾ oz/1 cup) fresh breadcrumbs
3 garlic cloves
3 tablespoons finely chopped flat-leaf
   (Italian) parsley
2 teapoons thyme leaves
½ teaspoon finely grated lemon zest
60 g (2¼ oz) butter, softened
250 ml (9 fl oz/1 cup) beef stock
1 garlic clove, extra, finely chopped
1 thyme sprig

1 Preheat the oven to 250°C (500°F/Gas 9).
Score the fat on the lamb racks in a diamond
pattern. Rub with a little oil and season.
2 Heat the oil in a frying pan over high
heat, add the lamb racks and brown for
4–5 minutes. Remove and set aside. Do
not wash the pan as you will need it later.
3 In a large bowl, mix the breadcrumbs,
garlic, parsley, thyme leaves and lemon zest.
Season, then mix in the butter to form a
smooth paste.
4 Firmly press a layer of breadcrumb mixture
over the fat on the lamb racks, leaving the
bones and base clean. Bake in a roasting tin
for 12 minutes for medium–rare. Rest the
lamb on a plate while you make the jus.
5 To make the jus, add the beef stock,
extra garlic and thyme sprig to the roasting
tin juices, scraping the pan. Return this
liquid to the original frying pan and simmer
over high heat for 5–8 minutes, or until the
sauce has reduced. Strain and serve with
the lamb.

COCONUT-CRUSTED LAMB CUTLETS

Preparation time 10 minutes +
Total cooking time 20 minutes
Makes 24

24 thin, lean lamb cutlets
1 large onion, grated
2 garlic cloves, crushed
2 teaspoons ground turmeric
1 tablespoon soft brown sugar
60 g (2¼ oz) desiccated coconut
2 teaspoons soy sauce
2 tablespoons lemon juice

1 Trim the lamb cutlets of excess fat and sinew. Combine all the remaining ingredients in a non-metallic bowl with 1 teaspoon salt and ½ teaspoon pepper. Stir until the coconut is thoroughly moistened.
2 Add the lamb cutlets to the bowl and press the coconut mixture onto the surface of each cutlet. Cover with plastic wrap and refrigerate for 2 hours.
3 Preheat a grill (broiler) and lightly oil the grill tray. Working in batches if necessary, cook the cutlets for 3–5 minutes on each side, or until crisp and golden brown. Serve with a green salad, if you like.

BEEF

Beef is one of the most popular meats in the world. It can be cooked in so many different ways, using a wide range of flavours, yet is also a favourite on its own. And if you follow a few simple rules when cooking with beef, you'll get great results every time.

BEEF BASICS

Beef refers to the meat of cattle such as heifers, cows, bullocks and bulls that have been raised and fattened for meat production. The quality of the beef varies according to breed, diet and farming technique.

Specialist beef, such as organic, grass-fed or Shimotun beef from Kobe in Japan (reared on beer and grains and massaged daily) produce higher-quality meat than mass-produced beef reared on grain. Often beef is hung for 2–3 weeks to allow it to mature in flavour and become more tender (in countries such as in South America, beef is eaten freshly killed). Prime cuts of beef are more expensive and have been aged to improve both flavour and texture, while cuts for stewing are sold younger. Classic beef dishes include beef Wellington, boeuf bourguignonne, beef en croute, roast beef, goulash and beef Stroganoff.

BUYING

A beef carcass is divided into sections from which numerous cuts are made (the names of these cuts vary from country to country). Choose cuts of meat that will suit your recipe and the cooking method. Don't buy expensive cuts of meat if you are going to use the meat in a stew or casserole: a less-expensive cut of meat will suffice.

Buy dark-red, moist meat with creamy white fat (bright red meat usually indicates that it has not been aged sufficiently).

Because of limited storage space, meat bought from the butcher will rarely have been hung for more than 1 week. If you intend buying a joint, if possible, order it ahead and ask the butcher to hang it for you.

STORAGE

Wipe any blood off the beef, put it on a plate, cover with plastic wrap and store in the fridge. Put larger cuts on a rack on a plate to allow the juices to escape. Keep raw meat away from cooked to stop cross contamination. To ensure beef cooks evenly, remove from fridge half an hour before use.

Oil small cuts of meat before storing to help stop the meat oxidizing.

Freeze beef either vacuum-packed or well wrapped in freezer wrap. It will keep for up to 1 year.

CUTS OF MEAT

Front cuts Cuts from the front contain the muscles that do the most work and are the toughest. Therefore, they need long, slow cooking (pot roasting, braising or stewing). Cuts include neck, clod, chuck, blade and shin.

Centre cuts Cuts from the top and centre are tender and can be cooked quickly (roasting, grilling or frying). Cuts include fore rib, wing rib, sirloin, fillet and rump. Cuts from the underside, like brisket and skirt, need long, slow cooking

Back cuts The back of the animal falls in between the first two cuts and needs a reasonably long cooking time (casseroling, braising or pot roasting). Cuts include topside, silverside and shin.

COOKING

Roasting Choose joints from the back, ribs, fillet or sirloin for roasting. Meat should be well marbled with fat and slightly larger than needed, as it will shrink slightly when cooked. A covering of fat will baste the meat well as you cook it. Beef cooked on the bone cooks faster than a rolled joint and the bones also add extra flavour. If you ask your butcher to chine (loosen the backbone from the ribs) your joint, it will be easier to carve it when cooked. Season and sear the joint before cooking.

To roast beef on the bone to medium, allow 20 minutes cooking per 500 g (1 lb 2 oz) plus 20 minutes; for beef off the bone, 25 minutes per 500 g (1 lb 2 oz) plus 25 minutes. Cook at 200°C (400°F/Gas 6) or start your roasting at 240°C (475°F/Gas 8) for 15 minutes, then reduce the temperature to 180°C (350°F/Gas 4) for the remaining time. When cooking is complete, rest for 15 minutes.

SLOW COOKING

Less expensive or tougher cuts of meat can benefit greatly from slowly cooking in liquid on a low temperature as the connective tissue melts, tenderizing the meat. Dishes such as boeuf bourguignonne and Hungarian goulash are slow-cooked to produce a rich, tender meat.

Methods of slow cooking include pot-roasting, braising, casseroling and stewing. Use a heavy ovenproof dish that comfortably holds the meat. Stews are traditionally cooked on the stovetop; casseroles on either the stovetop or in the oven. Pot-roasting is useful when cooking less tender cuts such as topside, silverside and top rump. Braising involves less liquid than casseroling or stewing and the meat is left whole. It is done in the oven in a dish with an airtight seal made by putting a piece of greaseproof paper between the lid and dish.

VEAL BASICS

The meat from unweaned or recently weaned male calves. The delicately flavoured flesh is finely grained, light pink to white with little marbling and fat. Traditionally veal is an expensive meat and the idea of killing an animal when it had not reached its full meat-producing potential is a luxury not available to many. Veal is used extensively in European cuisines, often as part of a dish along with other ingredients, in blanquette de veau or veal paupiettes (pieces of veal wrapped around a filling) for example. Veal is usually sold as escalopes; as roasting joints like leg and loin for use in braised dishes such as osso buco; and as chops. Common accompaniments include prosciutto or bacon and cheeses, which are melted on the meat, or sauces made with fortified wines such as Marsala and Madeira. Veal bones make very gelatinous stock.

Veal goes with — anchovies, capers, lemon, sage, sour cream, spinach, tomato

WHITE OR PINK VEAL?

Calves on a milk diet, and that have their movement restricted have firm white flesh. Slightly older animals, sometimes grain or grass fed and reared in a more open environment, have pink meat.

COOKING

To prepare an escalope, cut the meat from a piece of leg, best end or loin into thin slices across the grain of the meat. Lay a slice flat on a chopping board, bring a mallet down flat on the meat, then in one continuous motion, slide the mallet from the centre outwards. Repeat several times. Use the mallet to evenly stretch and thin out the meat rather than pounding it.

Because of the lack of fat and marbling, veal should be cooked quickly, usually pan-fried with butter or olive oil, or slow cooked with liquid to prevent it from drying out.

Joints of veal may need to be larded or barded to help moisten the meat as it cooks.

CUTS OF VEAL

Escalopes Also known as schnitzel, scaloppine and collop, a thin piece usually cut from the loin, leg or best end. Usually pan-fried, crumbed or stuffed and rolled.
Leg and shin Used for roasting, either stuffed or on the bone. Veal shin (osso buco) is sliced and used for stews like osso buco.
Shoulder Used for roasting and stuffing or diced.
Loin Used as a loin roast, cut into chops or sold as a piece of fillet. Slices of fillet are medallions.
Breast The belly of the calf, which is usually rolled and slow cooked or roasted.
Best end The ribs, sold as individual rib chops or may be joined as one piece. With the bones removed used for escalopes.

STEAK BASICS

A cut of meat, usually beef, but it can also refer to lamb, veal and fish. Cuts of steak vary from country to country, depending on the way the carcass is jointed.

The most tender meat comes from the least exercised parts of the animal—from the hind quarter to the loin. Tenderness and optimum taste of the steak depend on age and breed, feed (grain or pasture), how the animal is handled during slaughtering and whether it has been aged or hung to make it more tender.

In Britain, steak is usually named by the joint from which it is cut; in the United States, steaks are larger; French and Italian cuts also vary. The main steak cuts are from the fillet, also called tenderloin or undercut, which is tender rather than flavourful; sirloin, which has a superb flavour; and rump, for many, the best flavour of all.

BUYING

Choose steaks with a bright red colour, flecked through with tiny streaks of white intramuscular fat. The flesh should be firm and upstanding, and the selvage fat (on the edge of the steak) should be crisp and waxy, flaking on the outside, but firm enough so that it would carve easily into pieces.

COOKING

These cooking times apply to a steak that is about 2.5 cm (1 in) thick (its weight is irrelevant to the cooking time), has been brought to room temperature before cooking and is pan-fried in a heavy-based pan. If you want to grill your steaks, they will take about a minute longer.

For a blue steak, cook for 1–2 minutes per side. The steak will feel fleshy and soft when pressed. For a rare steak, cook for 2–3 minutes per side. The steak will spring back a little when pressed.

For a medium steak, cook for 3–4 minutes per side. The steak will spring back when pressed.

For well-done, cook for 4–5 minutes per side. The steak will feel very firm when pressed.

TYPES OF STEAK

Different steaks can be known by various names depending on what country you are from. We've listed the more commonly known types.

Châteaubriand A thick steak cut from the centre of the fillet. Serves two people.

Tournedos The tender 'eye' or centre of the fillet steak cut into small rounds.

Mignon A small round steak cut from the thin end of the fillet, sometimes called **filet mignon**.

Entrecôte Cut from between the ribs. It is boneless and thin with a marbling of fat. It is also known as **rib steak** and in America is served as **Delmonico** or **Spencer steak**, which is the eye of the rib.

Sirloin A boneless steak from the sirloin, which can be cut short or long. In America, this is not always boneless, depending on which part of the sirloin it is cut from. In Australia, a boneless sirloin with the fat removed is a **New York steak**.

Porterhouse A steak from the sirloin and the tenderloin separated by a bone. Often cut very thick (5 cm/2 in) and served for two people.

T-bone Cut across the sirloin and includes a piece of fillet.

Club steak (USA) A cut from the thin end of the loin, which includes no fillet.

New York (USA) A strip of steak cut from the loin when the fillet has been removed.

Rump A large steak from the top of the rump.

Minute A thin steak (sometimes called a **frying steak**) that has been tenderized so it cooks quickly — in a minute.

TRIMMING BEEF FILLET

Step 1 Try to buy a piece of beef fillet of even thickness. Using a small sharp knife, trim off any fat.

Step 2 Trim off any membrane by sliding the blade of your knife underneath while pulling the membrane taut. Neaten any straggly pieces.

Step 3 If your fillet is uneven along its length it won't cook at the same rate. Fold the thinner end back under the thicker end to make it an even thickness all the way along. If you are roasting it, tie it all the way along with kitchen string.

TESTING MEAT FOR DONENESS

Step 1 Steak can be tested for doneness by pressing it with your finger and then comparing the tenderness with the feel of the flesh at the base of your thumb.

Step 2 When meat is rare, it still feels very tender, much the same as the flesh at the base of your thumb when it is relaxed. When well cooked, it feels much firmer, like the base of your thumb if you press your thumb and little finger together.

Step 3 For large joints of meat you will have to use a meat thermometer or push a skewer into the meat. Leave the skewer there for 5 seconds, then pull it out and touch it carefully to the inside of your wrist or your lip — it should feel extremely hot when the meat is cooked through.

BARBECUED STEAK WITH CARAMELISED BALSAMIC ONIONS AND MUSTARD

Preparation time 15 minutes
Total cooking time 25 minutes
Serves 4

1½ tablespoons wholegrain mustard
200 g (7 oz) crème fraîche
2 capsicums (peppers), 1 red and 1 yellow,
    seeded and quartered
2 zucchini (courgettes), trimmed and sliced
    lengthways into strips
2 tablespoons oil
2 large red onions, thinly sliced
4 rump steaks (about 200 g/7 oz each)
2 tablespoons soft brown sugar
3 tablespoons balsamic vinegar

1 Heat a barbecue hotplate or large chargrill pan to hot. Combine the mustard and crème fraîche in a small bowl. Season. Cover and set aside.

2 Brush the capsicum and zucchini with 1 tablespoon oil. Cook the capsicum, turning regularly, for 5 minutes, or until tender and slightly charred. Remove and cover with foil. Repeat with the zucchini, cooking for 5 minutes.

3 Heat the remaining oil on the hotplate, then cook the onion, turning occasionally, for 5–10 minutes, or until softened. When nearly soft, push to the side of the hotplate, then add the steaks and cook on each side for 3–4 minutes (medium-rare), or until cooked to your liking. Remove the steaks, cover with foil and allow to rest.

4 Spread the onion over the hotplate once again, reduce the heat, sprinkle with sugar and cook for 1–2 minutes, or until the sugar has dissolved. Add the vinegar, stirring continuously for 1–2 minutes, or until it is absorbed. Remove at once.

5 Peel the capsicum, then divide among serving plates with the zucchini. Place the steaks on top, season and top with the balsamic onions. Serve with the mustard crème fraîche and a salad.

ROSEMARY AND RED WINE STEAKS WITH BARBECUED VEGETABLES

Preparation time 15 minutes

Total cooking time 30 minutes

Serves 4

12 small new potatoes

3 tablespoons olive oil

1 tablespoon finely chopped fresh rosemary

6 garlic cloves, sliced

sea salt flakes, to season

4 large, thick field mushrooms

12 asparagus spears

250 ml (9 fl oz/1 cup) red wine

4 scotch fillet steaks (about 260 g/9 oz each)

1 Heat a barbecue plate or chargrill pan to hot. Toss the potatoes with 1 tablespoon of the oil, half the rosemary and half the garlic and season with the sea salt flakes. Divide the potatoes among four large sheets of foil and wrap into neat packages, sealing firmly around the edges. Cook on the barbecue, turning frequently for 30 minutes, or until tender.

2 Meanwhile, brush the mushrooms and asparagus with a little of the remaining oil and set aside.

3 Combine the red wine with the remaining oil, rosemary and garlic in a non-metallic dish. Season with lots of freshly ground black pepper. Add the steaks and coat in the marinade. Allow to marinate for 25 minutes, then drain.

4 Cook the steaks and mushrooms on the barbecue for 4 minutes each side, or until cooked to your liking (this will depend on the thickness of the steak). Transfer the steaks and mushrooms to a plate, cover lightly and allow to rest. Add the asparagus to the barbecue, turning regularly for about 2 minutes, or until tender. Pierce the potatoes with a skewer to check for doneness. Season with salt and pepper. Serve the steaks with the vegetables.

CHINESE BEEF AND ASPARAGUS WITH OYSTER SAUCE

Preparation time 10 minutes +
Total cooking time 10 minutes
Serves 4

500 g (1 lb 2 oz) lean beef fillet, thinly sliced
   across the grain
1 tablespoon light soy sauce
½ teaspoon sesame oil
1 tablespoon Chinese rice wine
2½ tablespoons vegetable oil
200 g (7 oz) fresh thin asparagus, cut into thirds
   on the diagonal
3 garlic cloves, crushed
2 teaspoons julienned fresh ginger
3 tablespoons chicken stock
2–3 tablespoons oyster sauce

1 Place the beef slices in a non-metallic bowl with the soy sauce, sesame oil and 2 teaspoons of the rice wine. Cover and marinate for at least 15 minutes.
2 Heat a wok over high heat, add about 1 tablespoon of the vegetable oil and swirl to coat the side of the wok. When the oil is hot but not smoking, add the asparagus and stir-fry for 1–2 minutes. Remove from the wok.
3 Add another tablespoon of oil to the wok and, when hot, add the beef in two batches, stir-frying each batch for 1–2 minutes, or until cooked. Remove the meat from the wok.
4 Add the remaining oil to the wok and, when hot, add the garlic and ginger and stir-fry for 1 minute, or until fragrant. Pour the stock, oyster sauce and remaining rice wine into the wok, bring to the boil and boil rapidly for 1–2 minutes, or until the sauce is slightly reduced. Return the beef and asparagus to the wok and stir-fry for a further minute, or until heated through and coated in the sauce. Serve with steamed rice.

BEEF AND BAMBOO SHOOTS

Preparation time 10 minutes

Total cooking time 10 minutes

Serves 4

3 tablespoons oil

400 g (14 oz) rump steak, thinly sliced across
the grain

225 g (8 oz) tinned sliced bamboo shoots, drained
and rinsed

3 garlic cloves, crushed with about
¼ teaspoon salt

2 tablespoons fish sauce

8 spring onions (scallions), cut into 4 cm (1½ in)
lengths on the diagonal

40 g (1½ oz/¼ cup) sesame seeds, toasted

1 Heat a wok over high heat, add about
2 tablespoons of the oil and swirl. When the
oil is hot, add the beef in two batches and
stir-fry for 1 minute, or until it starts to turn
pink. Remove and set aside.

2 Add an extra tablespoon of oil if necessary,
then stir-fry the bamboo shoots for about
3 minutes, or until starting to brown. Add
the garlic, fish sauce and ¼ teaspoon salt and
stir-fry for 2–3 minutes. Add the spring
onion and stir-fry for 1 minute, or until
starting to wilt.

3 Return the beef to the wok, stir quickly
and cook for 1 minute until heated through.
Remove from the heat, toss with the sesame
seeds and serve with rice.

THAI BEEF SKEWERS WITH PEANUT SAUCE

Preparation time 10 minutes
Total cooking time 15 minutes
Serves 4

1 onion, chopped
2 garlic cloves, crushed
2 teaspoons sambal oelek
1 lemongrass stem, white part only, chopped
2 teaspoons chopped fresh ginger
1½ tablespoons oil
270 ml (9½ fl oz) coconut cream
125 g (4½ oz/½ cup) crunchy peanut butter
1½ tablespoons fish sauce
2 teaspoons soy sauce
1 tablespoon grated palm sugar or soft brown
    sugar
2 tablespoons lime juice
2 tablespoons chopped coriander (cilantro) leaves
750 g (1 lb 10 oz) round or rump steak, cut into
    2 cm x 10 cm (¾ x 4 in) pieces
2 teaspoons oil, extra

fresh red chilli, chopped, to garnish (optional)
chopped roasted peanuts, to garnish (optional)

1 Put the onion, garlic, sambal oelek, lemongrass and ginger in a food processor and process to a smooth paste.
2 Heat the oil in a saucepan over medium heat, add the paste and cook, stirring, for 2–3 minutes, or until fragrant. Add the coconut cream, peanut butter, fish sauce, soy sauce, sugar and lime juice and bring to the boil. Reduce the heat and simmer for 5 minutes, then stir in the coriander.
3 Meanwhile, thread the meat onto 12 metal skewers, and cook on a hot chargrill or in a non-stick frying pan with the extra oil for 2 minutes each side, or until cooked to your liking. Serve the skewers on a bed of rice with the sauce and a salad on the side. Garnish with chopped chilli and peanuts,.
Note If using wooden skewers, soak them for 30 minutes before grilling to prevent them from burning.

LEMONGRASS BEEF

Preparation time 10 minutes +
Total cooking time 22 minutes
Serves 4

300 g (10½ oz/1½ cups) long-grain rice
3 garlic cloves, finely chopped
1 tablespoon grated fresh ginger
4 lemongrass stems (white part only), finely
    chopped
2½ tablespoons oil
600 g (1 lb 5 oz) lean rump steak, trimmed and
    sliced thinly across the grain
1 tablespoon lime juice
1–2 tablespoons fish sauce
2 tablespoons kecap manis
1 large red onion, cut into small wedges
200 g (7 oz) green beans, sliced on the diagonal
    into 5 cm (2 in) lengths

1 Bring a large saucepan of water to the boil. Add the rice and cook for 12 minutes, stirring occasionally. Drain well.
2 Meanwhile, combine the garlic, ginger, lemongrass and 2 teaspoons of the oil in a non-metallic bowl. Add the beef, then marinate for 10 minutes. Combine the lime juice, fish sauce and kecap manis.
3 Heat a wok until very hot, add about 1 tablespoon oil and swirl to coat. Stir-fry the beef in batches for 2–3 minutes, or until browned. Remove from the wok.
4 Reheat the wok to very hot, heat the remaining oil, then add the onion and stir-fry for 2 minutes. Add the beans and cook for another 2 minutes, then return the beef to the wok. Pour in the fish sauce mixture and cook until heated through. Serve with the rice.

FRIED BEEF WITH POTATO, PEAS AND GINGER

Preparation time 15 minutes
Total cooking time 20 minutes
Serves 4

oil, for deep-frying
1 potato, cut into small cubes
2.5 cm (1 in) piece of ginger
500 g (1 lb 2 oz) beef rump steak, thinly sliced
3 garlic cloves, crushed
1 teaspoon ground black pepper
2 tablespoons oil, extra
2 onions, sliced in rings
3 tablespoons beef stock
2 tablespoons tomato paste (concentrated purée)
½ tablespoon soy sauce
1 teaspoon chilli powder
3 tablespoons lemon juice
3 tomatoes, chopped
50 g (⅓ cup) fresh or frozen peas

1 Fill a deep heavy-based saucepan one-third full with oil and heat to 180°C (350°F), or until a cube of bread dropped in the oil browns in 15 seconds. Deep-fry the potato cubes until golden brown. Drain on paper towels.

2 Pound the ginger using a mortar and pestle, or grate with a fine grater into a bowl. Put the ginger into a piece of muslin, twist it up tightly and squeeze out all the juice (you will need about 1 tablespoon).

3 Put the steak in a bowl, add the garlic, pepper and ginger juice and toss well. Heat the oil and fry the beef quickly in batches over high heat. Keep each batch warm as you remove it. Reduce the heat, then fry the onions until golden. Remove and set aside to keep warm.

4 Put the stock, tomato paste, soy sauce, chilli powder and lemon juice in the saucepan and cook over medium heat until reduced. Add the fried onion, cook for 3 minutes, add the chopped tomato and the peas, then stir well and cook for 1 minute. Add the beef and potato and toss well until heated through. Serve immediately.

TAMARIND BEEF, BEAN, AND HOKKIEN NOODLE STIR-FRY

Preparation time 15 minutes
Total cooking time 20 minutes
Serves 4

Tamarind sauce
1 tablespoon tamarind purée
1 tablespoon vegetable oil
1 onion, finely diced
2 tablespoons palm sugar or light brown sugar
2 tablespoons tamari

500 g (1 lb 2 oz) hokkien (egg) noodles
4 beef fillets
2 tablespoons vegetable oil
3 garlic cloves, crushed
1 small chili, seeded and diced
200 g (7 oz) baby green beans, trimmed
100 g (3½ oz) sugar snap peas, trimmed
1 tablespoon mirin
1 small handful cilantro, finely chopped

1 To make the tamarind sauce, dilute the tamarind in 250 ml (9 fl oz/1 cup) hot water. Heat the oil in a saucepan. Add the onion and cook over medium heat for 6–8 minutes or until soft and golden. Add the palm sugar and stir until dissolved. Add the tamarind liquid and tamari and simmer for 5 minutes or until thick.

2 Rinse the noodles in a colander with warm water to soften — separate with your hands. Drain well.

3 Season the steaks with salt and freshly ground black pepper. Heat half the oil in a large frying pan. Add the steaks and cook on each side for 3–4 minutes or until cooked to your liking. Remove from the pan and allow to rest in a warm place.

4 Heat the remaining oil in a wok and cook the garlic and chili over high heat for 30 seconds. Add the beans and peas and cook for 2 minutes. Stir in the mirin and cilantro. Add the noodles and toss through to heat.

5 Divide the noodles among four plates. Top with the steak and drizzle with the tamarind sauce.

SPANISH-STYLE BEEF KEBABS

Preparation time 20 minutes +
Total cooking time 5 minutes
Makes 18–20

1 kg (2 lb 4 oz) rump steak
3 garlic cloves, chopped
1 tablespoon chopped flat-leaf
   (Italian) parsley
4 tablespoons lemon juice
lemon wedges, to serve

Paprika dressing
2 teaspoons paprika
large pinch cayenne pepper
2 tablespoons red wine vinegar
4 tablespoons olive oil

1 Trim any excess fat from the beef and cut into 2 cm (¾ in) pieces. Combine the beef, garlic, parsley, lemon juice and ½ teaspoon pepper in a non-metallic bowl, cover with plastic wrap and marinate in the refrigerator for 2 hours. Meanwhile, soak 18–20 wooden skewers in water for 30 minutes to ensure they don't burn during cooking.
2 To make the paprika dressing, whisk the paprika, cayenne pepper, vinegar, oil and ½ teaspoon salt together until well blended. Heat a lightly oiled barbecue hotplate. Thread the pieces of marinated beef onto the skewers, then cook the kebabs, turning occasionally, for 4–5 minutes, or until cooked through. Drizzle with the paprika dressing and serve hot with lemon wedges.

STEAK BAGUETTE WITH ROCKET AND MUSTARDY MAYO

Preparation time 15 minutes
Total cooking time 30 minutes
Serves 4

3 tablespoons olive oil, plus extra for frying
1 red onion, sliced
1 teaspoon brown sugar
2 teaspoons balsamic vinegar
1 teaspoon thyme
1 tablespoon Dijon mustard
3 tablespoons mayonnaise
100 g (3½ oz) rocket (arugula)
500 g (1 lb 2 oz) beef fillet, cut into 4 thin slices
2 thick baguettes, cut in half, or 8 thick slices of
    good-quality bread
2 tomatoes, sliced

1 Heat 2 tablespoons oil in a small saucepan. Add the onion and cook very slowly, with the lid on, stirring occasionally, until the onion is soft but not brown. This could take up to 15 minutes. Remove the lid, add the sugar and vinegar and cook for a further 10 minutes, or until the onion is soft and just browned. Take the pan off the stove and stir in the thyme.
2 Meanwhile, make the mustardy mayo by mixing together well the mustard and mayonnaise in a small bowl.
3 Drizzle the rocket leaves with the remaining olive oil and season with salt and freshly ground black pepper.
4 Heat 1 tablespoon of the extra oil in a frying pan over high heat and cook the steaks for 2 minutes on each side, adding more oil if necessary. Season to taste.
5 To serve, put out the bread, along with separate bowls containing the onion, mustardy mayo, rocket leaves, steak and sliced tomatoes. Let everyone make their own baguette using all the ingredients.

HAMBURGERS WITH FRESH CORN RELISH

Preparation time 15 minutes
Total cooking time 15 minutes
Serves 4

700 g (1 lb 9 oz) minced (ground) beef
1 garlic clove
1½ onions, very finely chopped
2 tablespoons parsley, finely chopped
1 tablespoon tomato ketchup
¼ teaspoon Worcestershire sauce
2 corn cobs
2 tomatoes, finely chopped
1 tablespoon sweet chilli sauce
1 handful coriander (cilantro) leaves
lime juice
1 tablespoon oil
4 hamburger buns
baby cos (romaine) leaves, to serve

1 Turn on the grill (broiler). Put the beef in a bowl with the garlic, half of the onion, the parsley, tomato ketchup and the Worcestershire sauce. Season and mix well, then leave it to marinate while you make the relish.

2 Grill the corn cob on all sides until it is slightly blackened and charred around the edges. By this time it should be cooked through. Slice off the kernels by slicing down the length of the cob with a sharp knife. Mix the kernels with the tomato, chilli sauce, coriander and remaining onion. Add lime juice and salt and pepper, to taste.

3 Form the beef mixture into four large patties and flatten them out to the size of the buns (bear in mind that they will shrink as they cook).

4 Heat the oil in a frying pan and fry the beef patties for between 3 and 5 minutes on each side, depending on how well cooked you like them. While they are cooking, toast the buns.

5 Lay a lettuce leaf or two on each bun bottom, add some relish and top with a hamburger patty and the bun top. Serve any extra relish on the side.

FAJITAS

Preparation time 5 minutes +
Total cooking time 15 minutes
Serves 4

185 ml (6 fl oz/¾ cup) olive oil
2 tablespoons lime juice
4 garlic cloves, chopped
3 red chillies, chopped
2 tablespoons tequila (optional)
1 kg (2 lb 4 oz) rump steak, thinly sliced
  into strips
1 red and yellow capsicum (pepper), thinly
  sliced
1 red onion, thinly sliced
8 flour tortillas
ready-made guacamole, shredded lettuce, diced
  tomato and sour cream, to serve

1 Combine the oil, lime juice, garlic, chilli, tequila and some pepper in a large bowl. Add the meat, cover and marinate it for at least 1 hour.
2 Drain the meat and toss it with the capsicum and onion.
3 Just before serving, wrap the tortillas in foil and warm them in a 150°C (300°F/Gas 2) oven for about 5 minutes.
4 Cook the meat and vegetables in batches in a sizzling-hot heavy-based frying pan until cooked.
5 Scoop onto a large serving plate and place in the middle of the table. Serve the tortillas, guacamole, shredded lettuce, diced tomato and sour cream in separate bowls or plates at the table and let everyone assemble their own fajita.

PEPPER STEAK

Preparation time 5 minutes

Total cooking time 10 minutes

Serves 4

4 x 200 g (7 oz) fillet steaks
2 tablespoons oil
6 tablespoons black peppercorns, crushed
40 g (1½ oz) butter
3 tablespoons Cognac or brandy
125 ml (4 fl oz/½ cup) thick (double/heavy) cream
green salad, to serve

1 Rub the steaks on both sides with the oil and press the crushed peppercorns into the meat so they don't come off while you're frying. Melt the butter in a large frying pan and cook the steaks for 2–4 minutes on each side, depending on how you like your steak.

2 Add the Cognac or brandy and flambé by lighting the pan with your gas flame or a match (stand well back when you do this and keep a pan lid handy for emergencies). Lift the steaks out onto a warm plate.

3 Add the wine to the pan and boil, stirring, for 1 minute to deglaze the pan. Add the cream and stir for a couple of minutes. Season with salt and pepper and pour over the steaks. Serve with green salad.

STEAK WITH GREEN PEPPERCORN SAUCE

Preparation time 5 minutes

Total cooking time 10 minutes

Serves 4

4 x 200 g (7 oz) fillet steaks

30 g (1 oz) butter

2 teaspoons oil

250 ml (9 fl oz/1 cup) beef stock

185 ml (6 fl oz/¾ cup) whipping cream

2 teaspoons cornflour (cornstarch)

2 tablespoons green peppercorns in brine, rinsed and drained

2 tablespoons brandy

potato chips, to serve (optional)

rosemary, to garnish

1 First of all, bash the steaks with a meat mallet to 1.5 cm (⅝ in) thick. Next, nick the edges of the steaks to prevent them from curling when they are cooking.

2 Heat the butter and oil in a large heavy-based frying pan over high heat. Fry the steaks for 2–4 minutes on each side, depending on how you like your steak. Transfer to a serving plate and cover with foil.

3 Now add the stock to the pan juices and stir over low heat until boiling. Combine the cream and cornflour, then pour the mixture into the pan and stir constantly until the sauce becomes smooth and thick — a few minutes will do the trick. Add the peppercorns and brandy and boil for 1 more minute before taking the pan off the heat. Spoon the sauce over the steaks. Serve with potato chips and garnish with rosemary.

STEAK WITH MAITRE D'HOTEL BUTTER

Preparation time 5 minutes
Total cooking time 6 minutes
Serves 4

90 g (3¼ oz) unsalted butter, softened
2 teaspoons finely chopped parsley
lemon juice
4 steaks, about 1.5 cm (⅝ in) thick
1 tablespoon olive oil

1 Beat the butter to a cream in a bowl, using a wooden spoon, then beat in a pinch of salt, a pinch of pepper and the parsley. Next add about 2 teaspoons of lemon juice, a few drops at a time. Let the butter harden in the fridge a little, then form it into a log shape by rolling it up in greaseproof paper. Put it into the fridge until you need it.

2 Season the steaks with salt and pepper on both sides. Heat the oil in a large frying pan and, when it is very hot, add the steaks. Cook them for 2 minutes on each side for rare, 3 minutes on each side for medium, and 4 minutes on each side for well done. The timings may vary depending on the thickness of your steaks — if they are thin, give them a slightly shorter time and if they are thick, cook them for longer.

3 Cut the butter into slices and put a couple of slices on top of each steak. The heat of the steak will melt the butter. Serve with potatoes and vegetables or salad.

BEEF AND MOZZARELLA BURGERS WITH CHARGRILLED TOMATOES

Preparation time 10 minutes +
Total cooking time 25 minutes
Serves 4

500 g (1 lb 2 oz) minced (ground) beef
160 g (5¾ oz/2 cups) fresh breadcrumbs
1 small red onion, very finely chopped
4 garlic cloves, crushed
30 g (1 oz/½ cup) finely shredded basil leaves
50 g (1¾ oz) pitted black olives, finely
    chopped
1 tablespoon balsamic vinegar
1 egg
8 pieces mozzarella 2 cm x 3 cm x 5 mm
    (¾ x 1¼ x ¼ in)
olive oil spray

Chargrilled tomatoes
6 roma (plum) tomatoes
1½ tablespoons olive oil

1 Put the beef, breadcrumbs, onion, garlic, basil, olives, balsamic vinegar and egg in a large bowl and season well with salt and pepper. Use your hands to mix it all together, then cover and refrigerate the mixture for about 2 hours.

2 Divide the beef mixture into eight portions and roll each portion into a ball. Push a piece of mozzarella into the middle of each ball, then push the mince mixture over to cover the hole and flatten the ball to form a patty.

3 To make the chargrilled tomatoes, slice the tomatoes in half lengthways and toss them with the olive oil. Spray the flat plate with olive oil and preheat it to high direct heat. Cook the tomatoes, cut-side down, for 8 minutes then turn them over and cook for another 5 minutes or until they are soft.

4 Cook the patties on one side for 5 minutes then flip them and cook for 5 minutes or until they are cooked through and the cheese has melted. Serve the burgers and chargrilled tomatoes with a fresh green salad.

PEPPER STEAKS WITH HORSERADISH SAUCE

Preparation time 10 minutes
Total cooking time 15 minutes
Serves 4

4 sirloin steaks
3 tablespoons seasoned cracked pepper

Horseradish sauce
2 tablespoons brandy
3 tablespoons beef stock
4 tablespoons cream
1 tablespoon horseradish cream
½ teaspoon sugar

1 Coat the steaks on both sides with pepper, pressing it into the meat. Cook on a hot, lightly oiled barbecue grill or flat plate for about 5–10 minutes, until cooked to your taste.

2 To make the sauce, put the brandy and stock in a pan. Bring to the boil, then reduce the heat. Stir in the cream, horseradish and sugar and heat through. Serve immediately with the steaks.

BEEF WITH BLUE CHEESE BUTTER

Preparation time 15 minutes

Total cooking time 10 minutes

Serves 4

100 g (3½ oz) butter, softened
2 garlic cloves, crushed
100 g (3½ oz) Blue Castello cheese
2 teaspoons finely shredded sage leaves
1 kg (2 lb 4 oz) beef eye fillet (thick end), trimmed
1 tablespoon olive oil

1 To make the blue cheese butter, mash together the softened butter, garlic, cheese and sage until they are well combined. Form the mixture into a log and wrap it in baking paper, twisting the ends to seal them.

Refrigerate the butter until firm, then cut it into 5 mm (¼ in) slices and leave it at room temperature until needed.

2 Cut the beef into four thick, equal pieces and tie a piece of string around the edge of each so it will keep its shape during cooking. Brush both sides of each steak with the oil and season with freshly ground pepper. Heat a barbecue to medium–high direct heat and cook the beef on the chargrill plate for 6–7 minutes each side for medium, or to your liking.

3 Put two slices of blue cheese butter on top of each steak as soon as you remove it from the barbecue and remove the string.

Note Any leftover butter can be wrapped in baking paper and foil, and frozen for up to 2 months. It is also delicious with chicken and pork.

THAI BEEF SALAD

Preparation time 5 minutes
Total cooking time 8 minutes
Serves 4

4 tablespoons lime juice
2 tablespoons fish sauce
2 teaspoons grated palm sugar
   or soft brown sugar
1 garlic clove, crushed
1 tablespoon finely chopped coriander (cilantro)
   roots and stems
1 lemongrass stem (white part only), finely
   chopped
2 small red chillies, finely sliced
2 x 200 g (7 oz) beef eye fillet steaks
150 g (5½ oz) mixed salad leaves
½ red onion, cut into thin wedges
15 g (½ oz) coriander (cilantro) leaves

1 small handful torn mint leaves
250 g (9 oz) cherry tomatoes, halved
1 Lebanese (short) cucumber, halved lengthways
   and thinly sliced on the diagonal

1 Mix together the lime juice, fish sauce, palm sugar, garlic, chopped coriander, lemongrass and chilli until the sugar has dissolved.
2 Preheat a barbecue chargrill plate to medium–high direct heat and cook the steaks for 4 minutes on each side, or until medium. Let the steaks cool, then slice thinly across the grain.
3 Put the salad leaves, onion, coriander leaves, mint, tomatoes and cucumber in a large bowl. Add the beef and the dressing, toss them together and then serve immediately.

SESAME AND GINGER BEEF

Preparation time 10 minutes +
Total cooking time 25 minutes
Serves 4

3 tablespoons sesame oil
3 tablespoons soy sauce
2 garlic cloves, crushed
2 tablespoons grated fresh ginger
1 tablespoon lemon juice
2 tablespoons chopped spring onions
   (scallions)
60 g (2¼ oz) soft brown sugar
500 g (1 lb 2 oz) beef fillet

1 Combine the sesame oil, soy sauce, garlic, ginger, lemon juice, spring onion and brown sugar in a non-metallic dish. Add the beef and coat well with the marinade. Cover and refrigerate for at least 2 hours, or overnight if possible.

2 Brown the beef on all sides on a very hot, lightly oiled barbecue grill or flat plate. When the beef is sealed, remove, wrap in foil and return to the barbecue, turning occasionally, for a further 15–20 minutes, depending on how well done you like your meat. Leave for 10 minutes before slicing. Serve immediately.

3 Put the leftover marinade in a small saucepan and boil for 5 minutes. This is delicious served as a sauce with the beef.

FILLET STEAK WITH FLAVOURED BUTTERS

Preparation time 10 minutes

Total cooking time 15 minutes

Serves 4

4 fillet steaks

Capsicum butter

1 small red capsicum (pepper)

125 g (4½ oz) butter

2 teaspoons chopped oregano

2 teaspoons chopped chives

Garlic butter

125 g (4½ oz) butter

3 garlic cloves, crushed

2 spring onions (scallions), finely chopped

1 Cut a pocket in each steak.

2 For the capsicum butter, cut the capsicum into large pieces and place, skin-side up, under a hot grill (broiler) until the skin blisters and blackens. Put in a plastic bag until cool, then peel away the skin and dice the flesh.

3 Beat the butter until creamy. Add the capsicum, oregano and chives, season and beat until smooth.

4 For the garlic butter, beat the butter until creamy, add the garlic and spring onion and beat until smooth.

5 Push capsicum butter into the pockets in two of the steaks and garlic butter into the other two.

6 Cook on a hot, lightly oiled barbecue grill or flat plate for 4–5 minutes each side, turning once. Brush with any remaining flavoured butter while cooking. These steaks are delicious served with a green salad.

BEEF STROGANOFF

Preparation time 10 minutes

Total cooking time 15 minutes

Serves 4

400 g (14 oz) beef fillet, cut into 1 x 5 cm
  (½ x 2 in) strips
2 tablespoons plain (all-purpose) flour
50 g (1¾ oz) butter
1 onion, thinly sliced
1 garlic clove, crushed
250 g (9 oz) small Swiss brown mushrooms,
  sliced
3 tablespoons brandy
250 ml (9 fl oz/1 cup) beef stock
1½ tablespoons tomato paste (purée)
185 g (6½ oz/¾ cup) sour cream
1 tablespoon chopped flat-leaf (Italian)
  parsley

1 Dust the beef strips in flour, shaking off any excess.

2 Melt half the butter in a large frying pan and cook the meat in small batches for 1–2 minutes, or until seared all over. Remove. Add the remaining butter to the pan and cook the onion and garlic over medium heat for 2–3 minutes, or until they soften. Add the mushrooms and cook for 2–3 minutes.

3 Pour in the brandy and simmer until nearly all of the liquid has evaporated, then stir in the beef stock and tomato paste. Cook for 5 minutes to reduce the liquid slightly. Return the beef strips to the pan with any juices and stir in the sour cream. Simmer for 1 minute, or until the sauce thickens slightly. Season with salt and freshly ground black pepper. Garnish with the parsley and serve immediately with fettucine.

BEEF WITH MANDARIN

Preparation time 15 minutes +
Total cooking time 5 minutes
Serves 4

2 teaspoons soy sauce
2 teaspoons dry sherry
1 teaspoon chopped fresh ginger
1 teaspoon sesame oil
350 g (12 oz) rib eye steak, thinly sliced
1 tablespoon peanut oil
¼ teaspoon ground white pepper
2 teaspoons finely chopped dried mandarin or
　　tangerine peel
2 teaspoons soy sauce, extra
1½ teaspoons caster (superfine) sugar
1½ teaspoons cornflour (cornstarch)

4 tablespoons beef stock
steamed rice, to serve

1 Combine the soy sauce, sherry, ginger and sesame oil in a bowl. Add the beef and stir to coat in the marinade. Set aside for 15 minutes.
2 Heat the peanut oil in a wok, swirling gently to coat the base and side. Add the beef and stir-fry over high heat for 2 minutes, or until the meat changes colour. Add the white pepper, peel, extra soy sauce and sugar and stir-fry briefly.
3 Dissolve the cornflour in a little of the stock, then add to the wok. Add the remaining stock and stir until the sauce boils and thickens. Serve with steamed rice.

CORIANDER BAMBOO BEEF

Preparation time 10 minutes +
Total cooking time 10 minutes
Serves 4

6 coriander (cilantro) roots and stems
2 garlic cloves, crushed
1 tablespoon whole black peppercorns, dry
    roasted and crushed
2 tablespoons fish sauce
3 tablespoons vegetable oil
500 g (1 lb 2 oz) rump or fillet steak, thinly sliced
250 g (9 oz/1 cup) sliced bamboo shoots
2 tablespoons chopped coriander (cilantro) leaves

1 To make the marinade, combine the coriander, garlic, pepper, 1 tablespoon of the fish sauce and 1 tablespoon of the oil in a food processor and blend until a smooth paste forms. Put the beef and marinade in a non-metallic bowl, mix well, then cover and marinate in the refrigerator for 2 hours.

2 Heat a wok over high heat, add another tablespoon of oil and swirl to coat. Add the bamboo shoots and stir-fry for 1 minute, then stir in the remaining fish sauce and cook for an additional minute. Remove and set aside.

3 Heat the remaining oil, add the beef in batches and stir-fry for 3–4 minutes, or until browned. Return the bamboo shoots to the wok, then toss to combine with the beef. Remove from the heat, stir in the chopped coriander and serve immediately.

JAPANESE SAKE BEEF STIR-FRY

Preparation time 15 minutes
Total cooking time 10 minutes
Serves 4

1½ tablespoons toasted sesame seeds
600 g (1 lb 5 oz) rump steak, thinly sliced
2 garlic cloves, finely chopped
2 teaspoons grated fresh ginger
3 spring onions (scallions), finely chopped
1 teaspoon soft brown sugar
100 ml (3½ fl oz) Japanese soy sauce
a few drops of sesame oil
3 tablespoons mirin
3 tablespoons sake
1–2 tablespoons vegetable oil
4 spring onions (scallions), extra, diagonally
   shredded into 3 cm (1¼ in) pieces

1 Put 1 tablespoon of sesame seeds in a mortar and pestle and grind to a powder. Put the beef slices in a large non-metallic bowl. In a separate bowl combine the garlic, ginger, spring onion, sugar, ground sesame seeds, 1 tablespoon of the Japanese soy sauce and a few drops of sesame oil. Pour this mixture over the beef and mix gently to coat. Season with freshly ground black pepper and marinate for 2 hours in the refrigerator.
2 Drain the beef well, reserving the marinade. Add the mirin, sake and remaining Japanese soy sauce to the marinade and set aside.
3 Heat a wok over high heat, add 1 tablespoon of oil and swirl to coat. Stir-fry the beef in batches for 1 minute, or until just starting to brown. Remove and keep warm.
4 Pour the marinade into the wok, bring to the boil, then simmer for 3–4 minutes, or until reduced by half. Return the beef to the wok, stirring quickly for 1–2 minutes, or until it is heated through and well coated with the sauce. Serve, garnished with the remaining sesame seeds and shredded spring onion.

THAI BASIL, BEEF AND ASPARAGUS STIR-FRY

Preparation time 5 minutes

Total cooking time 5 minutes

Serves 4

3 tablespoons peanut oil

500 g (1 lb 2 oz) beef fillet or rump steak, thinly sliced

2 garlic cloves, crushed

1 small red chilli, finely chopped

175 g (6 oz/1 bunch) asparagus, sliced diagonally into thirds

1 large handful Thai basil leaves

1 tablespoon fish sauce

1 tablespoon oyster sauce

Thai basil leaves, extra, to garnish

1 Heat a wok over high heat, add 1 tablespoon of the oil and swirl to coat. Stir-fry the beef in batches for 2–3 minutes, or until almost cooked through. Remove and keep warm.

2 Heat the remaining oil. Add the garlic, chilli and asparagus and stir-fry for 1 minute. Return the beef to the wok. Toss in the basil, then add the fish sauce, oyster sauce and freshly ground black pepper to taste and stir-fry for 1 minute, or until heated through. Garnish with Thai basil leaves and serve.

VEAL SCALOPPINE WITH WHITE WINE AND PARSLEY

Preparation time 10 minutes

Total cooking time 5 minutes

Serves 4

4 x 175 g (6 oz) veal escalopes

30 g (1 oz) butter

3 tablespoons dry white wine or dry Marsala

100 ml (3½ fl oz) thick cream

1 tablespoon wholegrain mustard

2 tablespoons chopped flat-leaf (Italian) parsley

1 Place the veal between two sheets of baking paper and pound with a meat mallet or rolling pin until they are about 5 mm (¼ in) thick.

2 Heat the butter in a frying pan and cook the escalopes in batches for 1 minute on each side, or until just cooked. Remove and cover.

3 Add the wine to the pan, bring to the boil and cook for 1–2 minutes, or until reduced by half. Then add the cream, bring to the boil and reduce by half again. Stir in the mustard and 1 tablespoon parsley until just combined. Return the veal to the pan to warm through and coat in the sauce.

4 Serve the veal with a little sauce and sprinkle with the remaining parsley. Serve with potatoes and a green salad, if desired.

SHAKING BEEF

Preparation time 5 minutes

Total cooking time 5 minutes

Serves 4

750 g (1 lb 10 oz) beef eye fillet

1 tablespoon fish sauce

1 tablespoon light soy sauce

1 teaspoon caster (superfine) sugar

3–4 garlic cloves, crushed

2 spring onions (scallions), white part finely
   chopped

½ teaspoon freshly ground black pepper

2 tablespoons peanut oil

100 g (3½ oz) mixed frisee and red oak lettuce
   leaves

1 Cut the beef into 2 cm (¾ in) cubes and put them in a non-metallic bowl. Put the fish sauce, soy sauce, sugar, garlic, white part of the spring onions, black pepper and 1 teaspoon of the oil in a small jug, mix well and pour over the beef. Toss to coat the beef well, then cover and marinate in the refrigerator for at least 1 hour.

2 Heat a wok over high heat, add about 1 tablespoon of oil and swirl to coat. When the oil is hot, add half the beef in one layer, allowing it to sit without tossing for about 1 minute, so that a brown crust forms on the bottom. Stir-fry the beef quickly or use the wok handle to shake the beef vigorously, tossing it around the wok for 3–4 minutes for medium rare or longer if desired. Remove and repeat with the remaining oil and beef. Arrange the beef on a bed of salad leaves.

DOUBLE-FRIED
SHREDDED BEEF

Preparation time 10 minutes

Total cooking time 5 minutes

Serves 4

500 g (1 lb 2 oz) rump or sirloin, cut into thin strips

2 eggs, lightly beaten

40 g (1½ oz/⅓ cup) cornflour (cornstarch)

vegetable oil, for deep-frying

1 onion, sliced

1 carrot, cut into 5 cm (2 in) strips

2 garlic cloves, chopped

2 small red chillies, sliced

2 spring onions (scallions), sliced on the diagonal

4 tablespoons Chinese black vinegar

80 g (2¾ oz/⅓ cup) caster (superfine) sugar

2 tablespoons soy sauce

2 teaspoons toasted sesame seeds,
   to garnish

1 Combine the beef, beaten egg and cornflour in a bowl. Fill a wok one third full of oil and heat to 170°C (325°F), or until a cube of bread dropped in the oil browns in 20 seconds. Using your hands and working in batches, carefully drop strips of the beef into the oil, separating them as you go. Cook for 20–30 seconds, or until the strips are golden brown. Remove with a slotted spoon and drain on paper towels.

2 Remove all but 2 tablespoons of the oil from the wok (or use another wok). Heat the oil over medium heat and cook the onion and carrot for about 1 minute, or until softened. Add the garlic, chilli, and spring onion and stir-fry until aromatic. Add the fried beef strips, black vinegar, sugar and soy sauce and toss for 1–2 minutes.

3 Sprinkle the sesame seeds over the top and serve with steamed rice.

PEPPERED BEEF ON UDON NOODLES

Preparation time 10 minutes

Total cooking time 15 minutes

Serves 4

3 teaspoons cracked black pepper

3 teaspoons shichimi togarashi seasoning (see tip)

4 x 150 g (5½ oz) beef fillets

400 g (14 oz) udon noodles

oil, for brushing

2 baby fennel bulbs, trimmed and quartered

1 tablespoon vegetable oil

2 tablespoons light soy sauce

2 spring onions (scallions), finely sliced on the diagonal

1 Preheat a kettle or covered barbecue chargrill to low–medium indirect heat. Put the pepper and shichimi togarashi seasoning in a small bowl and mix well. Spread the mixture over both sides of the beef fillets, pressing in well. Cover with plastic wrap and refrigerate until ready to use.

2 Put the noodles in a heatproof bowl, cover with boiling water and leave for 3 minutes. (Alternatively, cook the noodles according to the packet instructions.) Rinse the noodles and drain well.

3 Brush the grill plate lightly with oil. Add the beef and fennel, then lower the lid and cook for 4 minutes. Turn the beef and fennel and cook for a further 3 minutes (the steaks will be medium to well done). Remove the steaks, cover loosely with foil and allow to rest for 5–10 minutes. Barbecue the fennel for several more minutes, or until soft and cooked. Slice the beef into thin strips and keep warm.

4 Heat a wok over medium–high heat, add the vegetable oil and swirl to coat. Add the noodles and stir-fry for 2 minutes, or until heated through. Arrange a nest of noodles on four serving plates. Top with the fennel, then the beef fillets. Drizzle with the soy sauce, sprinkle with the spring onion and serve.

TERIYAKI BEEF AND SOY BEAN STIR-FRY

Preparation time 15 minutes

Total cooking time 20 minutes

Serves 4

1 tablespoon mirin

2 tablespoons sake

2 tablespoons Japanese soy sauce

2 teaspoons sugar

400 g (14 oz) frozen soy beans (see Note)

1 tablespoon peanut oil

700 g (1 lb 7 oz) lean beef fillet, thinly sliced
   across the grain

6 spring onions (scallions), thinly sliced

2 garlic cloves, chopped

2 teaspoons finely chopped fresh ginger

50 g (1¾ oz) soy bean sprouts, tailed

1 red pepper (capsicum), thinly sliced

1 To make the stir-fry sauce, combine the

mirin, sake, Japanese soy sauce and sugar
in a small bowl or jug and set aside until it
is needed.

2 Cook the soy beans in a saucepan of
boiling water for 2 minutes. Drain.

3 Heat a large wok over high heat. Add
2 teaspoons of the peanut oil and swirl it
around to coat the side of the wok. Cook
the beef in three batches for 3–4 minutes per
batch, or until well browned. Remove from
the wok. Add the spring onion and stir-fry
for 30 seconds, or until it has wilted.

4 Return the beef to the wok, add the garlic,
ginger, soy beans, soy bean sprouts and
pepper, and stir-fry for 2 minutes. Add the
stir-fry sauce to the wok and stir-fry until
heated through. Serve hot with steamed rice.

Note Frozen soy beans are available in
packets, either in their pods or shelled. They
are available from Asian food stores. This
recipe uses the shelled variety.

BEEF STIR-FRY WITH GINGER AND LEMONGRASS

Preparation time 15 minutes +
Total cooking time 25 minutes
Serves 4

3 garlic cloves, finely chopped
1 tablespoon grated fresh ginger
4 lemongrass stems, white part only, chopped
2½ tablespoons vegetable oil
600 g (1 lb 5 oz) lean beef fillet, thinly sliced
   across the grain
1 tablespoon lime juice
1–2 tablespoons fish sauce
2 tablespoons kecap manis
1 large red onion, cut into small wedges
200 g (7 oz) green beans, sliced
steamed rice, to serve

1 Combine the garlic, ginger, lemongrass and 2 teaspoons of the oil in a large non-metallic bowl. Add the beef, toss well to coat in the marinade, then cover with plastic wrap and refrigerate for at least 10 minutes.
2 To make the stir-fry sauce, combine the lime juice, fish sauce and kecap manis in a small bowl and set aside until needed.
3 Heat a wok over high heat, add 1 tablespoon of the oil and swirl to coat the base and side. Stir-fry the beef in batches for 2–3 minutes. Remove and set aside.
4 Heat the remaining oil in the wok over high heat. Add the onion and stir-fry for 2 minutes. Add the beans and cook for a further 2 minutes, then return the beef to the wok. Pour in the stir-fry sauce and cook until heated through. Serve with steamed rice.

CHILLI PLUM BEEF

Preparation time 15 minutes

Total cooking time 15 minutes

Serves 4

2 tablespoons vegetable oil

600 g (1 lb 5 oz) lean beef fillet, thinly sliced
across the grain

1 large red onion, cut into wedges

1 red pepper (capsicum), thinly sliced

1½ tablespoons chilli garlic sauce

125 ml (4 fl oz/½ cup) plum sauce

1 tablespoon light soy sauce

2 teaspoons rice vinegar

good pinch of finely ground white pepper

4 spring onions (scallions), sliced on the
diagonal

1 Heat a wok over high heat, add about 1 tablespoon of the oil and swirl to coat the side of the wok. Stir-fry the beef in two batches for 2–3 minutes, each batch, or until browned and just cooked. Remove from the wok.

2 Heat the remaining oil in the wok, add the onion and stir-fry for 1 minute before adding the red pepper and continuing to stir-fry for 2–3 minutes, or until just tender. Add the chilli garlic sauce and stir for 1 minute, then return the meat to the wok and add the plum sauce, soy sauce, vinegar, white pepper and most of the spring onion.

3 Toss everything together for 1 minute, or until the meat is reheated. Sprinkle with the remaining spring onion.

VIETNAMESE BEEF SOUP

Preparation time 20 minutes +
Total cooking time 30 minutes
Serves 4

400 g (14 oz) lean rump steak, trimmed
½ onion
1½ tablespoons fish sauce
1 star anise
1 cinnamon stick
pinch ground white pepper
1.5 litres (52 fl oz/6 cups) beef stock
300 g (10½ oz) fresh thin rice noodles
3 spring onions (scallions), thinly sliced
1 small handful Vietnamese mint leaves
90 g (3¼ oz/1 cup) bean sprouts, trimmed
1 small onion, halved and thinly sliced
1 small red chilli, thinly sliced on the
    diagonal
lemon wedges, to serve

1 Wrap the steak in plastic wrap and freeze for 40 minutes.

2 Meanwhile, put the onion half, fish sauce, star anise, cinnamon stick, white pepper, stock and 500 ml (17 fl oz/2 cups) water in a large saucepan. Bring to the boil, then reduce the heat, cover and simmer for about 20 minutes. Discard the onion, star anise and cinnamon stick.

3 Put the noodles in a large heatproof bowl. Cover with boiling water and soak for 5 minutes, or until softened. Seperate gently and drain. Thinly slice the meat across the grain.

4 Divide the noodles and spring onion among four deep bowls. Top with the beef, mint, bean sprouts, thinly sliced onion and chilli. Ladle the hot broth over the top and serve with the lemon wedges — the heat of the liquid will cook the beef.

STIR-FRIED BEEF WITH SNAKE BEANS AND BASIL

Preparation time 10 minutes +
Total cooking time 10 minutes
Serves 4

3 fresh bird's eye chillies, seeded and finely
   chopped
3 garlic cloves, crushed
2 tablespoons fish sauce
1 teaspoon grated palm sugar
2 tablespoons peanut or vegetable oil
400 g (14 oz) lean beef fillet, thinly sliced across
   the grain
150 g (5 oz) snake beans, sliced into 3 cm
   (1¼ in) lengths
30 g (1 oz) fresh Thai basil
thinly sliced fresh bird's eye chilli, to garnish

1 Combine the chilli, garlic, fish sauce, palm sugar and 1 tablespoon of the oil in a large non-metallic bowl. Add the beef, toss well, then cover and marinate in the fridge for 2 hours.

2 Heat a wok to hot, add 2 teaspoons of the oil and swirl to coat. Stir-fry the beef in two batches over high heat for 2 minutes each batch, or until just browned. Remove from the wok.

3 Heat the remaining oil in the wok, then add the snake beans and 3 tablespoons water and cook over high heat for 3–4 minutes, tossing regularly until tender.

4 Return the beef to the wok with the basil. Cook for a further 1–2 minutes, or until warmed through. Garnish with chilli, then serve.

GINGER BEEF STIR-FRY

Preparation time 20 minutes +
Total cooking time 15 minutes
Serves 4

1 garlic clove, crushed
1 teaspoon grated fresh ginger
3 tablespoons kecap manis
3 tablespoons Chinese rice wine
1 teaspoon sugar
pinch of Chinese five-spice powder
500 g (1 lb 2 oz) lean beef fillet, thinly sliced
    across the grain
½ teaspoon cornflour (cornstarch)
3 tablespoons peanut oil
1 red onion, sliced into thin wedges
1½ tablespoons julienned fresh ginger
400 g (14 oz) Chinese broccoli (gai larn), cut into
    6 cm (2½ in) lengths

1 Combine the garlic, grated ginger, kecap manis, rice wine, sugar and five-spice powder in a large non-metallic bowl. Add the beef, toss together, then cover and marinate in the fridge for at least 15 minutes.

2 Mix together the cornflour with about 1 tablespoon water to form a paste.

3 Heat a wok over high heat, add about 1 tablespoon of the oil and swirl to coat the side of the wok. Remove half the meat from the marinade with tongs or a slotted spoon, add to the wok and stir-fry for 2–3 minutes, or until browned and just cooked. Remove from the wok. Repeat with more oil and the rest of the beef, reserving the marinade.

4 Add the remaining oil to the wok and stir-fry the onion for 2–3 minutes, or until it starts to soften, then add the julienned ginger and stir-fry for another minute. Stir in the gai larn and cook for 2–3 minutes, or until wilted and tender.

5 Return the beef to the wok, along with the reserved marinade and any meat juices. Add the cornflour paste and stir until thoroughly combined. Continue to cook for 1–2 minutes, or until the sauce has thickened slightly and the meat is heated through. Serve with steamed rice or noodles.

CHINESE BEEF AND BLACK BEAN SAUCE

Preparation time 15 minutes
Total cooking time 20 minutes
Serves 4

2 tablespoons rinsed and drained black beans,
    chopped
1 tablespoon dark soy sauce
1 tablespoon Chinese rice wine
1 garlic clove, finely chopped
1 teaspoon sugar
3 tablespoons peanut oil
1 onion, cut into wedges
500 g (1 lb 2 oz) lean beef fillet, thinly sliced
    across the grain
½ teaspoon finely chopped fresh ginger
1 teaspoon cornflour (cornstarch)
1 teaspoon sesame oil
steamed rice, to serve

1 Put the beans, soy sauce, rice wine and
3 tablespoons water in a small bowl and mix.
In a separate bowl, crush the garlic and sugar
to a paste, using a mortar and pestle.

2 Heat a wok over high heat, add 1 teaspoon
of the peanut oil and swirl to coat the base
and side. Add the onion and stir-fry for
1–2 minutes, then transfer to a bowl and
set aside.

4 Add 1 tablespoon of the peanut oil to the
wok and swirl to coat the base and side,
then add half the beef and stir-fry for
5–6 minutes, or until browned. Remove to
the bowl with the onion. Repeat with the
remaining beef.

3 Add the remaining peanut oil to the wok
along with the garlic paste and ginger and
stir-fry for 30 seconds, or until fragrant. Add
the bean mixture, onion and beef. Bring to
the boil, then reduce the heat and simmer,
covered, for 2 minutes.

4 Combine the cornflour with 1 tablespoon
water, pour into the wok and stir until the
sauce boils and thickens. Stir in the sesame
oil and serve with steamed rice.

SPICY DRY-FRIED SHREDDED BEEF

Preparation time 15 minutes +
Total cooking time 10 minutes
Serves 4

1 tablespoon light soy sauce
½ teaspoon sesame oil
1 tablespoon Chinese rice wine
400 g (14 oz) lean beef fillet, thinly sliced across
   the grain, then shredded
2–3 tablespoons peanut oil
2 garlic cloves, finely chopped
1 teaspoon grated fresh ginger
3 spring onions (scallions), finely chopped

Sauce
1½ tablespoons brown bean sauce
1 tablespoon chilli bean paste
½ teaspoon caster (superfine) sugar
½ teaspoon chilli oil
¼ teaspoon sea salt

1 Combine the soy sauce, sesame oil, about
2 teaspoons of the rice wine and ½ teaspoon
salt in a large non-metallic bowl. Add the
beef, cover with plastic wrap and marinate in
the refrigerator for at least 2 hours.
2 To make the sauce, combine all the
ingredients in a non-metallic bowl.
3 Heat a wok over high heat, add about
1 tablespoon of the peanut oil and swirl to
coat the base and side. Add the beef in two
batches, using your hands to break up any
clumps as you drop the beef into the wok.
Stir-fry each batch for 1 minute, or until the
beef is browned. Remove, place on crumpled
paper towel and drain off any liquid from
the meat.
4 Clean and dry the wok, then heat over
high heat, add the remaining oil and swirl to
coat. Add the garlic and ginger and stir-fry
for 30 seconds, or until fragrant. Return the
beef to the wok and cook for 2 minutes,
or until it is very dry. Add the remaining
2 teaspoons of rice wine and stir-fry for
30 seconds, or until all the wine is absorbed.
Add the bean sauce mixture and stir well
until the beef is well coated. Remove from
the heat, stir in the spring onion and serve.

PESTO BEEF WITH PASTA

Preparation time 30 minutes

Total cooking time 25 minutes

Serves 4

1 large red capsicum (pepper)
1 large yellow capsicum (pepper)
canola or olive oil spray
100 g (3½ oz) lean beef fillet steak, trimmed
125 g (4½ oz) penne
100 g (3½ oz) button mushrooms, quartered

Pesto
50 g (1¾ oz) basil leaves
2 garlic cloves, chopped
2 tablespoons pepitas (pumpkin seeds)
1 tablespoon olive oil
2 tablespoons orange juice
1 tablespoon lemon juice

1 Cut the capsicums into large flat pieces, removing the seeds and membrane. Put skin-side-up under a hot grill (broiler) until blackened. Leave covered with a tea towel until cool, then peel away the skin and chop the flesh.

2 Spray a non-stick frying pan with oil and cook the steak over high heat for 3–4 minutes on each side. Remove and leave for 5 minutes before cutting into thin slices. Season with a little salt.

3 To make the pesto, finely chop the basil, garlic and pepitas in a food processor. With the motor running, add the oil, orange and lemon juice. Season well with salt and freshly ground black pepper.

4 Meanwhile, cook the pasta in a large saucepan of boiling water for 10 minutes, or until al dente. Drain well and toss with the pesto in a large bowl.

5 Add the capsicum pieces, steak slices and mushroom quarters to the penne and toss well to coat thoroughly. Serve warm immediately.

BEEF SATAY

Preparation time 10 minutes
Total cooking time 15 minutes
Serves 4

650 g (1 lb 7 oz) rump steak, finely sliced
lime wedges, to serve
2 tablespoons chopped coriander (cilantro)
    leaves, to serve

Satay sauce
2 teaspoons peanut oil
1 small onion, finely chopped
2 tablespoons chopped lemongrass, white part
    only
2 tablespoons finely grated fresh galangal
1 red bird's eye chilli, finely chopped
140 g (5 oz) crunchy peanut butter
250 ml (9 fl oz/1 cup) coconut milk

1 Soak 12 bamboo skewers in cold water for 20 minutes. Thread the beef evenly onto the skewers.

2 To make the satay sauce, heat the oil in a small saucepan over medium heat and cook the onion, stirring, for 3 minutes, or until soft. Add the lemongrass, galangal and chilli and cook, stirring, for 1 minute, or until fragrant. Stir in the peanut butter and coconut milk and cook over low heat until well combined and heated through.

3 Heat an oiled barbecue grill plate or chargrill pan over high heat. Lightly brush the beef with oil. Cook the skewers for about 3 minutes on each side, or until browned and cooked as desired.

4 Serve the beef with the satay sauce and lime wedges and sprinkle with the extra coriander.

SALTIMBOCCA

Preparation time 15 minutes

Total cooking time 20 minutes

Serves 4

4 thin veal steaks
2 garlic cloves, crushed
4 prosciutto slices
4 sage leaves
30 g (1 oz) butter
170 ml (5½ fl oz) Marsala

1 Trim the meat of excess fat and sinew and flatten each steak to 5 mm (¼ in) thick. Nick the edges to prevent curling and pat the meat dry with paper towels. Combine the garlic with ¼ teaspoon salt and ½ teaspoon ground black pepper and rub some of the mixture over one side of each veal steak. Place a slice of prosciutto on each and top with a sage leaf. The prosciutto should cover the veal completely but not overlap the edge.

2 Melt the butter in a large heavy-based frying pan, add the veal, prosciutto side up, and cook over heat for 5 minutes, or until the underside is golden brown. Do not turn the veal. Add the Marsala, without wetting the top of the veal. Reduce the heat and simmer very slowly for 10 minutes. Transfer the veal to warm serving plates. Boil the sauce for 2–3 minutes, or until syrupy, then spoon it over the veal.

PARMESAN AND ROSEMARY VEAL CHOPS

Preparation time 15 minutes
Total cooking time 15 minutes
Serves 4

4 veal chops
150 g (5½ oz) fresh white breadcrumbs
75 g (2½ oz/¾ cup) freshly grated
    parmesan cheese
1 tablespoon rosemary, finely chopped
2 eggs, lightly beaten, seasoned
3 tablespoons olive oil
60 g (2¼ oz) butter
4 garlic cloves

1 Trim the chops of excess fat and sinew and flatten to 1 cm (½ in) thickness. Pat the meat dry with paper towels. Combine the breadcrumbs, parmesan and rosemary in a shallow bowl.

2 Dip each chop in the beaten egg, draining off the excess. Press both sides of the chops firmly in the crumbs.

3 Heat the oil and butter in a heavy-based frying pan over low heat, add the garlic and cook until golden. Discard the garlic.

4 Increase the heat to medium, add the chops to the pan and cook for 4–5 minutes on each side, depending on the thickness of the chops, until golden and crisp.

INDEX

Published in 2009 by Bay Books, an imprint of Murdoch Books Pty Limited.

Murdoch Books Australia
Pier 8/9
23 Hickson Road
Millers Point NSW 2000
Phone: + 61 (0) 2 8220 2000
Fax: + 61 (0) 2 8220 2558
www.murdochbooks.com.au

Murdoch Books UK Limited
Erico House, 6th Floor
93–99 Upper Richmond Road
Putney, London SW15 2TG
Phone: + 44 (0) 20 8785 5995
Fax: + 44 (0) 20 8785 5985
www.murdochbooks.co.uk

Chief Executive: Juliet Rogers
Publishing Director: Kay Scarlett

Design manager: Vivien Valk
Design concept and design: Jo Yuen
Photographers: Alan Benson, Craig Cranko, Jared Fowler, Ian Hofstetter, Chris Jones
Stylists: Jane Collins, Mary Harris, Cherise Koch
Production: Monique Layt
Recipes developed by the Murdoch Books Test Kitchen

ISBN: 978 1 74196 392 2

Printed by Sing Cheong Printing Co. Ltd. PRINTED IN CHINA.

IMPORTANT: Those who might be at risk from the effects of salmonella poisoning (the elderly,
pregnant women, young children and those suffering from immune deficiency diseases) should
consult their doctor with any concerns about eating raw eggs.

OVEN GUIDE: You may find cooking times vary depending on the oven you are using.
For fan-forced ovens, as a general rule, set the oven temperature to 20°C (35°F) lower than
indicated in the recipe.